The Battle for the Bs

The Battle for the Bs

1950s Hollywood and the Rebirth of Low-Budget Cinema

BLAIR DAVIS

RUTGERS UNIVERSITY PRESS

NEW BRUNSWICK, NEW JERSEY, AND LONDON

LIBRARY OF CONGRESS CATALOGING-IN-PUBLICATION DATA

Davis, Blair, 1975–
    The battle for the Bs : 1950s Hollywood and the rebirth of low-budget cinema /
Blair Davis.
        p.   cm.
    Includes bibliographical references and index.
    ISBN 978–0–8135–5252–1 (hardcover : alk. paper) — ISBN 978–0–8135–5253–8
(pbk. : alk. paper) — ISBN 978–0–8135–5324–5 (e-book)
    1. B films—United States—History and criticism.   2. Motion pictures—United
States—History—20th century.   I. Title.
    PN1995.9.B2D38 2012
    791.430973—dc23

                                                                    2011023489

A British Cataloging-in-Publication record for this book is available from the
British Library.

Visit our Web site: http://rutgerspress.rutgers.edu

Manufactured in the United States of America

For Erin

CONTENTS

ACKNOWLEDGMENTS

Many people contributed to the realization of this book—first and foremost my wife, Erin Davis, who has never known a time when I was not working on this project in some capacity, and whose love makes everything in life better. Leslie Mitchner has been a fantastic editor, and I am very thankful for all of her help and guidance. Paul Heyer has been an incredible mentor and friend for many years and taught me how to be a better student and scholar (and how to shoot a recurve bow and throw a boomerang, and many other useful skills). Dana Polan has been extremely encouraging of this project since its early stages, offering many suggestions that made this a better book. Thank you to David Culbert and my other anonymous reader, whose comments and suggestions proved extremely valuable to the revision process, as did those of Paul St. Pierre. Mary Francis has my gratitude for helping me place this work at Rutgers University Press.

Thanks are due to numerous supervisors and colleagues at several institutions: Will Straw, Darin Barney, and Marc Raboy at McGill University; Charles Acland and Haidee Wasson at Concordia University; Jen Marchbank, Robert Anderson, and Jan Walls at Simon Fraser University; Steffen Hantke at Sogang University; Scott Preston, Murray Linton, and Allan Reid at the University of New Brunswick.

I draw on the interviews of Tom Weaver at several points and am grateful for his diligence in conducting them. I am also indebted to those who have gone before me in the study of B-movies, including Don Miller, Jeffrey Sconce, Eric Schaeffer, Kevin Heffernan, Brian Taves, Wheeler Dixon, Mark Thomas McGee, Charles Flynn, and Todd McCarthy, among others. Special thanks to David Taylor for the Ramar lobby cards.

Chapter 5 contains material that was revised and expanded upon from two previously published essays: Blair Davis, "Small Screen, Smaller Pictures: Television Broadcasting and B-Movies in the Early 1950s," *Historical Journal of Film, Radio and Television* 28, no. 2 (June 2008): 219–238; and Blair Davis, "Made-from-TV-Movies: Turning 1950s Television Into Films," *Historical Journal of Film, Radio and Television* 29, no. 2 (June 2009): 197–218. Reprinted with permission.

Much love and appreciation to my family and friends: my father, Stephen Davis; Allison and Graham Knights; Mhairi and Steve MacKenzie; Rita and George Thorpe; Rob, Sheena, and Shannon Maybin; Kelly and Greg Pombert; Carole Akazawa; Guy Neill.

Finally, this book is dedicated to the memory of my Mum, Mrs. Wilma Davis, whose love and support helped me get to where I am today. The news that this book would be published brought her great joy, and she is dearly missed.

The Battle for the Bs

The Bs Take Flight

An Introduction

B-movies are frequently labeled as simply being "bad" films, both historically within the film industry and by many modern critics and fans. What this overlooks is how vital B-films have been overall to cinema, particularly from a business perspective. Despite often being ridiculed or dismissed as inconsequential trash, Bs were important commercial entities, not only in how they allowed the major Hollywood studios to solidify their control over the marketplace in the 1930s and 1940s as the double bill emerged, but also in how they allowed 1950s independent filmmakers to change the very way in which low-budget filmmaking was understood.

Many film historians see the B-movie as a product of 1930s/1940s Hollywood, where the sometimes meager yet generally reliable profits generated from the Bs served as a support mechanism to the larger-budgeted A-films of the major studios. Yet low-budget filmmaking endured even after the double-bill format that necessitated B-filmmaking in the first place waned in the 1950s. Indeed, with many producers, directors, studio executives, and journalists still regularly using the term "B-movie" throughout this decade, it can be seen how the Bs did not simply die out in the 1950s—instead, they evolved. In the process, low-budget filmmaking secured a new role within the film industry, one that was no longer purely secondary but instead often innovative.

Originating as a largely subordinate and supportive entity to the Hollywood A-film, B-movies were made with the intent of generating predictable profit margins from modestly budgeted films that satisfied a marketplace need for increased quantities of cinematic entertainment. While B-movies stem from a system of distribution choices that typically placed them in exhibition contexts limiting their earning potential in prior decades (although there were often exceptions), the Bs pioneered new methods in the 1950s by which such fiscal restraints could often be overcome. Although the B-movie emerged within the framework of the double bill and a relationship with A-pictures in the studio-system era of filmmaking in the 1930s and 1940s, its role within the film industry evolved as both the overall cinematic marketplace and Hollywood filmmaking practices began to change. B-films didn't disappear at the end of the 1940s despite industrial transformation; the film industry itself commonly used such terms as "B-movie" and "Poverty Row" to describe films produced on low budgets throughout the 1950s. This was even true of the tradition of "underground" filmmaking, in which films are made more for the purpose of artistic expression than profit-driven entertainment—the latter notion being central to B-filmmaking.

This book chronicles the ways in which the B-film was understood as a low-budget product (which saw patterns of production, distribution, and exhibition that typically differed from those of higher-budgeted major studio releases) within the film industry throughout the 1950s, at a time when such filmmaking reinvented itself. Increasingly the result of newly formed independent companies, 1950s B-movies innovated such industrial components as new genre cycles, demographic patterns and marketing approaches. With both major and minor studios questioning the economic viability of low-budget production, B-movies regularly existed in opposition to the cinematic mainstream—a legacy that was passed on to independent filmmakers of subsequent decades.[1]

On May 3, 1948, the United States Supreme Court handed down its infamous Paramount decree ruling, placing major Hollywood studios in violation of antitrust laws. The decision signaled the end of the classical Hollywood studio system of the 1930s and 1940s, altering the corporate organization of these studios and in turn modifying how they made films. It also meant the end of the B-movie—at least in the traditional sense, as they would soon become a distinctly different product.

Prior to the antitrust ruling, movie theaters were largely required to show whatever films the studios gave them due to the policy of block booking, whereby a distributor would offer certain films to an exhibitor only on the provision that an additional group of films would also be bought. Essentially, in order for exhibitors to get the films they really wanted, they had to take a lot of unwanted films as well. The antitrust ruling prohibited the practice of block booking as well as the process of vertical integration, whereby movie studios owned the theaters in which their films were shown. With studios forced to divest themselves of their theaters and no longer able to sell their films in blocks, their total control over the marketplace was at an end. The guaranteed connection between production and exhibition now severed by the Paramount decree, filmmaking suddenly became a far more uncertain venture than it had been.[2]

Block booking had created a new category of films in the 1930s—the B-movie. An all-or-none approach to selling films allowed the studios to give exhibitors a handful of top-quality films along with a multitude of second-rate titles. Films became commonly shown as double bills, with a marked difference in quality typically evident between the two films screened in a given movie theater each night. An A-level film with a major cast and relatively expensive production values was normally followed by a B-movie with lesser-known actors, a lower budget, and reduced production values.

The double bill (and in turn the rise of the B-movie) originated as a response by some exhibitors to the economic effects of the Great Depression. By 1933, one in four Americans was unemployed, leading to an overall decline in movie theater attendance from the 1920s.[3] Reacting to decreasing revenues, many theater owners tried new marketing approaches to lure more viewers. Ticket prices began to drop at the start of the decade, as audiences grew increasingly less affluent. Lower-cost matinee screenings were offered, often outselling evening performances. Recent developments in air-conditioning made the technology cost-effective for exhibitors, and it became a widespread attraction in theaters and often a bigger draw than the films themselves in summer months. Some exhibitors resorted to various gimmicks such as a lottery that gave away a car, as well as bingo and other games with cash prizes. "Bank night," for instance, offered the chance to win up to $250, while a nationwide "movie quiz contest" offered the chance to win up to $50,000 (to those who could answer at least thirty questions about recently released films). Giveaways were also common, with one of the most popular being glass dinnerware that prompted many families to return week after week in the hopes of collecting a full dining set.[4] In short, the attempt was made in the early 1930s to turn moviegoing into a more marketable commodity in light of the fact that the public had less money to spend on entertainment.

Central to the changing cinematic experience in the 1930s was the coming of the double bill, with many exhibitors offering two feature-length films for the price of one to give audiences more value for their money. In previous decades, screenings regularly had the added attraction of live vaudeville performances, a practice that nearly all theaters eliminated with the coming of sound cinema and the start of the double bill. Two-for-one screenings can be traced back to 1915 with the Triangle Film Corporation, but few exhibitors utilized this strategy throughout the 1920s.[5] Double bills gained prominence in New England in 1930, becoming standard practice in many theaters across the country the following year. Most of the earliest adopters were independent exhibitors, with the major studios following suit in greater numbers once the trend's popularity solidified. By mid-1932, double features were the norm in 40 percent of theaters, increasing to 85 percent by 1936 (with the remaining 15 percent being the prestigious downtown first-run theaters, which could afford to keep screening single features).[6]

In addition to two feature films, audiences were offered a miscellany of items such as short films, cartoons, trailers, serials, and newsreels, which varied depending on the theater. This practice was also common in the silent era, though once it was integrated into the double-bill format many viewers increasingly sought the cumulative effect of the total package rather than any one particular feature serving as the main draw. A variety of programming also meant more frequent intermissions, resulting in higher concession-stand sales for exhibitors.[7]

While such programming diversity was often an asset to exhibitors, the larger industrial implications of the double bill were equally considerable. As Paul Kerr has written, double bills

> had the additional—and, as it proved, crucial—advantage of enabling independent exhibitors to accommodate their programme policies to the majors' monopolistic distribution practices (such as blind selling and block booking) and allowed them to exhibit more independent productions at the same time. Of the 23,000 theatres operating in the United States in 1930, the five majors (MGM, RKO, Fox, Warners, and Paramount) either owned or controlled some 3,000—most of that number being among the biggest and best situated of the first-run theatres; these 3,000 theatres, though comprising less than 14 per cent of the total number then in operation, accounted for nearly 70 per cent of the entire industry's box-office takings that year. This left the independents with some 20,000 theatres in which to screen what were either second-run or independent films.[8]

Double bills can therefore be seen as a response by independent theaters seeking to compete with the larger, studio-owned theaters. MGM, Warner Bros., Twentieth Century–Fox, Paramount, and RKO all controlled the means of exhibiting their films, in addition to their production and distribution. As a result of this vertical integration, these studio-owned theaters were guaranteed the newest films from each respective studio. This unequal distribution prompted some exhibitors to try new strategies such as double features in order to lure audiences with quantity (if not necessarily quality).[9]

Whereas Hollywood studios could turn out enough product to satisfy demand in a single-feature marketplace, the rise of the double bill resulted in a doubling of demand for new films. Some of the major studios tried countering the dual format by producing single films that were approximately two hours or longer, such as Warner Bros.' *A Midsummer Night's Dream* (1935), *Anthony Adverse* (1936), and *Charge of the Light Brigade* (1936), as well as MGM's

David Copperfield (1935) and *A Tale of Two Cities* (1935). Many found such efforts to be far too long: one reporter complained in 1935 that "stories which could be recited with telling directness in eighty minutes" were being "padded into a swollen two hours."[10] The major studios also feared that certain exhibitors hoping to preserve a double-bill format without making their program overly long might edit these longer films down to a shorter running time.

Double bills were not immediately popular with everyone, however, and opponents conducted various surveys showing how most audiences were seemingly against dual features. A 1933 poll conducted by Hal Roach studios found 80 percent of viewers disapproving of double bills for such reasons as lacking diversity and being too long, with a preference stated instead for a single feature accompanied by numerous short films. In 1936, Warner Bros. sent out form letters seeking responses about double-bill preferences from thousands of clubs, newspapers, and colleges. The letters they received back opposing twin bills saw a wide range of complaints: the double-bill format "injured the eyes, it necessitated cutting good pictures to make room for bad ones, it caused headaches and aching joints and it engendered a distaste for movies generally." One viewer even wrote a letter to the editor at the *New York Times* stating that he had "often suspected" that double bills were responsible for headaches, heart problems, "and other allied diseases," and sought a law passed banning the dual bills. "Only the best pictures would be chosen" as a result, he argued, and "it would do away with many headaches and perhaps many cases of heart trouble."[11]

Despite such protests, most of the major studios had resigned themselves by 1935 to the fact that the double bill would remain. In October of that year, two of the biggest theater chains in New York—Loew's and RKO—announced plans to convert all of their first-run theaters to a double-bill policy. The decision quickly proved successful, with one reporter writing in 1936 that "picture audiences insist upon their bargains. Experiments in both the Loew's and RKO circuits have demonstrated that two bad pictures will outdraw one good picture."[12] The fiscal reality of the new marketplace conditions made it economically unfeasible for the majors to produce twice as many films of a similarly high quality, since it was beyond their resources in terms of both production facilities and available actors and crew. It was also not financially advantageous for the studios to offer two expensive productions for the same single admission price. Hence, the studios devised a new mode of production to capitalize on the changed state of film exhibition. Production was divided into two groups, "class A and class B," and special production units were formed to create the latter.[13]

Double bills became associated with a divide between A-pictures and B-pictures, with theaters showing a package typically featuring one of each. The former was thought to be more prestigious because of its larger budget

6 THE BATTLE FOR THE Bs

and more popular actors, while the latter became synonymous with low-budget filmmaking. A-pictures traditionally played the first half of the pairing, followed by the B-picture in what became known as the lower half to the A's top half of the double bill. The average running length of a B-movie in the 1930s was between fifty-five and seventy minutes; hence most Bs were approximately six reels in length, while A-films were at least seven reels long. Shooting schedules were also reduced, with most Bs made in approximately three weeks, but sometimes as quickly as one week or less. A-pictures were also allowed the privilege of rehearsal time before shooting and multiple retakes during production, luxuries typically not afforded by the reduced budgets of the Bs.[14] At the major studios, A-films were typically budgeted at $350,000 and upwards. Bs were usually budgeted closer to $200,000, with a few even approaching $300,000. At smaller studios like Columbia Pictures and Republic Pictures, B-movies cost even less, between $50,000 and $125,000. Republic was part of a group of studios collectively termed Poverty Row, with the most minor of such companies often making films for between $10,000 and $20,000 or less.[15]

Given such wide discrepancies in budget, the Bs were clearly subject to variations in their mode of production from studio to studio. As the B-film became a regular feature in theaters, the *New York Times* offered a four-tier structure in 1935 to help explain the differences among all of the various B-movie producers in the marketplace. "As an executive on one major lot stated, 'It's getting so you don't know whose throat to cut,'" explained journalist Douglas W. Churchill. He designated "four production classes" for the Bs:

1. "Major lots," as represented by the major studios such as MGM, RKO, Warner Bros., and their peers, and described as "those in high places."
2. "Individual operators," which consisted of independent producers like Jesse L. Lasky, Sol Lesser, Charles R. Rogers, and Walter Wanger, who often made films that were distributed by the majors but were not under an exclusive contract to any one studio (and therefore not beholden to their particular methods of filmmaking).
3. "Large independents" such as Monogram Pictures and Republic Pictures, described as being in a "competitive position" through possession of a large program of films they could sell "en bloc" for much less than small companies could sell the same number of films.
4. "Small independents," the most impoverished of Poverty Row studios that made films "costing upward from $12,500" and on four-to-six-day production schedules. Churchill describes their films as "quickies," with the success of larger independents such as Republic contributing to a certain level of volatility at this level of production.[16]

Between the first two of these production levels also lies the phenomenon of the "programmer"—a B-film that could be played in either half of a given double bill. This decision depended upon the theater involved and the strength of the second film with which the programmer was paired. Typically featuring a cast with minor stars as opposed to the more generic casts of lower-tiered productions, programmers were usually on the higher end of the budgetary scale afforded to the Bs at a given studio, so their production values were usually not far off from those of the lower-budgeted A-films (if there was even a noticeable difference).[17] Sometimes a film originally intended as a B-movie even turned out so well that it was promoted to A-film status, or at least what trade publications called "the 'sub-A' class": just because it may have been made on a lower budget "doesn't mean . . . that a picture that is produced as a 'B' can't pan out to be an 'A'—in which case nobody is mad," Twentieth Century–Fox producer John Stone explained.[18]

By 1937, nearly two-thirds of all films made in Hollywood were B-movies, taking both major and minor studios into account. Some exhibitors even began to fear that, despite the double bill's perceived value for money, the Bs would eventually drive customers away once they began to notice the difference in quality. Industry rhetoric soon began referring to low-budget films as "C" and even "Z" pictures, and many actors, producers, and directors reportedly "rebel[led] against being associated with the short money films." Critics of the B-film believed that its contrast with the A-film was often so pronounced that "the entire institution suffers in consequence" and would lead viewers to "ask about quality before they lay their money down." Audiences who had previously "been loyal to all product" would presumably begin to question whether a film was made on a high or low budget before buying a ticket. "Everywhere the warning is being sounded," wrote one cautionary reporter, "that the quickies eventually will drive the customers from the theaters and instead of queues in front of ticket windows there will be large vacant spaces."[19]

The major studios ultimately embraced the Bs because their profits were essentially guaranteed in a new era of block booking. When asked what he liked best about B-films, Stone offered the simple fact that they "don't lose money."[20] The reason for this was that B-movies were subject to different patterns of distribution than their A-picture counterparts. A-films were rented to theaters on a percentage basis, whereby the studio (serving as producer and distributor) and exhibitor split the box office revenue. The split with most films was approximately 60/40, with the distributor receiving 60 percent and the theater getting 40. The split often went up to 80/20 or 90/10 for more popular films, such as those with actors who were proven box office draws. B-movies were rented on a different basis, being offered to exhibitors for a flat rental fee. This meant that, unlike with A-films, the profits made by the studios on Bs were not solely determined by popularity at the box office. Producers could therefore predict with high degree of accuracy the minimum amount of revenue that any given B-movie would generate. In order to make a profit on each film, a producer simply had to ensure that the budget was suitably lower than the expected minimum profit from the flat fee.[21]

With the risk of going over budget being the potential difference between profit and loss, the phrase "time is money" has always been particularly true of B-movie production. Edward Dmytryk, director of such 1940s Bs as *Confessions of Boston Blackie* (1941), *The Devil Commands* (1941), and *Captive Wild Woman* (1943), said that B-directors were hired primarily for their speed and efficiency in shooting a film: "They could make a picture on time, that's the main thing. At RKO and Columbia, you could make a picture in 12 days; at Paramount, because they had more theaters, you had a little longer; and MGM was about the same as Paramount. And [B] directors were hired for that purpose." B-movie directors "were simply people who had a reputation for making it in 12 days," said Dmytryk, "or whatever it was at that particular studio."[22]

Shooting schedules were even more intense at the smaller Poverty Row studios, given that their profit margins were even smaller than those of the major studios: Monogram made an average profit of $1,932.12 per film, while Producers Releasing Corporation's (PRC) films averaged $1,750.[23] Along with Monogram and Republic, PRC became one of the more relatively successful independent studios in the 1940s by using more extreme methods of cost-effectiveness than the major studios. Many of its films were shot at night, a common B-movie production method that allowed producers to maximize set and equipment rental time and facilitate shorter shooting schedules.[24] PRC, like many other smaller studios, also limited the amount of footage shot on any given production, often only allowing directors to shoot between twenty and forty additional minutes of footage beyond the film's sixty- to eighty-minute running time.[25] This allowed for precious few retakes and led some directors—such as Edgar G. Ulmer, who made the acclaimed film noir *Detour* for the studio in 1945—to adopt some creative shooting strategies.

Ulmer shot most of his films for the studio on a six-day schedule, achieving up to eighty camera setups a day. To keep up such a frantic pace, he developed what he called the "perfect technique" for shooting B-movies with extremely limited resources:

> No set of mine existed in these pictures where one wall was not without any paintings, without anything, just a plain wall in gray. I shot my master scene, but left for the last day the close-ups. They would play against that one flat, blank wall, and I would say "camera left," "camera right." They would say two sentences, I would hold my hand in front

of the lens [using it in place of a slate] not to stop the camera, and he would go into the second speech, because I couldn't afford to go through. I had to cut with the camera, because I was only allowed 15,000 feet [of film stock] for a feature. No more.[26]

In 1943, wartime rationing measures saw the government limit the amount of film stock that all studios were allowed, initially mandating 25 percent below 1941 usage. B-filmmaking units were the most affected by such measures, with the use of montage sequences becoming more common as a result. This forced some filmmakers to rely more heavily on stock footage—or as B-director Nick Grinde explained it, "You borrow or buy about twenty pieces of thrilling moments from twenty forgotten pictures."[27] This meant less original footage needed to be shot, hence less raw film stock used, and more money saved.

B-movies were a key part of the mode of production utilized in the classical studio system, and due in part to their role in the double-bill structure the film industry saw a period of great success that lasted between fifteen and twenty years, from the early 1930s to the late 1940s, often referred to as the golden age of Hollywood. Ultimately, however, B-movie production began to change at studios of all sizes. June 1, 1946, saw a federal district court rule against the major Hollywood studios for antitrust violations, a decision that was upheld by the Supreme Court two years later. The effects were quickly felt in Hollywood, with some major studios either reducing the number of Bs they produced or eliminating them entirely. Poverty Row studios also began producing fewer films after seeing increased production during the war years. Between 1940 and 1944, Monogram made an average of forty-six films per year, but that fell to an average of thirty-seven films each year between 1945 and 1950.[28] In the hopes of revitalizing the company, PRC changed its name to Eagle-Lion Studios in 1946, but by 1951 the studio was bought out by United Artists.

The fate of PRC was just one of the many changes that B-movies in particular and the film industry as a whole underwent in the late 1940s. As the decade came to a close, Hollywood faced the consequences of the 1948 antitrust ruling, theaters began selling fewer tickets, and audiences became far more discriminating in the wake of television's rising popularity, with moviegoing becoming a less frequent habit. When the golden age of Hollywood ended, low-budget filmmaking was subsequently forced to evolve.

While the B-film was a small (yet important) cog in the Hollywood studio machine in the 1930s and 1940s that allowed A-films to command top dollar, it would become a key industry player by the end of the 1950s, influencing both the major studios and underground filmmakers alike. With the end of block booking, Hollywood studios no longer had a guaranteed market for their B-movies, hence no longer the same economic incentive to keep producing so many of them. The 1950s was consequently a period of tremendous change for filmmakers, as existing companies struggled or went out of business. New independent companies emerged to fill the void, bringing with them a style of filmmaking that was decidedly rawer and inherently more risky.

No longer explicitly tied to the Hollywood studio system, the patterns of production, distribution, and exhibition established by B-movies in the 1950s created new opportunities for independent filmmakers for decades to come. While minimum profits were no longer guaranteed, the potential for greater reward in this new era of risk was substantial, and many independent B-films ranked among the highest-grossing releases of the year. In 1950, Eagle-Lion's science fiction film *Destination Moon* earned $5 million domestically, while the 1952 American Pictures cold-war thriller *Invasion, USA* earned $1.2 million. The latter half of the decade saw the 1956 rock 'n' roll entry *Rock Around the Clock* from Clover Productions earn $4 million, while the 1958 horror film *I Was a Teenage Werewolf* grossed $2 million for American International Pictures (AIP).

Low-budget films were certainly capable of substantial profits in the 1930s and 1940s, just as many big-budget A-films failed to turn a profit. *The Wizard of Oz* lost over a million dollars in its initial 1939 release, while both *Hitler's Children* and *Behind the Rising Sun* were made for under $240,000 at RKO, with each earning well over a million dollars in 1943. Similarly, MGM produced numerous entries in the *Andy Hardy* series in the late 1930s and early 1940s that cost little more than $200,000 each but earned over a million dollars per film.[29] Such examples demonstrate the programmer phenomenon at work, with studios promoting titles that were produced with B-unit budgets to the level of percentage distribution.

Even a film intended as a B for flat-rate sales could sometimes bring in sizable returns; RKO's *Cat People*, for instance, earned $183,000 between 1942 and 1943 (although some sources see the film as earning much more than this).[30] The potential for success would increase exponentially in the 1950s, however, as the rules changed entirely for what independent low-budget films could earn—AIP's films regularly made net profits of $100,000 or more, and multimillion-dollar returns also became a regular possibility. B-movies would often prove to be among a studio's biggest earners in the 1950s and no longer served as just a revenue supplement whose primary value was to offset losses from big-budget A-movies that failed to make a profit. Furthermore, whereas Poverty Row producers had to be content with meager flat-rate sales in prior decades, the industrial changes in the 1950s allowed independent producers the chance to make a film for under $20,000 and earn a million dollars at the box office, which is exactly what the 3-D film *Robot Monster* did in 1953 for producer-director Phil Tucker and distributor Astor Pictures.

Independent producers could also now land a lucrative distribution deal with one of the larger Hollywood studios once their film was made, in turn seeing their product reach wider audiences than it might have through other means. This was the case when Paramount bought the rights to *The Blob* from Tonylyn Productions in 1958, with the film earning over $4 million, while the Italian-made *Hercules* earned $5 million with distribution from Warner Bros. in 1959. Many low-budget films were able to find as much first-run screen time as their big-budget major studio peers if audience demand (or a studio's expectations thereof) proved sufficient. Whereas the programmers of old merely benefited the major studios, the new state of low-budget filmmaking allowed the independents the chance to benefit financially when a B-film found success with mass audiences.

The 1950s B-film was the turning point between the vanishing era of Poverty Row and the modern-day version of low-budget filmmaking in which a small independent film can find itself to be an unexpectedly huge hit. Somewhere between the Bowery Boys and Range Busters films of the 1940s and high-grossing independently made horror films such as *The Texas Chainsaw Massacre* (1974) and *The Blair Witch Project* (1999) lie the films of Phil Tucker,

Robot Monster (Three Dimension Pictures/Astor Pictures Corporation, 1953)

Roger Corman, and their contemporaries—filmmakers who pioneered a new way of making films outside of the major Hollywood studios on an extremely reduced budget. The B-movie label often gets applied to everything from 1960s Russ Meyer films and Mario Bava Euro-horror to 1970s blaxploitation films, 1980s slasher films, and 1990s direct-to-video entries. With the films that make up all of these categories being so far removed from the Bs of the 1930s/1940s and their studio-system-driven mode of production, the 1950s stands as a key transitional era in low-budget filmmaking—a period in which the B-movie's role in the film industry was fought over by major and minor studios alike.

Given the wide range of such films, the question of how B-movies are to be defined and exactly which films should and should not be classified as Bs looms large. Certainly one of the most complex aspects of studying the B-movie is trying to arrive at its exact definition. The term is often a loosely used one, inspiring a multitude of interpretations (including this book's notion of the B-film as profit-minded entertainment operating within a relatively reduced fiscal context in comparison to that of higher-budgeted major studio product).[31] Undoubtedly, certain films that some people would readily label a B-film, others would surely not, with the term generally used in two different ways: either in a historical and economic context, or else from a perspective that is more content-driven and focusing largely on such aesthetic elements as acting and directing. The first approach frequently views the antitrust ruling of 1948 as marking the end of the Bs as a product of the classical Hollywood studio system and its reliance on block booking and the double-bill format. The emphasis in this case is primarily on the economic context of these films, rather than on any issues surrounding their lurid or sensational content. In contrast, much of what is written about the Bs by nonhistorians is generally concerned with their aesthetics (i.e., how "bad" they are) and the often provocative nature of their content.

The difference between these two approaches can be understood in the parallel approaches to studying cultural commodities set forth by John Fiske in his book *Understanding Popular Culture*—cultural products may be analyzed according to both their "financial economy" and "cultural economy." The former "circulates wealth," and the label can be applied to the B-movie as an economic product of 1930s/1940s Hollywood. Cultural economy, however, "circulates meanings and pleasures" rather than wealth and is produced by the audience rather than a production studio.[32] Fiske's model of cultural economy is intrinsic to those definitions of the B-movie that are primarily concerned with the meanings and pleasures of the Bs rather than analyzing them as an economic product.

Rather than focus primarily on the B-movie's mode of production as a result of larger filmmaking practices in 1930s/1940s Hollywood, what we might call cultural definitions of the B-movie encompass not only those decades but everything up to the present as well, with new B-movies seemingly released each month. For example, critics called the 2005 Wes Craven thriller *Red Eye* a "brisk, efficient B-movie," "a B-thriller wrapped up in the glossy package of an A-movie," and "a modest B-movie thriller," while the 2007 film *Fracture* starring Ryan Gosling and Anthony Hopkins was described as "just a cheap B-movie with expensive A-list talent."[33]

Critics routinely label even films with extremely high budgets as B-movies. 2007's *X-Men: The Last Stand* cost over $200 million, and 2008's *The Incredible Hulk* had a budget of $150 million, yet the former was described by *New York Magazine* as being "just another big-budget B-movie . . . a fast and enjoyable B-movie, though," while *Entertainment Weekly* referred to the latter as "just a luridly reductive and violent B movie."[34] To call a film such as *X-Men* that grosses nearly half a billion dollars worldwide a B-movie seems entirely ridiculous given that the financial scope of such filmmaking is so vastly different than that of B-movies made in decades past.

For certain viewers, however, B-movies elicit a pleasurable response based on an enchantment with the combination of earnestness and ineptitude (in acting, screenwriting, or directorial ability, or in overall intent or tone) displayed in these films. As one modern newspaper article entitled "The Return of the B-Movie" put it, these are "movies so bad, they're good": "B-movies feature awful acting, bad dialogue and cheap special effects. So, what's not to like?" Journalists frequently employ derisive rhetoric in praise of B-movies, which serves to create such paradoxical evaluations as so-bad-it's-good.[35]

In turn, there has been a tendency among some scholars to discuss 1950s B-movies with an undertone of condescension or bemusement—or treat them as quaint anomalies at best. In *Film History: An Introduction*, Kristin Thompson and David Bordwell acerbically describe Corman's films as featuring "dime-store special effects" with monsters "apparently assembled out of plumbers' scrap and refrigerator leftovers."[36] Even Greg Merritt's *Celluloid Mavericks: A History of American Independent Film*, a serious attempt at chronicling the pioneering efforts of early independent directors, uses condescending rhetoric toward AIP's films in such phrases as "a lot of hokum about the subconscious," "it's good for a few laughs," and "no-budget dreck."[37]

This facetious attitude became crystallized in the late 1970s with the appearance of such books as Harry and Michael Medved's *The Golden Turkey Awards* and Harry Medved and Randy Dreyfuss's *The 50 Worst Films of All Time*. These books present a thoroughly patronizing attitude toward B-movies, despite the authors' profession that such films are "neglected gems" and that they hope their work "will encourage bad-film freaks to come out of the closet and declare themselves." The end result is that such efforts damage the overall status of B-filmmaking, despite what good intentions may have spurred their creation.[38]

This dismissive stance undermines the B-movie's importance to the film industry, viewing its major contribution as offering viewing pleasures of the so-bad-they're-good variety. Within such an approach, B-movies become considered worthy of the attention of camp theory, a predominant framework through which 1950s Bs have been understood in recent decades. Camp functions as what Jeffrey Sconce calls both "a reading strategy that allowed gay men to rework the Hollywood cinema through a new and more expressive subcultural code" and "an aesthetic of ironic colonization and cohabitation." Paul Roen's *High Camp: A Gay Guide to Camp and Cult Films*, for instance, contains entries on such 1950s B films as *The Bride and the Beast* (1958), *Dragstrip Girl* (1957), *Frankenstein's Daughter* (1959), *Glen or Glenda?* (1953), *Hot Rod Gang* (1958), *Jail Bait* (1954), *Queen of Outer Space* (1958), and *Wrestling Women vs. the Aztec Mummy* (1959).[39]

This approach toward the study of B-movies and low-budget films is a limited one, however, given the subjective nature of taste cultures inherent in camp-based criticism. As Greg Taylor notes:

> Cultism and camp are fundamentally aesthetic procedures steeped in highbrow taste, and directed toward the assertion of highbrow distinction—by highbrows themselves, or by those who wish to appropriate such distinction within the middlebrow arena. Yet what makes them somewhat problematic, ultimately, is that as *vanguard* procedures, they carefully veil their aesthetic biases behind an overriding pragmatism and seek to naturalize aesthetic value in the elevated sensibilities of the vanguard critic. The critic's own tastes . . . are not questioned but assumed to be inherently justified and above all useful for getting to the job of artistic reconstruction. Unlike critics of inherent aesthetic value, who at least must confront and gauge the aesthetic assumptions of artists under scrutiny, vanguard critics draw on—but rarely question—their own aesthetic biases, which are used to help create the value of the objects they appropriate.[40]

Since camp theory is a reading strategy and a form of aesthetic response, it has largely concentrated on the surface elements of the B-movies it examines. The focus, in other words, is primarily on the "badness" of these so-called bad movies, with viewers taking an ironic or satiric stance in their assessment of a given film. Yet camp theory is a limited analytic strategy for studying B-movies because it generally does not take into account economic contexts of filmmaking. If these films are bad (some may be, some may not), then they are largely bad due to the fiscal prudence of their creation. Such criticisms of the 1950s B-movie that are rooted in mockery—be it dismissive or playfully affectionate—have served to suppress the importance of these films to the history of cinema. These B-movies may often feature ridiculous plots and characters, but regardless of their particular content it is the patterns of low-budget independent filmmaking they established that proved key to future developments in the film industry as the move away from the classical Hollywood studio system offered room for new talent to emerge from the margins.

The Battle for the Bs is an attempt to steer discussions of the B-movie away from taste-based critical assessments of its seemingly questionable aesthetics and move toward a fiscally oriented understanding of how and why those aesthetics were formed. Notions surrounding the economic aspects of the unique nature of the B-filmmaking process become vital to understanding these films, and how their role in film history was a complex one: How exactly does the low-budget nature of independent cinema determine its mode of production? How is a B-movie limited and/or defined by the low-budget nature of its mode of production, and how does this affect the film's aesthetics? How did B-movies function in, and what is their value to, the changing film marketplace of the 1950s?

Answering these questions can be achieved by way of examining how economic mode of production shapes cultural aesthetics. It has become increasingly difficult to separate considerations of cultural products from their economic implications. "Arguably, what we call culture," says Alan Warde, "and how we separate culture from economy, is almost entirely a function of the general models that we use to characterize societies. We might distinguish between economy and society; or base and superstructure; or economy, civil society and the state; or the economic, the political and the social. Increasingly we seem to distinguish between economy and culture, only to say that there are scarcely separate spheres any more because they are collapsing into one another."[41]

All cultural industries therefore function in an economic context and are subject to fiscal matters that influence the creation of their products and the resulting aesthetics. How films are made (and for how much) inevitably affects what kinds of stories they can tell and how those stories are told. Focusing on the "industrial determinants" of film production, distribution, and exhibition is central to studying the low-budget cinema of the 1950s, as it is these determinants that are at the core of the independent filmmaking process.[42] The mode of production for major studio films is obviously very different from that used by independent filmmakers, who possess much smaller budgets. When filmmakers work with a fraction of the budget used in a typical Hollywood production, everything from script decisions to casting and location choices is determined by cost-effectiveness.

Cinematic aesthetics are therefore often highly influenced by monetary factors, even determined by them in many cases. In turn, my work here seeks to include issues of form and style in its examination of the business of 1950s B-movies. My analysis of individual films often uses economic considerations as a basis for aesthetic analysis. This approach is undertaken in order to demonstrate that what are often considered to be aesthetic questions in film studies may perhaps be better understood by examining the economic factors and industrial context surrounding a given film. A film's content, in other words, is inevitably affected by how that film is made—stylistic choices to do with lighting, camerawork, and set design, among other things, are influenced by a film's budget and what kind of equipment and amenities can be afforded therein. How a director handles his or her actors is similarly affected—the amount of time and resources available for rehearsals and multiple takes also comes down to what the budget allows. Analyzing the film industry's economic mode of production in the 1950s, specifically how films are produced, distributed, and exhibited, is crucial to an understanding of the 1950s B-movie—where it came from, what it was, and what it would lead to.

Film history is an evolving process and has been subject to past revision with such critical movements as the rise of genre theory and auteur theory. The 1950s has been chronicled as an era of change in Hollywood, a time in which filmmakers were forced to adapt in the face of internal pressures such as the antitrust rulings and external pressures such as the growing competition from television. The role of the B-movie in particular during this era of change has not been fully examined, and it is my hope that this book will begin to address this need and allow other scholars to build upon my work here. This book presents its account of the transitions that occurred in low-budget filmmaking in the 1950s largely in the form of a historical narrative, given that this kind of approach has rarely been attempted by other authors in a full-length format (and given that many books written about the B-movie are now long out of print). This approach was born partially out of my own frustrations teaching university film courses and wanting to assign to my students a book that approached the B-film as an industrial entity, but finding nothing available.

This book is therefore written primarily as a historical account of a particular cinematic entity within a period of significant and fairly rapid industrial change. Several chapters draw extensively on a wide range of trade publications from the period such as *Variety*, the *Hollywood Reporter*, *Motion Picture Daily*, and *Motion Picture Herald*, along with such journalistic sources as the *New York Times*, *Newsweek*, and *Business Week*. These sources, along with numerous published interviews with key B-film creators, are used not only to capture a sense of how the industry's mood toward B-movies evolved throughout the 1950s but also to uncover new information about the practices of numerous smaller film companies, given that little actual archival material relating to them exists publicly. When documents no longer remain from a low-budget company that may never have kept thorough records in the first place, it becomes necessary to consult trade publications while trusting that the facts presented therein are accurate. I have attempted to overcome the problem of potentially unreliable reporting by cross-referencing information with other publications whenever possible.

While the use of archival research conducted through accessing both private collections (a logistically difficult task) and public institutions such as university library collections (in which information is available only for certain major studios) would undoubtedly have turned up valuable information and allowed for further cross-referencing of trade publication material, I ultimately decided that this approach was beyond the scope of this current project (and beyond the resources of this particular young scholar). My work here is therefore intended as an entry point to the study of B-filmmaking, in the hopes that more scholars might turn their attention to the Bs and continue to unearth new facts and perspectives that such archival research might provide.

At the same time, the decision to use trade publications was made in the hopes of providing an industry-wide overview of the changes that occurred in the 1950s, in the voices of those journalists covering the industry and of those whom they interviewed. The rhetoric of the trades can tell us much about the prevailing attitudes to do with B-films and the industry as a whole, and about where many saw it going—especially concerning the ebb and flow of confidence and doubt that occurred throughout the highly transitional era of 1950s Hollywood. I have therefore attempted to preserve as much of the original articles as possible rather than paraphrase them, in order to allow the reader to engage with what was written about the 1950s B-movie in the particular rhetoric of its time—something that becomes especially significant when looking at the ways in which the terminology itself surrounding low-budget filmmaking was understood throughout the decade.

The 1950s B-movie is vitally important to the study of film, serving as a bridge between its previous incarnations in the classical Hollywood studio system of prior decades and the many new forms of low-budget filmmaking that would emerge in the 1960s and beyond. To fully understand its role in the film industry, it must be considered first and foremost as an economic product—a framework that is rarely the preferred way in which viewers approach films: "Movie buffs tend to be as ignorant about the movie industry as they are knowledgeable about its products," says David Gordon. "The very word 'product' is one they find distasteful, reminding them as it does of a manufacturing process churning out items for mass consumption. People who love films seem to need to bless the object of their affection with the sacred title of art."[43]

Yet an understanding of the economic framework of any cinematic product—be it art, trash, or otherwise—is crucial to its full comprehension, given how the study of a film's mode of production can prove essential to analyzing its aesthetics. B-movies are something that many see as being part of the cinematic underbelly, a notion that may evoke either delight or displeasure according to one's personal tastes. B-movies might be considered trashy, cheesy, corny, funny, amusing, entertaining, and/or so-bad-they're-good, but any consideration of the B-film must start with the acknowledgment that they are low-budget films, and that fiscal concerns are crucial to how such films are made. Everything that is good, bad, or otherwise about the Bs stems from their economic context, and this edict is at the heart of this book's examination of how the 1950s B-movie established new forms of independent low-budget filmmaking.

1

Hollywood in Transition

The Business of 1950s Filmmaking

The 1950s B-movie became something that stood apart from its predecessors—not a mere continuation of what came before, but an entity with its own unique role in the history of cinema. While stemming from the production, distribution, and exhibition patterns of the B-movies of previous decades, in the wake of industry-wide change 1950s Bs established innovative ways of making films and getting them before audiences. With the end of block booking, B-movies were no longer necessarily subject to flat-rate rentals, and by the end of the decade many B-films would command the same percentage-based distribution deals in first-run markets that their A-film counterparts routinely enjoyed. The catalyst for the B-movie's transformation was the 1948 Supreme Court antitrust ruling, which brought about a film industry wherein financial risk became much more palpable, but in which independent filmmakers would find a wealth of opportunities that were largely unattainable in prior years.

Although the 1948 ruling was the most consequential of its kind in the history of American cinema, it was not the first time that Hollywood was faced with an antitrust lawsuit. In essence, the major studios had decades to prepare for the effects of the 1948 ruling, with the Federal Trade Commission investigating Hollywood's business practices as early as 1921. Previous attempts at ending vertical integration, while often producing a temporary impact, were ultimately unsuccessful. The Antitrust Division of the Justice Department first began focusing on the problem of vertical integration among the major Hollywood studios in 1938, resulting in such government lawsuits as *United States v. Fox West Coast Theatres Corp.* in 1939 and *United States v. Paramount Pictures* in 1940. While the former was withdrawn, the latter saw the five studios that owned theaters sign a three-year consent decree permitting them to keep their existing theaters while acquiring no further ones, and limiting their distribution practices to selling blocks of only five films at a time. In place of harsh organizational reform, an arbitration board was established and the studios were instructed to work together in developing a new economic model that would eliminate the monopolistic problems of vertical integration.[1]

This 1940 decree proved ineffectual because its provisions were extremely favorable to the major studios, essentially drafted so as to allow them "escape clauses" should any major hardship be felt.[2] In a 1942 letter entitled "Shall Block Booking of Motion Pictures Be Permitted to Return?" the Society of Independent Motion Picture Producers addressed their concerns to Thurman Arnold, the assistant attorney general of the United States. They argued that the method of film distribution required of the five integrated major studios by the 1940 ruling "no longer is binding upon such defendants." The letter concludes:

> It is incredible that the Department of Justice, having already achieved signal success in abolishment of certain phases of block booking and having in mind the public interest, will subscribe to any retrogressive, substitution sales scheme that incorporates any of the objectionable features of the present five picture group plan, or countenances the revival of licensing feature films in advance of their completion. On the contrary, the protection of the public, the exhibitor and the producer against any kind of group selling is what the situation demands. Let each feature picture be sold on its individual merits, after its content is known to the prospective buyer through obligatory trade showings.[3]

In light of such concerns, the government reopened *United States v. Paramount Pictures* in 1944 with the intent of fully divorcing the studios' exhibition channels from their production-distribution activities. The case went to trial in federal district court in 1945, and the court ruled against the studios in June of 1946. The decision was appealed but ultimately upheld on May 3, 1948, by the Supreme Court, which found "a marked proclivity for unlawful conduct" on behalf of the major studios.[4]

Sixty-four theatrical film distributors existed in 1944, and thirteen more in 1946, yet only eleven distributed their films nationwide. Eight of these eleven distributors were Hollywood studios—Paramount, Twentieth Century–Fox, Warner Bros., Loew's/MGM, RKO, Columbia, Universal, and United Artists—while the remaining three distributors were from Poverty Row: Monogram, Republic, and Producers Releasing Corporation. The first five of these eleven studios were considered the true Hollywood majors since they were fully integrated, owning production facilities, distribution channels, and significant theatrical chains in which to exhibit their own films. Despite their only releasing approximately 40 percent of all feature films, the combined power of the five majors controlled overall distribution practices within the industry and ensured that the availability of cinematic product was not equal to all theaters.

For distribution purposes, the major studios established thirty different markets across the country for what was known as a "run-zone clearance" system: each market contained numerous different zones, with each zone's theaters being classified by run (first, second, third, etc.). Downtown theaters in major cities were designated as first-run and played the newest films at the highest prices. Second-run theaters charged less and were located in a city's business districts, while subsequent-run theaters charged even less and were located in communities outside of the city. Films would typically move between zones after a period ranging between two and six weeks, although larger markets could see films remain in circulation for up to a year.[5]

This distribution system, known as "admission price discrimination," was a dominant factor in the major studios' control over the marketplace. While owning only approximately 15 percent of all national theaters, the majors were still able to use block booking with the remaining independent theaters, most of which actively sought subsequent-run distribution. In this way, despite the fact that the majority of theaters across the country were not vertically integrated, the major studios were able to establish control over cinematic distribution practices.[6]

Block booking, the fixing of admission prices by nonexhibitors, uniform systems of runs and clearances, licensing terms favoring affiliated theaters, and joint ownership of theaters by major studios, or by a major and an independent theater owner, were all made illegal by the 1948 decision.[7] As a result, the major studios entered into consent decrees aimed at eliminating the practice of vertical integration. A report prepared by the Antitrust Division of the Department of Justice stated that "the granting of equal opportunity to independent exhibitors" was the chief success of the 1948 ruling, which would "give every exhibitor the same opportunity to license product as that enjoyed by his competitor." Whereas vertical integration had "created a power on the part of the defendants to exclude competition from the distribution and exhibition markets," the new ruling would instead "create an open market for the distribution of pictures" through "opening up all closed competitive situations and by requiring the divestiture of theaters" by Paramount, RKO, Loew's/MGM, Warner Bros., and Twentieth Century–Fox.[8]

Although it would eventually have enormous consequences, the Paramount case did not prompt Hollywood to take immediate action, perhaps due to the belief that this antitrust ruling would ultimately prove to be as ineffectual as those in past years. Yet in the years that followed, exhibitors and executives alike would have much to say as the effects began to take hold within the industry—bringing important changes in how B-films functioned in Hollywood, and in how the growing profits being reaped from low-budget product frequently went to companies other than the major studios.

The Old Order Changeth

One major shift in the cinematic landscape of the 1950s came in the downward trend in theater attendance. The year 1946 saw a record high of 82 million paid admissions per week, but by 1955 it was down to less than 46 million weekly, a decline of 45 percent during a time when the population rose in the United States by 26 million.[9] The reasons for this steep decline are manifold, but the end result was a change in industry organization. In previous decades, Hollywood films were produced under the studio system, which entailed a standardized mode of production and the division of specialized labor within a factory-like environment. The studio system existed in its purest form for a period of fifteen to twenty years, from the early 1930s to the late 1940s. As such, the classical studio system only represents approximately one third of Hollywood's entire history up until 1950. Since its origins in the early twentieth century, Hollywood has gone through several versions of corporate organization, each with its own distinct mode of production. While directors held primary control between 1907 and 1914, producers soon began to take control as the major Hollywood studios emerged. By the early 1930s the "producer unit" system that exemplified classical Hollywood's assembly-line mode of production became dominant, while the "package-unit" system emerged in the 1940s and became established practice in the 1950s.[10]

As a result of this evolving structure of industrial organization, the mode of production of Hollywood filmmaking was constantly changing. Hollywood was, is, and will continue to be an unstable set of relations between various institutions: between bureaucratic organizations and production units, between production companies and distributors, between distributors and exhibitors, and other such variations. Balances of power and degrees of control shift over time, but the economic imperative behind these relationships remains absolute. With the antitrust ruling and the end of studio system filmmaking—along with increasing competition from the new television medium—new patterns in production and distribution emerged in the 1950s in the face of newfound marketplace uncertainty.

Some patterns proved easy for Hollywood to adapt to, such as the increasing growth of distribution to foreign countries. In the early 1940s, foreign markets accounted for between 20 and 25 percent of all film rentals, whereas by the mid-1950s Hollywood saw nearly half of its income deriving from foreign markets.[11] Other new patterns proved to be relatively more radical for the industry because they were more systemic. Where Hollywood's product was once characterized by an integrated system, the emphasis was soon placed on the individual units as the move was made to a package-unit system of production that concentrated on single films:

> Rather than an individual company containing the source of the labour and materials, the entire industry became the pool for these. With the old producer-unit system, a producer had a commitment to make six to eight films per year with a fairly identifiable staff. The package-unit system, however, was a short-term film-by-film arrangement. . . . Instead of a filming unit owning the entire means of production for use in film after film, the unit leased or purchased the pieces for a particular project from an array of support firms. Costumes, camera, special effects technology, lighting and recording equipment were specialties of various support companies, available for component packaging.[12]

As Hollywood responded to new marketplace challenges, the move to a package-unit system allowed studios to significantly reduce their operating costs. With the industry facing a rapid series of social, economic, and technological changes, studios were forced to constantly adapt if they were to survive. One of the biggest changes that studios faced was accepting the fact that their products now entailed a far greater amount of financial risk than in the days of vertical integration—a factor that also brought with it new potentials in financial reward for studios of all sizes.

The notion of risk is central to understanding the economics of filmmaking, a business that is regularly portrayed as being inherently uncertain. The Motion Picture Association of America, the film industry's primary trade association, emphasizes this financial danger by stating: "Moviemaking is an inherently risky business. Contrary to popular belief that moviemaking is always profitable, in actuality, only one in ten films ever retrieves its investment from domestic exhibition. In fact, four out of ten movies *never* recoup the original investment."[13]

Studio executives were all too aware of such risks in the 1950s. Charles M. Reagan, vice president and general sales manager of Loew's, summed up the new state of economic risk faced by the studios in 1956:

> We are presented with a most difficult problem when we undertake the production of a picture which will not be released for many months after production begins since its measure of public acceptance is not yet known. This risk, now increased greatly by changes in public tastes, and made still greater by increased costs and unusual expenses of experimentation, limits even our boldest attempts to make more motion pictures. In the past, the failure of a picture costing $2 million

or $3 million might be offset by public acceptance of a number of less costly productions. Today, outstanding pictures are for the most part very expensive productions and if for unforeseeable reasons one or two do not meet the final test of public acceptance, the success of a whole year's production effort can be seriously affected.[14]

Many considered the film industry to be in a state of financial crisis at the start of the 1950s. While in 1946 "net theater profits on admissions alone amounted to more than $290 million; by 1953, admission receipts had fallen off so that total theater expenses exceeded admissions by more than $165 million."[15] Ticket sales rapidly declined as the decade began, with *Motion Picture Daily* reporting in March of 1950 that box office receipts were off by 17 percent in the previous four months as compared to the same period just a year earlier.[16] By the middle of the decade, an estimated 5,200 theaters were not making a profit, with another 5,700 more barely breaking even. Some exhibitors were only able to endure due to the strength of their concession sales, making them little more than glorified popcorn merchants. Indoor theaters in rural areas and smaller towns as well as those playing subsequent-run films in larger cities were most affected, and by 1956 total theater expenses were still exceeding ticket sales in America, forcing thousands of exhibitors to close their doors.[17]

While the rise of television is typically offered as the primary reason for the decline of theater attendance, at the time some within the film industry doubted whether the new medium would be a threat, presuming that the television set was "basically only a movie projection machine in the home."[18] Despite any initial beliefs that it would be merely supplementary to the film industry, most exhibitors and studios quickly accepted the fact that television was strong competition. Producer Samuel Goldwyn stated in 1949, "The thoroughgoing change which sound brought to picture making will be fully matched by the revolutionary effects (if the House on Un-American Activities Committee will excuse the expression) of television upon motion pictures. I predict that within just a few years a great many Hollywood producers, directors, writers, and actors who are still coasting on reputations built up in the past are going to wonder what hit them."[19]

Goldwyn's predictions proved astute concerning television's ultimate impact on the film industry (although, as chapter 5 will demonstrate, the relationship between the two media—and the role of the Bs therein—was often far more complex than many realized). A study conducted by Sindlinger & Co. reported that in the first four years of television audience growth, from 1948 to 1952, "in those areas where television reception was good, 23 percent of the theaters closed compared to only 9 percent of the theaters closing in areas where television was not available." One hundred and eight stations were active in this period due to a Federal Communications Commission freeze on new stations in 1948, lifted in April of 1952. During these four years, audiences spent 40 percent less on movies in areas with television reception, while ticket sales actually rose by 3 percent in those areas without television. Even more tellingly, the Sindlinger study noted that prior to the debut of television in a given area, "roughly 60 percent of the adults attend the movies more than once a month while this number drops to less than 30 percent when television ownership in an area approaches 70 percent."

The study concluded that "once an area becomes saturated with television, theater closings come to practically a halt; but during the period in which television is building up in an area, the rate of theater closings is high," estimating that "40 to 45 percent of the theaters close in an area by the time a city or State becomes completely saturated with television."[20] In 1946, nearly 20 percent of money spent on entertainment by the American public was on movie tickets, as compared to less than 15 percent on radio, television, and music records. By 1957, however, Americans spent only 7 percent on films and 23 percent on rival media.[21]

Hollywood studios contributed to this trend by selling portions of their film libraries to the television networks. As audiences became accustomed to seeing feature films at home at no additional cost, many viewers no longer felt the need to pay money to see them in theaters. By 1956, all of the major Hollywood studios except Paramount and Universal had sold films to television. In an eight-month period during 1955 and 1956, more than 2,600 films were sold to networks. MGM accepted $50 million for a portion of its film library, a move that prompted actor Clark Gable to offer his opinion on the studios' ready acceptance of big payoffs for their older films: "It is a direct invitation to the public to stay at home by their TV sets, and I know it is going to hurt my box office as well as other players earning their livelihood from this business." With his older films now shown on television, Gable noted that when his new films were released in theaters he was essentially in competition with himself.

Some studio executives realized the fact that viewers would not pay to see the same product they could get at home, and so believed that Hollywood had to make better pictures than those of years past. Y. Frank Freeman, vice president of Paramount, described how audiences "will no longer buy tickets at the theater, except to see the very highest form of entertainment, far superior to what they can see on television free. For this type of entertainment they will pay an admission price. For anything less they will not."[22] In a move toward creating a seemingly higher form of motion pictures (a notion implying that lower-budgeted films were suddenly a lower form of entertainment—or perhaps that they always were), Hollywood began using new technologies in order to differentiate its product from that shown on television. The strategy was to play upon the perceived weaknesses of the television medium—its reduced screen size, often-diminished picture quality, and lack of color. Widescreen cinema became prevalent with the development of anamorphic cinematography, in which an anamorphic camera lens condenses the filmed image and a similar-lensed projector expands the image onto a rectangular screen. This process entailed an aspect ratio (width to height) different from the older, squarish 1.33:1, which became the approximate dimensions of the television screen. Twentieth Century–Fox developed a widescreen process called CinemaScope for 1953's *The Robe* featuring an aspect ratio of 2.35:1, almost twice as wide as the former ratio. Paramount in turn created VistaVision, a nonanamorphic widescreen process with an aspect ratio of 1.85:1.

The term "flat films" entered industry terminology during this period, designating those films with a smaller aspect ratio than the new widescreen productions. When CinemaScope debuted in 1953, Twentieth Century–Fox chairman Spyros Skouras told shareholders that "the studio's library of over 900 flat films would soon be sold to television" because the success of new widescreen processes "would render the flat format obsolete and thus destroy the theatrical marketability of these pictures."[23] (It would be two more years, however, before Fox and the other major Hollywood studios began to sell their films to television in 1955.) Along with such widescreen processes, an increased use of color cinematography served to create a more spectacular product as well. In 1952, Eastman Kodak advanced previous developments in Technicolor by creating a process known as Eastman Color. Its faster and cheaper film stock allowed color cinematography to suddenly become more affordable and produce a better image quality.

With these and other technological changes affecting cinema in the 1950s, films were rapidly becoming a different product than they had been in years past. In turn, the major studios actively began to change their approach to filmmaking, concentrating on blockbusters by making fewer and bigger films—a lower number of total films per year, but with bigger budgets for each individual film. This situation soon resulted in an overall product shortage that allowed many new independent companies to thrive as the B-movie marketplace readjusted itself to these new conditions.

Declining attendance numbers meant that 1950s audiences were becoming more selective, with many people choosing only to go to films with the biggest stars or most spectacular production values.[24] One way that Hollywood sought to lure audiences was through the technology of 3-D films, which used stereoscopic cinematography to create the illusion of greater image depth and a spatially separated foreground. 3-D films such as *Bwana Devil* (1952), *House of Wax* (1953), *It Came from Outer Space* (1953), and *Creature from the Black Lagoon* (1954) were extremely popular with audiences and were considered by many executives and exhibitors as the key to boosting sagging revenues. One Atlanta theater-chain owner told a meeting of the Theatre Owners of Georgia in 1953 that "regular films have reached their zenith" and 3-D would be "a sorely needed shot in the arm." He saw 3-D films as further indicative of the trend toward fewer but bigger films, predicting that this practice would result in higher box-office grosses as well.[25]

While the blockbusters were indeed generating extraordinary box office numbers, films of more average budgets were simultaneously proving unsuccessful. As one 1951 *Variety* headline put it, the industry faced a new marketplace wherein films "Gotta Be Smash Hits, or Else." The article posits that there was "No In-Betweens on Pic Product," claiming that filmmaking had now become "a 'business of hits.'" Films "of the caliber which had been drawing moderate b.o. return in the past [were] now resulting in deficit operations, particularly in first-run locations."[26] The trend continued throughout the next year, with *Variety* proclaiming 1952 a year of "Big Grosses, Low Profits" and "dramatic transition," in which the "watchwords were Experimentation and Novelty," as marked by such emerging trends as 3-D, widescreen processes, and "super-epic Hollywood productions."[27]

With this increased focus on producing "greater" pictures, the majority of films actually failed to make a profit. In fact, *Variety* reported in 1951 that only 20 percent of all films made by both major and independent studios were currently showing a profit. This situation was not as problematic for the major studios, "since they have a whole program to fall back on," and "the profits of the 20% winners normally overcome the losses on the other 80%." Independent filmmakers, however, often found this state of affairs to be devastating due to their smaller release schedules: "They don't have enough product to assure that the law of averages will work to give them their share of nut-toppers. As a result, there's heavy turnover in indie production ranks."[28] While such turnover continued to varying degrees throughout much of the decade, several of the new independent companies that emerged found success—in turn signaling a shift in the industrial role of low-budget filmmaking.

Independent Production

The rise of the package-unit system was declared to be the "End of an Era" in a 1956 *Films in Review* article: "Until recently, it was standard operating procedure for a major studio to produce its own motion pictures," as opposed to films being made by "autonomous or semi-autonomous, independent units. A major studio, in addition to being a prime contractor, is now a sub-contractor also."[29] If it truly was the end of an era, then it was also the beginning of an entirely new age for independent filmmaking. Writing in 2004, producer

Barbara Boyle described how the "contemporary independent movement can be traced to the 1950s," whereby movies are created outside of the traditional confines of Hollywood filmmaking. In describing what she calls "the independent spirit," Boyle points to directors such as Roger Corman, Russ Meyer, and John Cassavetes as key creators working outside of "the traditional studio pipeline."

Their productions, like modern independent filmmaking, were inherently more risky than those made by the major studios, entailing radically different production methods. With financial risk far greater than it had been in recent years, independent filmmakers often struggled to fund their films—a symptom of their maverick status within the industry. "Economy of means continues to be an independent hallmark," says Boyle, describing a condition as true today as it was in the 1950s. "The truly independent producer today cobbles together financing from several sources in exchange for distribution rights defined not by media but by territory. . . . The producer of an independent film is much more responsible for obtaining financing than the studio-hired producer."[30]

The process of financing independent films in the 1950s typically involved three monetary categories—first money, second money, and completion money. First money usually comprised 60 percent of a film's budget and was obtained via a bank loan at a 6 percent interest rate. It was generally the last source of financing obtained by producers but took its name from the fact that it was the first money to be repaid. Second money, therefore, was the first to be raised but the second to be repaid. Coming from private capital, it represented 40 percent of a film's budget. Given that many films do not make a profit (up to 80 percent, as noted), second money constituted the most risk for a producer since bank loans were the first to be repaid. A common second-money arrangement came in the form of deferrals, whereby artists or technicians defer their salaries in return for a percentage of the film's net profit.

Once a producer raised second money for a film, there were usually few problems in obtaining first money from a bank, which kept the second money as a deposit. Both the bank and the private-capital group required completion guarantees from a producer, to ensure that the film they invested in was finished. If a film went over budget, completion money became a third source of financing that a producer had to obtain. This source of funding was wide-ranging with no standard arrangement, although completion-money groups typically demanded a 5 to 15 percent share of the producer's profits.

In order for an independent film to make a profit, however, it must obtain distribution. Therefore, it is important to distinguish at this point between what Boyle designates as "truly independent" filmmakers and those Hollywood producers, directors, and even actors who established their own production companies. Writing in 1955, indie director Terry Sanders defined independent films in that decade as those "produced by comparatively small organizations which are financed individually (picture by picture), as opposed to films produced by large companies (MGM, Warner Bros., Paramount, Twentieth Century–Fox, Columbia, Universal, and RKO) operating on capital raised on a corporate basis."[31]

By 1954, *Variety* began to notice a difference between independent producers working outside of the Hollywood "pipeline" and those who worked in conjunction with the major studios under the package-unit system. "When You Say 'Indie' Use Quotes," cautions one headline: "In large measure, the term independent production will now have to be written in quotes. For the independent, with few exceptions, is more and more wrapped up in partnership with major-scale production and distribution." In response to the problems that independents often have in securing financing, the article notes, the major studios "are arranging for all or part of the financing as a way of luring indies . . . to their lots." The benefit to the Hollywood majors is that "studio activity is maintained and overhead costs held down," while they take "a cut of the picture profits and [provide their] distribution affiliates with added releases."[32]

Various articles from this period highlight the impact that independent filmmaking was beginning to have within the film industry at the time, demonstrating the distinctions between the emerging varieties of "indies" as well as the disparity surrounding how this term was used within the industry. In 1947, Fredric Marlowe called independent filmmaking a "powerful new force [that] has shaken the majors as they haven't been jolted since the advent of sound." He noted that there were 160 independent production companies making films in 1947, fifteen times the number of those operating in 1940. Collectively, these independent producers had "a production schedule of 285 features during the next year, or about 50 per cent of Hollywood's total feature output."

Included among Marlowe's list of independents, however, are such familiar names as David O. Selznick, Howard Hughes, Walt Disney, and Charlie Chaplin, along with directors William Wyler, Leo McCarey, Fritz Lang, George Stevens, and Preston Sturges. All of these men had previously either worked for or had their films distributed by major Hollywood studios, hence the need to "use quotes" when referring to them as independents. Furthermore, Marlowe lists such actors as James Cagney, Bing Crosby, John Garfield, Paulette Goddard, Burgess Meredith, and Ginger Rogers as being among those who had joined the ranks of independent producers.[33] Such examples are more symptomatic of the change from the producer-unit to the package-unit mode of production in Hollywood than of Boyle's "independent spirit," with the latter indicative of those creators operating outside of traditional institutional structures, many of whom were producers and directors making B-films in the 1950s.

In contrast with these quote-unquote independents, Hall Bartlett and Stanley Kramer made the case in respective *Films in Review* articles in 1951 and 1955 that becoming an independent producer essentially means working in opposition to Hollywood filmmaking. "A truly independent motion picture producing company is a fighting company," said Bartlett.[34] Similarly, Kramer— himself an independent producer—argued that the true indies consist of those willing to become "a self-styled originator and quadruple-threat man who can move in several directions at the same time and wind up the day's work by expertly sweeping out the studio after everyone else has gone home."[35] Here, Kramer paints the picture of an operation that is decidedly smaller in scale than that typically mounted in Hollywood. The notion of the producer sweeping up the lot at the end of the day is more exemplary of low-budget filmmaking than of the "independents-incorporated" described by Marlowe.

In analyzing the indies' mode of production, Bartlett offered a list of various conditions that independent producers must consistently face. First, in terms of financing one's film, "you learn to look at your project with a banker's cautious and commercial eye." Furthermore, one must be "willing to gamble on getting a salary only after all other charges have been met." Independent producers must also possess "the courage to gamble, within limited budget restrictions, on [their] own inventiveness." An inordinate amount of time and money spent on marketing is often required, as a "key part of independent production is publicity and exploitation, particularly when the subject is unusual."

What's more, said Bartlett, independent filmmakers face poorer odds in getting their films shown to the public, because "the independent does not usually have a fifty-fifty chance for a fair deal in distribution":

> It is a fight all the way. The first thing that happens is that a major tries to buy the picture at practically cost, allowing only a very small profit, which is supposed to be sufficient reward for the independent producer who delivers them a picture to complete their programs which had cost them nothing in the terms of risk. The major companies know the independent does not have a great deal of money, and they feel they have the winning hand. Some companies will make contracts they know they will never live up to, and dare the independent to sue them, knowing they can tie him up in a costly suit for a long time, and gambling he will either settle for a part of what is due him or will not fight at all. Therefore, when the all-important trip to New York comes, you find yourself on your knees again, hoping and praying you will get a deal the picture deserves.[36]

The acrimony evidenced in Bartlett's rhetoric here is symptomatic of the struggles that true independents faced in getting their films made and distributed. It is doubtful, for example, that such "independents" as Bing Crosby and James Cagney were ever down on their knees in apprehension about their financial future.

The economic strength of independent filmmaking was highly disputed in the early 1950s, with trade publications regularly publishing conflicting information as to the relative strength or weakness of independent productions as a whole during this period. *Variety* reported in November of 1950 that independent filmmaking had "reached such a low ebb that producers haven't even been calling to seek loans." According to one bank executive, "Declining grosses, the question mark about distributors and the unavailability of second money . . . have created a situation in which it is not propitious for the independent flower to blossom."[37]

Similarly, *Motion Picture Daily* quoted producer Joseph Kaufman's more succinct summation that independent filmmaking needed a "shot in the arm."[38] Other reports detailed how financing was becoming difficult to obtain even for those independent producers who wanted it. In reference to the ongoing war in Korea, a January 1951 *Variety* article noted how a rise "in financing requests for war industries is making it increasingly difficult for indie producers to get bank coin for production. While bankers will continue to take care of their old customers, the door virtually is being closed to newcomers, according to bank sources."[39] On April 3, 1951, in response to decreased production and overall industry decline, a group called the Theatre Owners of America declared that its members were prepared to do "everything possible to encourage independent production, even to the point of underwriting the financing for the independent producer."[40]

While these sources describe a critical shortage in independent production, other reports from the same period contradict this notion, heralding an era of extraordinary growth and opportunity for independent filmmakers. *Variety* declared that while "most indies were scratching for coin and many went out of business" between 1947 and 1949, 1950 saw an "anticipated upturn" of independent production. Citing increased competition among major studios for independent product, the article noted that funding was becoming easier to obtain, with most studios "offering indies completion bonds and other aids to financing."[41]

Confidence was still high in February of 1951, with the report that the "volume of independent films channeled through majors in participation deals is hitting a new high as the companies are increasingly reaching out to bolster releasing schedules." In such deals the studio "supplies second money and guarantees for production. With this accomplished, indies have little trouble at all obtaining initial coin from the banks."[42]

In fact, *Variety* declared 1951 to be a "Banner Indie Year" in one headline, going on to describe how the "number of independent films seriously slated already tops 50 and more are expected in the spring when the blossoming greenness of easier financing is expected to become apparent. If they all come to bud, 1951 may go down in film history as the year of the independent renaissance. And at the very worst, it will be known as the year of the most optimistic announcements."[43]

Further optimism was soon displayed when *Variety* reported that "distribs this year are supplying the market with the greatest volume of films since before WW2." Along with an increase in production from the Hollywood studios themselves, "accounting for the overall boost is the fact numerous indie producers are swinging back into action after a long hiatus."[44] *Motion Picture Daily* confirmed this trend, with a headline stating, "25% Rise in Independent Films Seen." The article accounts for this growth by arguing that it "is traditional for independents to make good pictures at costs well below what the majors must pay in view of their large overhead"; hence the indies "have 'more inducement' than the majors have to increase their output."[45]

Whether independent production was in need of a "shot in the arm" or was in the midst of a "renaissance" in the early 1950s, there was generally agreement that if independent filmmakers were going to be successful, they ultimately needed to be different from the major studios. In order to succeed in a changing marketplace, Kramer declared in 1949, "the independent producer must take a run at something different, and also be prepared to take a fall. If the independent can keep going, he will be in a better position to satisfy the public. If the independent can stay in business through the transition, he will be better able to cope with the new medium better than the majors with their overheads." He further stressed that the independent producer "who attempts these days to challenge the majors studios must have a creative approach."[46]

Producer Philip A. Waxman echoed this emphasis on originality, stating that the market in the 1950s required independent filmmakers to have a "fresh story approach." "Since he cannot compete with the majors," said Waxman, "the independent must start out with an 'offbeat' story." Rather than adhere to formulaic genres that had been successful in the past, a producer could achieve success "from the different manner in which he makes the picture rather than from conformance to conventional story patterns."[47] The kinds of films that had drawn audiences to theaters in prior decades were no longer proving as profitable. New approaches and "offbeat" strategies were becoming a necessity in the new marketplace of the 1950s—a philosophy that the Bs would take in many innovative directions by decade's end.

Audience Patterns

Above all else, independent and major studio filmmakers alike in this period sought to connect with their audience at a time when demographics were shifting rapidly. In 1950, two books summarized the patterns and perceptions surrounding audiences at the start of the decade: Gilbert Seldes's *The Great Audience* and Leo Handel's *Hollywood Looks at Its Audience: A Report of Film Audience Research*. Seldes took a critical, often cynical approach to the film industry, beginning the book by declaring, "Except for the makers of baby foods, no industry in the United States has been so indifferent to the steady falling away of its customers as the movies have been." Referring to statistical research on audiences done over the previous five years, Seldes concluded, "In one generation the movies have lost two thirds of their customers," adding that the film industry has "survived only because a satisfactory birth rate provides new patrons for the seats left empty when people arrive at the years of discretion and stop going to the movies." He went on to compare the reason babies outgrow baby food to the reason film audiences were dwindling in the late 1940s—"in each case the formula no longer satisfies."

Pointing to a series of Gallup polls done by the "Audience Research Institute," Seldes argued that the number of regular moviegoers attending theaters in 1950 was far less than previously imagined:

> The dazzling (and inflated) figure of four billion paid admissions a year dwindles into a probable thirty million separate moviegoers, chiefly young people, many of whom go several times a week; and at the end of the statistical hocus-pocus stands the gaunt figure of a mere thirteen to fifteen million individuals who actually see the basic staple commodity of Hollywood, the A feature-picture. (This is three million less than in 1946—a drop of twenty per cent.) The Audience Research Institute estimates that eight of these thirteen million people are under thirty, so that something like two-thirds of the population is contributing to only one-third of the A-picture audience.[48]

In contrast to this critical study, Handel's book appears incredibly optimistic, at times to the point of naïveté. For example, while Samuel Goldwyn had predicted in the previous year, 1949, that television would have an enormously negative impact on theater attendance, Handel concluded that while "television is beginning to make itself felt in the field of entertainment," the medium was still "too new to permit a prediction of how it will affect the motion picture attendance of tomorrow." Despite the statistics showing steady decline in moviegoing, Handel confidently predicted a rise in theater attendance in the years to come. He noted that consumer spending on recreation was estimated to increase by 32 percent in 1950 as compared to 1940, and to further increase nearly 60 percent by 1960. "Films, as the single largest economic factor in recreation and entertainment," he claimed, "can be expected to absorb nearly a fifth of all money spent on recreation."[49]

Seldes, however, offered statistical information contradicting this prediction. He noted that while families had nearly twice the take-home pay at the end of the 1940s that they did at the start of the decade, "they spent a smaller share of their total income on the movies in 1948 than they had spent at any time in the previous twenty years." He concluded:

> Every inquiry into the reasons why people go less frequently to the movies brings the same answer: there aren't as many good movies as there used to be. According to Elmo Roper, thirty per cent of those who still go to the movies gave this reason. It isn't a scientific statement, but its meaning is clear: people are not sufficiently attracted to the movies that are offered, they do not feel that they have to see them. More than twice as many people say that going to the movies is too expensive, and while this may mean they 'can't afford to go to any movies,' it also includes the meaning that they 'can afford to go only to the movies that seem best' to them.[50]

"The public shops for its pictures as never before," confirmed Louis Phillips of Paramount in 1956.[51] Determining what audiences would respond to proved to be challenging for producers throughout the 1950s—"Public Taste Is Crazy Guesswork," read one *Variety* headline accompanying a Fred Hift article in 1957. In the midst of the uncertainty defining this transitional era, trying to determine audience tastes in a new media landscape made filmmaking an even riskier business. "Vacillating response to certain types of films has company executives in a quandary," wrote Hift, "as to what kind of features they want and need for their release schedules." He blamed "unpredictable audience reaction" for the current crisis, yet this condition would largely persist in the decades to come, making unpredictability a new marketplace reality for Hollywood that continues to endure into the present.

Marketing films in this situation becomes especially difficult. Hift quoted one 1950s "publicity man" as saying, "You never really know what's the right way of publicizing a picture nowadays. . . . Ignore what the picture is about and stress some other angle which you think will appeal to the audience, and you may expire at the box office. Then you kick yourself for not having presented the film for what it really is. But then take it the other way 'round. You tell the truth about a picture, about its art, its appeal, etc. And then it dies. Everybody will be down on you, complaining you didn't make it attractive enough. You almost can't win in this game—unless you have a winner."[52]

Part of the confusion lay in trying to determine exactly who was going to the movies in the 1950s—and how often. One of the most notable reasons for the decline in theater attendance was "not that fewer individuals go to the movies . . . but rather that fewer people go frequently to the movies than before." In 1946, 61 percent of adults went to the movies more than once a month, while that number fell to 26 percent by 1955.[53] This trend worsened in the years immediately following, with *Newsweek* reporting in 1958 that 54 percent of moviegoers "now go to the movies less often than they did 3 years ago." The article did provide a glimmer of hope for the film industry, though, noting that "fully 20% of all moviegoers attend the local palace without knowing beforehand what picture is being shown, which suggests that no matter how bad a film might be, there will always be *some* people to see it."[54]

Of concern to producers, however, was a 1957 survey of *Saturday Evening Post* readers revealing that nearly a quarter of respondents went to the movies once a year or less. In his article entitled "Who Goes to the Movies . . . and Who Doesn't," *Motion Picture Herald* editor Martin Quigley Jr. says of the survey findings: "There was a time when a movie patron was not considered a good one if he or she did not attend a theater once a week, or at the worst, once every two weeks. Taking the entire cross-section in the survey only 43.6 percent attend now once a month or more frequently. Approximately the same percent—44.1 percent attend only quarterly or less frequently."[55]

Audience demographics changed substantially in the 1950s, not least because of suburban development. "America's great inland urban centres are moving away from themselves," wrote Ned Armstrong in *Variety* in 1952. "A major shift in the population centre of gravity has occurred in recent years, and the great residential areas, formerly close to downtown, have gone out to the country," he noted in explanation of why theater attendance had been falling in America's major cities. For those who moved out of the city, downtown theaters were "now an hour or more from the new suburban residential communities which have been built five, 10 and 20 miles distant from 'the loop.'" The article's headline asks, "Suburbia—Key to Legit Future?" while surmising that by the early evening the "new city has gone home, miles away from its daytime centre of activity."[56]

Hollywood eventually came to realize that what urban audiences desired was not the same as what those outside of the major cities wanted. Even rural audiences became the focus of attention as studios pondered how "to lure the so-called 'lost audience' back to theatres." In what *Variety* pithily termed the battle of "Grass vs. Class"—namely "a serious schism between the smalltown rural communities and the large key cities"—exhibitors were demanding "pictures that appeal to family groups." The article speculates that Hollywood might soon be seeing "a return to the type of filmmaking which only recently was considered boxoffice poison."[57]

As studios and exhibitors pondered who their target audiences were and what kinds of films they desired, various changes at the level of exhibition occurred in the 1950s that would profoundly affect B-film programming patterns. Numerous downtown theaters went out of business, and the industry saw a shift away from the presentation of double bills, at least in first-run urban theaters. As B-movie production declined, so too did the need for dual bills, although those exhibitors that specialized in the Bs, such as rural or neighborhood independent theaters, typically continued to program double bills throughout the 1950s. Walter Brooks, director of the International Association of Motion Picture Showmen, saw the decline of the double bill as a positive factor: "Today's problem is to get them to 'go out to the movies' in the first place," he said, "and the top picture is what you have to sell, on the basis that motion pictures are bigger and better than ever. To admit a second choice is diminishing."[58]

When exhibition trends change, cinema spectatorship is also altered. The addition of widescreen processes, 3-D, and Technicolor, and the return of the single feature equated to a change in the product that audiences paid to see, while population shifts and increasing competition from television led to changing audience demographics. In sum, Hollywood was forced—as Handel puts it—to "look at their audience" more closely than ever before.

Drive-In Theaters

One trend in the 1950s that Hollywood eventually embraced was the growing popularity of the drive-in theater, which brought further change to film spectatorship patterns (and proved to be an enormous asset to most of the new B-film studios that emerged in this period). Although drive-ins originated in 1933, they did not begin to flourish until the postwar era. With the car becoming a status symbol, a "car culture" emerged, and the 1950s are commonly referred to as a golden age for drive-ins. While 4,696 indoor theaters—commonly referred to as "hard-tops" in industry rhetoric—closed between 1946 and 1953, with 851 new ones built, this period saw 2,976 drive-ins (or "ozoners") built, with only 342 shutting down.[59]

In July of 1950, one in eight moviegoers saw a film in a drive-in.[60] By 1952, ozoners accounted for 10 percent of total film rentals—*Variety* declared that they were "no longer being looked on by Hollywood as industry stepchildren."[61] Just one year later, that figure would double; drive-ins accounted for over 20 percent of total box office in 1953.[62] The *New York Times* noted in that year that until recently "drive-ins were both scarce and joked about . . . referred to as 'passion pits,' supposedly suitable mainly for convenient parking by amatory twosomes; but if that was ever the case, it certainly is not these days."[63] While many in the industry may have seen drive-ins as being primarily a haven for lusty teenagers as the decade began, *Advertising Age* declared that this was no longer true by the end of the 1950s. The "drive-in viewer is above average in income and education and has a larger than average family," it states.[64] Audiences were also thought of by many in the industry as being distinctly middle-class, with the following advice offered to potential drive-in owners:

> Your first step is to familiarize yourself thoroughly with the area which you think is a likely one for a profitable drive-in operation. Why does it appear a likely one? Perhaps you have noted that it contains a preponderance of wage earners and small salaried "white collar" workers of pretty steady employment, with a plentiful sprinkling of young folks, including teen-agers and small children. If so, you are on the right track. . . . [Also pay] special attention to the number of young married people with small children, and their economic status. They shouldn't be people of means, but they should have the wherewithal to go out once or twice a week in the family automobile.[65]

In order to further appeal to family audiences, many drive-ins provided additional attractions such as children's playgrounds. The *New York Times* reported in 1957 that the drive-in theater was "growing into a miniature amusement park" as the first stage of "evolution into pleasure palaces" and cited particular theaters as featuring "children's centers with swings, slides and other diversions, as well as cafeterias the size of supermarkets."[66] Drive-ins tried many different marketing gimmicks over the course of the decade, such as one Miami theater in 1953 that featured stage shows with circus performers. As a way of luring patrons early, the shows ran before nightfall, at 2:30 in the afternoon, and included "aerialists, trapeze artists and trampolinists." In 1956, one Canadian theater in Winnipeg offered a more practical approach, providing each car with a gallon of free gas.[67]

Nineteen fifty-six proved to be the year that drive-in theaters reached the peak of their popularity, with new records broken on an almost weekly basis in summer months. By the beginning of August, ozoner attendance was estimated at 19 million per week. A number of aspects contributed to the growth: "A larger number of strong boxoffice pictures has been a helpful factor, according to many drive-in operators. An increasing number of ozoners also have been able to outbid hardtops for important first-run showings. Another trend reported is toward larger drive-ins, with a considerable number now accommodating 1000 or more cars."[68]

Just a few weeks later, attendance numbers had risen by over 60 percent, setting a new record with an estimated 31 million patrons per week. In fact, this number was likely much higher, given that "estimates are based primarily on paid admissions and do not entirely reflect car-load attendance where each car buys only one ticket."[69] The following year saw this trend reverse, however, with the *Hollywood Reporter* labeling the 1957 drive-in season as "the worst in years" as attendance fell by 30 percent. The decline was blamed on severe storms and floods closing numerous theaters for extended periods, premature seasonal closings due to the early arrival of cold weather, and later screening times (due to daylight saving time) limiting the number of families attending.[70]

By 1958, it appeared that the car culture alone was no longer enough to bring audiences out to the ozoners, as viewers were becoming more discerning in what films they wanted to see. "Drive-In Patrons Now Choosy Like Hardtops," declared *Variety*, noting that drive-in operators were "now in the same boat as four-wall exhibitors—their patrons, too, have become selective and shop for their pictures":

> Whereas until this year it didn't see to matter to a large segment of ozoner patronage what was holding forth on the screen . . . [it] now is a predominating box office factor. . . . Prior thereto the portion of the public attracted to the drive-ins seemed to come no mater [*sic*] what was showing, just as the film fans did in the good old pre-television days for the four-wall houses. . . . Principal attendance influencing factors as far as the drive-ins were concerned were their novelty, the opportunity they afforded to be outdoors for a few hours on a warm night, etc. So that now it behooves the drive-ins to book skillfully and display the utmost in showmanship the same as indoor houses.

The article concludes by cautioning both producers and exhibitors that the films, "not the drive-ins themselves, must now be sold."[71] While drive-in theaters were one of the most significant—and profitable—changes in cinema spectatorship in the 1950s, their enormous popularity steadily declined in the decades that followed.

I Was a Teenage Spectator

One particular audience demographic became increasingly key to the popularity of drive-ins in the 1950s, as producers discovered that they could find success if they targeted teenage viewers, who had largely been neglected up until then. In *Hollywood Looks at Its Audience*, however, Handel claimed that a decisive factor in his projected rise in theater attendance in the 1950s would be older audience members, not younger ones. His reasoning behind this prediction was that "many of today's older persons could not acquire the movie habit when they were young because they had no chance to see pictures then. This holds especially true for the foreign-born population." He then confidently—but erroneously—boasted of how it "may be safely assumed that a larger population of older people will attend motion pictures in the years to come because of conditioning to this form of entertainment in their youth."[72] Yet as the decade progressed it became clear that the youth market was the one that would prove far more important. *Motion Picture Herald* found, for example, that "52.6 percent of those who attend movies once a week or more are 10 to 19 years of age."[73]

Producer Samuel Arkoff of American International Pictures contended that his studio was quicker than the majors to realize the untapped potential of the teenage audience in the mid-1950s. *Variety*, however, had reported on the trend as early as 1952 in a headline declaring "Teen-agers Best Film Audience." The findings were the result of various research surveys stating that teenagers "rate films as their favorite entertainment," largely because "they're in the 'dating' years and want to go out more often than parents and young marrieds." Most significantly, it states that "regular movie attendance seems to begin around the age of 12. After 19 it falls off sharply. Relatively few persons attend the movies with any regularity after the age of 35."[74] *Variety* later chose a different way of describing older audiences: "Anybody above age 35 is supposed to be home in his or her rocking chair."[75]

The mid-1950s were declared "Hollywood's 'Age of the Teens,'" whereby the film industry had finally become "teenage conscious." *Variety* noted, however, that the major studios were not doing enough to reach what it referred to as "the Coke set," adding that new stars with youthful appeal were needed:

The influence of the teeners—from the bobbysoxers of the Frank Sinatra era to the bluejean worshippers of the late James Dean—has been a social phenomenon of the past 15 years, perhaps reaching its peak during the last decade. The potential of this market has been recognized by the record industry and non-entertainment businesses. Hollywood, however, is regarded as lax in catering to this all important segment of the population whose buying power and king-making ability have reached astronomical proportions in recent years. To be sure, the teen set has not been completely neglected by the film solons. On the other hand, no determined effort has been made to extract the full capacity of the age 13 to 19 group by making pictures especially geared for the youngsters or building performers with "built-in" teen appeal.[76]

Exhibitors were also calling for the film industry to target younger audiences, and to promote new stars with teenage appeal. In 1957, theater-chain owner Norman Rydge declared: "The industry's one objective is to concentrate our selling upon the children, the teen-agers, the adolescents and younger people generally."[77] Leonard Goldenson, president of American Broadcasting–Paramount Theatres, further described a need "for pictures and players with definite appeal to young adults." In explanation, he added, "People in their teens and 20's have an innate need for stories in which they can visualize themselves and for players with whom they can 'associate' and admire as 'buddies.'"[78] Such patronizing rhetoric is perhaps symptomatic of why most within the film industry were so late in reaching younger audiences in the 1950s as compared with the music industry.

Using survey research, the Bureau of Advertising of the American News-paper Publishers Association addressed the buying power of the teenage market in 1956. They determined that there were over 16 million people in the thirteen-to-nineteen age bracket, representing $9 billion in dispos-able income. The study predicted further growth in both figures, estimating 24 million teenagers by 1965, and $14 billion worth "of spending money in their jeans."[79] Furthermore, a portion of revenues generated by teenage film viewers go unaccounted for, given exhibitors' reports that "when youngsters like a picture, they tout it to their parents, a good percentage of whom leave their TV sets to attend the theatre."[80]

As the decade progressed, Hollywood producers eventually realized that audience demographics were skewing decidedly younger than in prior years. By June of 1957, MGM producer Lawrence Weingarten was acknowledging that "fifteen to twenty four is the audience we are aiming at. Those are the kids who don't want to stay home in the first place." Yet rather than listen to the existing research of the previous five years, major studios like MGM apparently had to find out for themselves: "We have arrived at that grouping through audience preview cards," said Weingarten. "It always is 60 to 75 per cent of our audience."[81] United Artists planned a twelve-picture slate of films for 1957, all targeting viewers between the ages of thirteen and twenty. Executive producer Aubrey Schenck noted, "We aren't excluding adult interest by any means . . . but all our pictures will have problems and situations that youngsters recognize and will pay money to see. Let's face it," he added. "Teenage support, in today's market, spells the difference between profit and loss at the box office."[82]

RKO launched a unique marketing campaign aimed at teenagers for its 1956 film *Young Stranger*, which featured seventeen-year-old actor James MacArthur: "High school and college leaders and editors, after viewing the film, will be invited to write reviews of it, with best writeups appearing in metropolitan papers and winning a cash prize, followed later by selection of a national winner from among the local winners."[83] A similar approach was developed in 1959 with the participation of Twentieth Century–Fox and the Cleveland Board of Education. Screenings of new films were held for educators, followed by open discussions that were to "be taped and sent in [their] entirety to the studio which produced the film." Teenagers themselves were also involved in the process; students could "write reviews for their high school papers," with "a contest to select the best one" each term. Winners received a plaque in recognition of their efforts, as did their school.[84] These types of grassroots marketing and research strategies are entirely different, as subsequent chapters will show, from those that many independent studios were concurrently attempting.

The new focus on teenage audiences, however, brought with it some problems for exhibitors, ranging from mild to severe. A relatively uncomplicated issue was whether to charge teenagers at youth or adult rates. One chain of theaters announced an "intermediate price plan for teenagers in the 12-through-17 age bracket," whereby teenagers purchased "laminated plastic cards of identification" in order to receive the discount.[85] Another dilemma came in the form of protest over what films teenagers should be allowed to see. The Diocesan Councils of Catholic Men and Women declared that as "the rule of thumb that may permit some exceptions, high school students should not attend movies which have been evaluated in the A-2—objectionable for adults—category," as determined by the Catholic Legion of Decency organization. Concerning their fears about teenagers being exposed to objectionable content in movies, one leaflet recommended that "you, the parent, can best tell when your son or daughter is no longer an adolescent but a grown-up. We might hazard the general statement that in our culture, this time will hardly come before the completion of high school."[86]

By late 1956, some exhibitors had different fears about teenage audiences that had nothing to do with the content of the films. Vandalism was becoming an epidemic among some teenage audiences—"Berserk Teenagers Close Theatre," read one *Variety* headline. "Rowdyism and vandalism on the part of the youngsters" led one theater in Wenatchee, Washington, to temporarily close down and then to hire security for Friday night screenings. The article describes how "the exhibitors were spending thousands of dollars extra yearly to repair knifed seats and carpeting, remove scratched obscenities from walls and mirrors and replace equipment and fixtures that were stolen or rendered inoperative."[87] Such events led *Variety*'s Hy Hollinger to evaluate what his article's headline called a "Paradox in [the] New 'Best Audience.'" In weighing potential profits from youth audiences against the cost of vandalism—or as the headline put it, "Teenage Biz vs. Repair Bill"—Hollinger concluded:

In recent months exhibitors have clamored for films that would appeal to teenage audiences whom they regarded as their best customers. They called for pictures with built-in teen appeal; that is, product based on subjects that arouse the interest of youngsters. In this category, rock 'n' roll features prominently. Now that many theatres have had the opportunity to display some of these so-called teen features, they're wondering if it's worthwhile. On the basis of recent experience, many theatremen are doing some serious soul-searching and asking themselves if the "monster" they've created is a good thing after all. In their appraisal of the situation, their thoughts are somewhat schizoid. On the other hand, the teen films, many of them obvious "quickies" and "cheapies" made to take advantage of the market demand, succeeded in fulfilling a theatreman's prime purpose—bringing customers to the box office. The returns aren't sensational, but when weighed realistically, they're superior to what can be obtained with a lot of regular product.[88]

The "quickies" and "cheapies" that Hollinger describes are the many B-movies produced during the 1950s, mostly by independent producers. The various changes seen in the film industry over the course of the decade had an enormous effect on the B-movie, which became a volatile entity. Major and minor studios alike questioned the economic viability of low-budget production as the decade progressed, and the amount of combative rhetoric used within the industry both in support of and against B-movies soon made it apparent that a battle for the Bs was emerging.

2

The Battle Begins

Hollywood Reacts, Poverty Row Collapses

At stake in the battle for the Bs in the 1950s was the very survival of B-filmmaking itself. Although many low-budget films established new trends throughout the decade, several Hollywood studios quickly abandoned the B-movie in the decade's early years, while a few others were (tentatively) dedicated to its ongoing viability. At the same time, Poverty Row studios such as Producers Releasing Corporation, Republic, and Monogram underwent substantial changes as the industrial role of the B-movie continued to evolve throughout the decade. The battle would significantly affect all three of these studios, with two of them going out of business and another transforming itself into one of the industry's leading independents.

The battle over B-movies actually began in Hollywood soon after World War II, with the trend toward fewer but bigger pictures beginning at a few studios as early as 1946. Soon after the district court's antitrust ruling of that year, the *New York Times* reported that some studios were "reducing, or stopping altogether, production of modest budget pictures in the expectation of a tougher selling market" in light of the consent decrees.[1] That same year, Universal's merger with International Pictures saw the newly formed Universal-International Productions immediately attempt to distinguish itself from its former incarnation by favoring quality over quantity. Four B-production units were shut down in late July of 1946, and when the merger occurred at the end of that month it was announced that Universal would eliminate "Westerns, serials and low-budgeters," since the "new type of selling under the antitrust decision . . . would also make more difficult sale of B product."

To emphasize its new direction, Universal fired nine of its B-movie producers on the day of the merger. This soon put an end to Universal's long-running cycle of low-to-modestly budgeted horror films, despite the fact that the last major entry, *House of Dracula* (1945), was a financial success even while playing on the bottom half of double bills. Trade publications and newspapers commenting on the film's box office performance described its run as a "remarkably strong session," using such expressions as "excellent," "terrific," "potent," and "smash" in reference to its earning power.[2] Regardless of this success, Universal had all but eliminated horror films by the end of 1946 (a policy that continued well into the next decade) after such entries that year as *The Cat Creeps*, *The Spider Woman Strikes Back*, and *She-Wolf of London* failed to rejuvenate the genre for the studio.[3]

Not all of the major studios eliminated low-budget films, however, as Twentieth Century–Fox announced plans in September of 1947 to distribute films from independent producers in the $100,000 to $200,000 range, in the hopes that such films would absorb any potential losses on the studio's other, larger films. Spurred by the success of its film *Crossfire* (1947), RKO announced a program of Bs that it hoped "would differ from routine B-pictures in their experimental nature," including *The Boy with the Green Hair* (1948), which it estimated would cost $300,000.[4] MGM added a new B-filmmaking unit in 1948 that would specifically produce low-budget action films using a semidocumentary style. The studio also told its heads of story development to "find material for 'Exploitation' pictures that could be produced for as little as $400,000"—with the word "exploitation" being defined by MGM executives as "newsworthy, violent and even controversial subjects which lend themselves to documentary treatment and can be specifically advertised to sell a picture."[5]

Warner Bros. also announced a new slate of low-budget films in 1948 but was hesitant to call them outright Bs. "The reason for the studio's official silence on the subject," wrote Thomas F. Brady, was "the chronic fear that exist[ed] in Hollywood of the label B pictures—a term which primarily designates a low cost category but has acquired a derogatory qualitative significance, secondarily." One actor under contract to Warner Bros., James Davis, even refused his assignment to the film *The Big Punch* (1948) because he was reportedly afraid of the "B-stigma" carried by its $300,000 budget. The studio subsequently laid him off, but his actions demonstrate just how uncertain the fate of the B-movie was in the immediate postwar Hollywood era.[6]

By the early 1950s, a general state of confusion remained regarding the state of the Bs, and whether they still had a continuing viability. Trades such as *Variety* saw a steady parade of headlines in the 1950s proclaiming the end of major studio B-movies altogether, such as the 1952 article "B's Buzzing Out of Business?": "B's—at least those films consciously produced with that designation—may well buzz right out of the industry picture if present exhibition conditions continue. More and more of them are failing to pay for themselves, and they're becoming an increasing headache for distributors to book."[7]

This dilemma had been a long time coming, yet was ignored until its full implications began to be felt. While Hollywood knew that the 1948 Supreme Court ruling spelled the end of its block-booking practices, the consequences were not immediately felt at most studios. The implications of the antitrust ruling were largely disregarded in the late 1940s, but as the extent of the industry's changes began to be felt the B-movie would find itself in a state of rapid transition—abandoned by many studios of all sizes, and quickly adopted by a new crop of independent producers who would soon find unprecedented success with the Bs in the wake of Poverty Row's collapse.

The State of the Bs in Hollywood, 1950–1953

By some accounts, B-movies were performing relatively well at the box office in the early 1950s, particularly those made by smaller studios. A 1951 *Variety* headline declared "'B' Pictures Join Top Product in Upturn at B.O.," explaining how "[box office] improvement for lesser pic product has extended right down to Westerns," with such studios as Columbia, Republic, and Monogram all reporting increased grosses.[8] On a month-by-month basis, many B-movies were not financial failures in 1950 and 1951, and even saw brief periods of relative prosperity. Yet this success achieved by minor studio Bs did not translate into confidence from the majors. Two months later, *Variety* examined the tentative future of B-filmmaking in an article entitled "Hollywood's to 'B' or Not to 'B': Majors Cutting Program Films," describing how the major studio consensus was that "the picture industry can best withstand the slings and arrows of outrageous fortune by turning out top product only and leaving the B to the smaller lots and independent producers."

This reference to emphasizing "top product" was symptomatic of the growing trend toward making fewer but bigger pictures that was already under way in Hollywood by the start of the decade. The increasingly volatile nature of the industry was not lost on *Variety*, which saw a new mode of production emerging: "Persistent indications of a general increase in quality are cuing predictions that the next 12 months will set the basic pattern for future production in a changing motion picture economy."[9]

This forecast was further supported by Paramount executive Frank Freeman's proclamation the following month that "formula pictures are on their way out of major film lots," and that "the death knell of the low-cost B production" had sounded. Predicting that the industry would be "better off than it is today" if it focused primarily on "fewer but better pictures," he explained how "big pictures are doing better business at the box-office than ever," but that "production costs today impose a genuine problem in maintaining the entertainment magnitude required by current standards."[10]

In other words, Freeman proposed to funnel all resources previously used by his studio to make B-movies into making fewer but more spectacular A-pictures, betting that higher-budgeted films with more lavish production values could create this sense of "magnitude and generate a much greater cost-to-earnings ratio for Paramount."

Another result of this trend toward bigger films was the fate of the "medium budgeter," which was of particular concern to independent producers. *Variety* noted a "lack of market" at the start of the decade "for pix between the real quickie category and those in the lower-budgeted 'A' classification. That is generally in the field of product costing between about $120,000 and $500,000." The result of this new box office trend was a further disparity between the remaining Poverty Row studios and the major studios in 1950. Under such market conditions, independent producers were forced to either make due with the minuscule profits attainable from turning out "quickie" films or else join the majors in making fewer but bigger films.

The problem with the latter option for the independents, however, was the increased—and typically unattainable—degree of capitalization required, a financial risk made even greater by the fact that the minor studios did not release enough product to beat the law of averages when only 20 percent of films turned a profit. This created a further solidification of power by major studios, with the independents unable to take large creative risks in light of having to rely on conservative market strategies:

> Prevalence of this situation hits the lower-medium cost product hardest. The westerns and actioners that can be made by the shoestring-row contingents under the $120,000 figure have a ready market in subsequents and as dual-bill fodder in many situations. Their budgets are designed in recognition that they are going to be sold to exhibs at flat rental. . . . Furthermore, there's small chance taken in making them since variations in quality are minor and mean little. Producers are discovering that if they want to make anything better than that style of canned goods, they've got to jump to a budget classification that would allow their product to qualify at least as a 'lazy A.' That is in contrast to pre-war and the early war years when considerable profit was made in the category of pix which were frankly 'B's' and would come in for $250,000 to $350,000 or there abouts.[11]

The sharp decline in the immediate postwar years led *Life* magazine to declare in a 1951 headline that "Now It Is Trouble That Is Supercolossal in Hollywood." In the article, Robert Coughlan speculated as to the industry's future, yet unlike many other journalists and executives he did not see the end of the B-movie as a certainty. "B, C and Z pictures," he said, would not "disappear from local movie screens. The quickie western, jungle adventure and horror films, for instance, are likely to go on for a long time, perhaps forever, for they are cheap to make and they have an audience." Rather than make "safe" pictures, he saw the studios as beginning to focus on films that are "different," with the potential result being "a great increase in the number of good pictures. It could mean the return of the lost audience."[12]

The *New York Times* also put forth this correlation between "bad" films and decreasing revenues as 1951 began. Citing Gilbert Seldes's position that "Hollywood's 'bad' pictures had killed off the adult habit of going to the movies," the *Times* cautioned that "merely avoiding movies is no way to apply pressure for better pictures." Arthur L. Mayer of the Council of Motion Picture Organizations shared this position, urging the public "to follow the recommendations of reviewers and attend films of merit so as to indicate support for this better type."[13]

The major studios could perhaps be accused of believing that bigger films were therefore better by default than the more modest B-films of years past, particularly as Hollywood began relying on new technological advancements such as widescreen processes and 3-D to draw audiences simply by virtue of their spectacle. *Variety* declared in 1953:

> The major studios' once-buzzing 'B' hives—where fledgling talent was developed for better things—are growing more and more inactive as the independent producers take over the task of turning out low-budget productions, leaving the majors to concentrate on more expensive films embracing the recently developed technical processes. Most of the majors have all but discarded their low-budget units, although retaining and in some cases expanding their deals with independents to make the supporting product. The trend, however, is away from the companion film and the changing situation in both production and exhibition may cue the long-heralded demise of the supporting picture.[14]

Most major studios removed B-movies from their release schedules by the end of 1951. Warner Bros.' slate of films contained no self-professed Bs by this point; Universal declared it was "constantly striving for bigger names and better pix to carry the top half of the bill in all situations." While MGM had no obvious Bs, the studio still retained some product that "comes close to that classification and is frankly aimed at the supporting market." RKO declared that it "would eliminate all low cost films to concentrate on important productions." Paramount decided it was "abandoning the B as far as regular studio production is concerned," instead relying on independents such as Nat Holt for low-budget films for its release schedule. Not surprisingly, given that it had historically been the smallest of the major Hollywood studios, Columbia stuck to the steady release of B-product that had been its staple for years, with a continuing emphasis on westerns such as its Charles Starrett series.

The surprising holdout among the majors was Twentieth Century–Fox, with Darryl Zanuck declaring that the studio had "no plans to 'single grade' its schedule. Rather, it [would] continue to meet the story market, gearing each production expenditure to the individual subject."[15] Zanuck's divergent position would only last for two more years, as the studio's introduction of CinemaScope changed its attitude toward the Bs. With the debut of the new widescreen process in 1953, the studio "abandoned all its plans to turn out lower-budgeted films in favor of spectacle and lavish production." Twentieth Century–Fox announced that it would "use Cinemascope exclusively," rationalizing its abandonment of B-movies in that "the widescreen process isn't figured as lending itself to the smaller film." Instead, the studio contracted out several medium-budgeters to independent producer Leonard Goldstein, with an arrangement to produce ten films in the range of $500,000 each.[16]

By 1953, Hollywood had fully entered into the "smash hit or else" era, with little room for modest films earning modest profits—circumstances affecting the smaller studios most severely:

> [The] result of this new phenomenon of hit-or-flop is further revolution of an industry which is already in the throes of tremendous change. It means the finale of a whole, large class of films which formerly were not only important profit-makers for producers, but have been a necessity for theaters. Furthermore, while it hits indies harder, lack of return on the medium-low budget product is also important to the lesser of the big studios. They have to go on making pix in this category because of overhead and other problems, but they must depend on hits among their bigger films to bring them real profits. They're happy if the smaller ones just break even.[17]

Columbia was particularly affected by this state of affairs, being one of these "lesser" Hollywood studios. By 1953, Columbia's production schedule still contained a significant amount of low-budget films, the majority of which were either from producer Sam Katzman or the result of deals with other independents. Even Universal, which two years prior had tried to dissociate itself from the Bs, continued to make such series as the Ma and Pa Kettle and the Francis the Talking Mule films. Each bore a strong resemblance in both look and cost to the B-movies of the previous decade, but despite the fact that they were neither "better pix" nor featured "bigger names," their strong box office performance was enough that Universal occasionally ignored its own new emphasis on quality over quantity.

Overall, however, the fate of the Hollywood B-movie was still a highly uncertain one by late 1953. *Variety* surmised in August that the following twelve months would "cue a definite industry decision on the pix which once occupied so much of the Hollywood schedule." The public's long-term reaction to the introduction of widescreen cinema and 3-D films was deemed to "play an important part in the eventual fate of the 'B.' Meanwhile, it buzzes with less vigor."[18]

Poverty Row Goes Bankrupt: PRC/Eagle-Lion

In the midst of the battle for the Bs, Poverty Row studios struggled to maintain their small niche in the marketplace. By the end of the 1950s, however, the original denizens of Poverty Row were no more—either having transformed themselves into new entities, or else folding altogether while their share of the B-movie market went to new independent filmmakers who had recently entered the industry.

The 1930s saw the emergence of dozens of independent companies that were collectively known as Poverty Row, called such because many of these studios were located together in one specific region of Hollywood, Gower Gulch. Often renting the same studio space as other failed companies had done before them, the companies of Poverty Row included such now familiar names as Monogram and Republic and such lesser-known entities as Empire Pictures Corporation, Majestic Pictures Corporation, and Spectrum Pictures. The Poverty Row moniker was also earned by the extreme cheapness of production practiced at these studios. While Hollywood Bs were frequently made for a few hundred thousand dollars, Poverty Row Bs were often made for as little as $8,000 to $10,000 and filmed as quickly as a mere four days. Almost from their inception, these companies and their films were largely looked down upon within the industry and by journalists, as one 1934 article from the *New York Times* illustrates: "The quickie is a motion picture made in Poverty Row on a shoestring; the creature on a double bill the neighborhood movie is ashamed to advertise. . . . Stories are rehashes of the current major lot's success. Never do they deviate from the paths of mediocrity, manufacturing unflinchingly miles of rubber-stamp celluloid under the guise of entertainment."

Such companies—or, as dubbed by one Poverty Row producer, "the snatch racket"[19]—flourished between 1934 and 1936, until the major studio B-unit productions began to increase. The marketplace for B-movies soon became flooded, resulting in mergers between certain Poverty Row studios. Major studio B-movies soon took control of the market as many smaller companies struggled to secure financing, with several (including Beaumont Pictures, Diversion Pictures, and Resolute Pictures) going out of business by 1937.[20]

Given that they did not own movie theaters, Poverty Row companies often found the distribution process to be more difficult than the production process: "'Our real job was not making our films," one Gower Gulch alumnus explained, "it was the task of getting our pictures into all the side street theatres of the nation."[21] Larger independents such as Monogram and Republic were often successful enough in arranging their own distribution in major cities. The majority of Poverty Row firms, however, used the states' rights process whereby the distribution rights to a film were sold to autonomous distributors that circulated their films in various territories, largely to theaters in rural areas.[22]

Most Poverty Row studios were short-lived, and almost all of those that found some lasting success in the industry went out of business by the end of the 1950s. One of the more relatively enduring Poverty Row studios was Producers Releasing Corporation, which got its start in 1939. The company was initially divided into two entities, Producers Pictures Corporation and Producers Distributing Corporation, although this corporate structure was quickly altered when the Pathé Corporation took control in 1940, at which point the PRC name was adopted. PRC has been described as "shabby and slipshod" and "the cheapest of all Hollywood studios," routinely making films in a mere six to ten days, on budgets less than $40,000 and using minimal production facilities.

The company further evolved in 1947, with British film mogul J. Arthur Rank acquiring PRC in the hopes of expanding worldwide. Trade publications announced on August 8, 1947, that a merger with Eagle-Lion Films was being considered, and the deal was in place by month's end. Under Rank's Eagle-Lion banner, the studio's output improved substantially. While ceasing to produce its own films in 1948, Eagle-Lion still maintained a stable release schedule by serving as a distributor for (and often offering financing to) independent producers.[23]

Perhaps as a way of distinguishing the studio's new entity as being more reputable than its former incarnation, the decision was made to acquire films with higher budgets and more recognizable Bs stars. Director Phil Karlson described Eagle-Lion as "a little higher in their standards" than other low-budget studios of the era and said it "seemed to have very good taste in directors."[24] Celebrated film noir director Anthony Mann, for instance, made several movies for the studio, including *Railroaded* (1947), *T-Men* (1947), *He Walked by Night* (1948), and *Raw Deal* (1948). Other examples of films either produced or distributed by Eagle-Lion include Abbott and Costello's *The Noose Hangs High* (1948); *The Amazing Mr. X* (1948), starring former Universal horror regular Turhan Bey; *Trapped* (1949), starring Lloyd Bridges and Barbara Payton; *Tulsa* (1949), starring Susan Hayward; and *The Jackie Robinson Story* (1950). Particularly notable was the 1950 film *Destination*

Moon, produced by George Pal, who later produced *When Worlds Collide* (1951) and *War of the Worlds* (1953) for Paramount, along with *The Time Machine* (1960) and *Atlantis, the Lost Continent* (1961) for MGM. Pal first found success making a film with extensive effects work at Eagle-Lion, however, as *Destination Moon* was not only a pioneering effort in the new cycle of science fiction films that would soon dominate the decade but also one of the biggest box office hits of the year. The film even won the Academy Award for best special effects and was nominated for best art direction, due in large part to Pal's use of painter and architect Chesley Bonestell as a technical consultant.

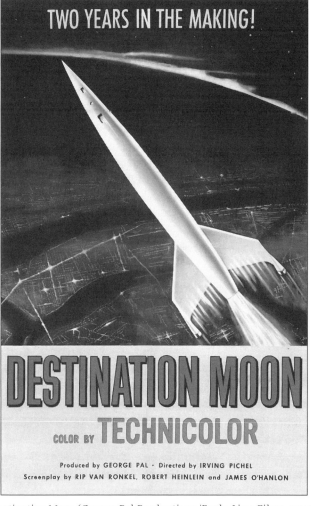

Destination Moon (George Pal Productions/Eagle-Lion Films, 1950)

Bonestell had previously worked for RKO on matte paintings for *The Hunchback of Notre Dame* (1939), *Citizen Kane* (1941), and *The Magnificent Ambersons* (1942), but he is best known for his career as a painter of astronomy-themed art. His matte paintings for *Destination Moon*, along with the film's highly detailed exterior and interior rocket-ship sets, lend the film a large degree of technical sophistication for which it was widely lauded. Using actual telescopic photos of the moon taken from the Mount Wilson Observatory, Bonestell painted a faithful representation of the crater Harpalus that was enlarged into a 45-by-370-foot backdrop for the set of the rocket's landing site. In turn, many saw the film as Hollywood's most realistic attempt to date at depicting outer space, with the *New York Times* noting how the film was "'a documentary view into the future'" and "regarded as something of a triumph in astronomical and scientific accuracy."[25]

While these successes could have feasibly prompted a move toward higher-budgeted films similar to those of the majors, Eagle-Lion still maintained the position that B-movies were a necessary factor in the overall strength of the film marketplace, a tenet that proved true by the end of the 1950s even though the company failed to last that long. Executive producer Aubrey Schenck noted in July of 1949: "Many producers in Hollywood are too interested in making Academy Award pictures and have all but forgotten how to make 'bread and butter' pictures with strong box office ingredients at reasonable budgets. . . . We at Eagle-Lion are in a particularly advantageous position . . . since we are geared right now to make budget pictures, the kind of pictures that conform with exhibition experience and don't take the shirt off the theatre man's back."

He added, "Producers have a lot to learn about the exhibitors' and distributors' part of the business." While realizing the value of the Bs, Eagle-Lion still sought to balance its release schedule by again returning to production with a full slate of its own bigger-budget films as well. The studio hoped to reach an output of approximately fifteen A-pictures per year within the months to come. By September of that year, however, Eagle-Lion was implementing a different strategy entirely. Executive vice president William MacMillan began soliciting deals with outside producers for their films, indicating a move toward distribution rather than production. The move is further symptomatic of the highly uncertain nature of independent filmmaking, where business plans can change in just a few months. As a result, the studio found itself unable to initiate any new production programs unless new financing became available.[26]

September 18, 1949, saw these new distribution deals implemented, with the announcement of five independent films for production in the immediate future. Titles included *Sunken Treasure*, *The Monster*, *The Boy from Indiana*, and *The Bone Is Pointed*, with each being financed either in whole or in part by the individual producers. MacMillan stated that the deals "assure Eagle-Lion of top product for early 1950 and at the same time greatly ease the company's position as regards product." In other words, Eagle-Lion had a product shortage and was forced to turn to producers as far away as England and Australia in order to secure enough product for release. While these films did not prove to be nearly as successful as *Destination Moon*, it was the studio's determined focus on "bread and butter" pictures that allowed it to be in a financial position to release its more notable films that followed.

In addition to these five films, several others were also being considered at the time. The studio's financier, N. Peter Rathvon, was reviewing various properties that had been submitted by independent producers, most with completed screenplays that could begin production relatively quickly.[27]

By 1950, Eagle-Lion enjoyed the industry-wide upturn in independent filmmaking and renewed bank financing thereof. "The key to the entire situation of indie production is the ability to offer a bank loan," said MacMillan. Whereas the films it distributed in 1949 were primarily financed by the individual producers, Eagle-Lion found itself in a better financial position in 1950 and therefore able to offer financing directly: "With our money, we are able to give a producer a straight 60% of his film budget in place of the banks," said MacMillan. "That is first money, of course. In return, we ask for 10% of the profits plus a fair distribution deal for Eagle-Lion." Due to the upswing in independent production in 1950, MacMillan now felt more comfortable in his studio's role as distributor, with no immediate pressure to return to production: "If we decide to produce in the future or if we can arrange for simultaneous shooting of a number of films on the lot by independent producers, we will reopen the studio," he declared.[28]

On June 12, 1950, Eagle-Lion's corporate identity again changed when the studio merged with Film Classics, creating a new company called Eagle-Lion Classics (ELC). This allowed for the acquisition of what one trade called "'substantial' new financing" from the banks, which ELC used to "retire outstanding obligations of both companies" and to provide further first money to more independent producers.[29] ELC board chairman Joseph Bernhard stated that the new company "will remain strictly a distributor of independently produced films," and that his "principal duty under the new set-up will be to seek out new product." Not all of this product was Bs, however, as ELC now found itself "geared to handle one big 'A' picture a month, together with a 'minimum' of program features." This minimum would include a deal for fifty films over five years with Harry Sherman and Neil Agnew, which "provides for delivery of six westerns and four features annually."[30]

Even while ELC was making strides in securing a steady flow of product, the company soon took more drastic measures in attempting to safeguard its future. Serving as a sign that the 1948 antitrust ruling was not having an immediate benefit to independent studios, MacMillan filed a $15 million triple-damages lawsuit on behalf of ELC against the Loew's and RKO theater circuits on October 3, 1950: "The complaint alleges that the two circuits have by their persistent collusive practices continued to virtually exclude independently-produced pictures from the New York market." Also named as defendants "but without damage claims are: Paramount, Warner, [Twentieth] Century–Fox, Columbia, 'Big U' Exchange and United Artists."

> The complaint claims that Eagle Lion was "driven out" of the distribution business in consequence of the alleged practice, and that ELC will be "driven out" if the defendants "continue to deny ELC all-competitive access to the prior-run market in the New York metropolitan area."
>
> Said MacMillan: "Since this market represents some 14 percent of the potential U.S. motion picture income, they have, in effect, deprived the independent producer of the chance to make the profit he needs to stay in business. They have also deprived the public of seeing pictures which even now would be doing a great deal to keep the movies in better favor with their declining audiences."
>
> The action, he said, "evidences Eagle-Lion Classics' determination that there shall be a free market in the sale of motion pictures to insure the future of independent motion picture production and distribution. That such a free market has not existed in our industry is proven by the decision of the Supreme Court of the U.S. to force divorcement of certain theatres by large producers and distributors, and to compel them to abandon their monopolistic practices. One would have expected that in the face of such a decision the law would be respected, but such has not been the case in Metropolitan New York."[31]

While the suit was pending, ELC continued its agenda of pursuing both A- and B-films into the early months of 1951, with increasing success. On March 21, *Variety* declared that ELC was "threatening to break into the bigtime with numerous 'A' pictures under its new policy."[32] Weeks later, a *Motion Picture Daily* headline affirmed "1950–51 Will Be ELC's 1st 'Profit' Year." The company was expected to make a net profit of $200,000 in the fiscal year. MacMillan described how this profit "compares with an $800,000 loss for the preceding 18 months," noting "that during 1950–51 when the box-office generally was off 15–20 per cent, ELC's gross was up 15 per cent and totaled approximately $18,000,000 worldwide. The gross for the previous fiscal year was $16,000,000. It was this increase in gross plus a slashing of costs by 25–30 per cent that enabled the company to come through with a profit this year."

Furthermore, it was predicted that if this profit could be maintained ELC would eventually be able to resume producing its own films. "The ELC studios are being retained," said MacMillan, "looking to that day [when production begins again] and, meanwhile, are bringing in rental revenue." The company also sought an increase in its distribution fees through applying a sliding scale formula. While currently at 30 percent, ELC proposed to raise this by taking on "a share of an increased cooperative advertising budget if the producer will share the increased cost by allowing a higher distribution fee and if the exhibitor will either share equally in the increased expenditure or allow the company better rental terms."

"It is surprising," MacMillan observed, "how little increase in rental is needed to increase the cooperative advertising to the point where that will produce a substantial increase in income." He further noted that while only 20 percent of all films in the current market were profitable, "a large part of the remaining 80 percent 'don't lose much, and many break even.'"[33] Hence it still seemed possible for a small independent studio to make a profit if it was able to withstand enough of the break-even films until a genuine hit emerged.

Despite the upsurge of positive coverage in the trades in March of 1951, ELC's future would be a brief one. Signifying that the company's financial health was not nearly as strong as MacMillan had indicated, ELC was bought out by United Artists within a matter of weeks. While United Artists had faced its own financial difficulties in recent years, and lost money at the rate of $100,000 per week in early 1951, the studio was making rapid strides to correct the problem. On February 7, 1951, control of the studio was given to Robert S. Benjamin (former head of the J. Arthur Rank organization in America) and Arthur B. Krim (former head of Eagle-Lion Films Inc.). Within a single day of gaining control, Krim and Benjamin had borrowed $500,000 from Twentieth Century–Fox head Spyros Skouras. From there, they needed product to distribute, with Krim offering half a million dollars for ELC's library of three hundred films. The deal was completed in April, with the films soon earning United Artists $200,000 per week.[34]

MacMillan had admitted in March that "as a distributor of independently-produced films, ELC's problems have been intensified by the resurgence of United Artists," presumably referring to the financial moves that United Artists had made in February. Yet MacMillan still felt confident that "ELC's advantage is that from a producer's standpoint, its financing terms are 'better than UA's.'"[35] The sale of ELC to United Artists came as a surprise to other independent companies and producers, who scrambled to fill the sudden gap in the marketplace: "Absorption of Eagle-Lion Classics by UA is looked upon by some industry observers as a starting signal for other indie distribs to hypo activities in order to move into the spot left open by the exit of ELC from the active market," reported *Variety*.[36]

ELC's demise added further uncertainty as to the overall fate of the B-movie in the early 1950s but did not stop other studios from attempting to be successful in the B-movie marketplace in the meantime: "Despite the number of indie producers who are left bloody and beaten, there are always new ones popping up out of nowhere to fill the ranks. However, the fact that only a small handful—such as Samuel Goldwyn, Edward Small and Sol Lesser—have been able to turn out profitable product year after year, means that there can be no real continuity in indie distribution."[37]

The Thrill Factory Shuts Down: Republic Pictures in the 1950s

Republic Pictures had a longer term of success than most in producing B-films, and although it outlasted Producers Releasing Corporation/Eagle-Lion by a few years, the studio ultimately failed to survive the changing cinematic marketplace in the 1950s because its approach to the Bs remained largely rooted in the past. Officially known as the Republic Studio Organization, its nicknames ranged from derogatory ("Repulsive") to endearing ("the Thrill Factory"). Founded by Herbert J. Yates, Republic began production in 1935, after merging with Mascot, Liberty, Supreme, and Monogram Pictures (the latter soon reemerging as a productive studio in its own right). Fittingly, the first film Republic produced was a western entitled *Westward Ho!* (1935), since the studio would be best known for this genre in the coming decades.[38] Republic established a solid market share in the 1940s, balancing its specialization in "horse operas" with a mix of other genres, as well such varied formats as short subjects, serials, cartoons (1947–1949), and army training films (1941–1945). In the late 1940s, the studio introduced a policy of making one "prestige film" per year, with the intention of enhancing Republic's status within the film industry. The most notable of these A-pictures were Orson Welles's *Macbeth* (1948) and John Ford's *The Quiet Man* (1952), but while adding to the studio's reputation, these higher-budgeted efforts were not always financially successful.

Production expanded slightly as the 1950s loomed, leading Yates to believe that his company was well positioned to compete in the new decade. In September of 1949 it was announced that the studio would release three more feature films in the 1949–1950 fiscal year than in the one prior. Fifty-three feature films, four serials, and four short subjects were scheduled, with Yates declaring his confidence "in the forward march of the industry."[39]

Although his optimism was ultimately misguided, Republic endured for several more years and even enjoyed the overall upturn in independent production in the early 1950s. Yates described his expectations in February of

1950 of a "substantial improvement" in business that year. *Variety* supported his prediction, noting that this view was "shared by many other execs of smaller distribs in the wake of greater flow of indie product plus the effects of cost-savings in Hollywood and in the field."[40] His enthusiasm, however, did not stop Yates from selling large portions of his film library to television in order to raise some immediate capital for the studio.

Republic tried several new production methods in its final years in the hopes of remaining competitive. The year 1952 saw the studio follow the lead of the majors, deciding to make fewer but bigger pictures. Yates estimated that upcoming budgets would be between 35 and 50 percent higher for each production, and later determined that the average budget would be doubled for the 1952–1953 season.[41] The move proved to be a successful one in the short term, as profits rose by over $100,000 in six months: Republic "reported net profit of $473,150 for the 26 weeks ending April 24 [1953], compared with $379,550 earned in the similar period last year."[42]

This financial upturn allowed Republic to take the same approach as Eagle-Lion once did, providing financing to independent producers in order to secure new product for distribution. Yates announced that his studio would bankroll any independent producer, director, or author with an outstanding story to turn into a film, believing this would benefit the entire industry. "The present formula of picture making," declared Yates, "is antiquated and belongs to an antiquated era. The future of this industry depends on the sympathetic understanding by the company of the creative work of the independent producers, directors and writers, functioning in an atmosphere free of interference." He saw this arrangement as resulting in "a continuous supply of great box-office motion pictures."[43]

While awaiting these "great" pictures, Republic continued producing minor ones in the meantime—although its success with the Bs was steadily evaporating as each year passed. The studio continued to make several serials per year until 1955, despite the fact that the format had itself become some-what antiquated by the 1950s. Universal ceased producing serials in 1947 in its move away from low-budget filmmaking, while Columbia produced fewer serials each year into the 1950s. Still, *Variety* noted in November of 1950 that although the format was in decline, it was still a desirable commodity to some exhibitors seeking to lure youth away from the new television medium: "Video's boxoffice inroads are providing a modest upbeat for film serials, as an increasing number of exhibs are starting to book cliffhangers as means of attracting the moppet trade—which has been particularly attentive to tele and consequently frequenting theatres less often."[44]

The decade began with Republic releasing four serials in 1950; this amount was amount cut in half by 1953. With each passing year, the economic viability of the serial became less certain. Bookings rapidly declined as the decade progressed, with distributors charging less for subsequent-run distribution in rural and neighborhood theaters. While in previous decades there had been an entire team of writers and producers working on Republic's serials, the 1950s saw this staff dwindle down to only one of each.[45]

Republic's steady decline continued through the mid-1950s and, with the exception of director Nicholas Ray's *Johnny Guitar* (1954), none of the films released between 1953 and 1959 is particularly well remembered by film historians or the public. B-movie director Ed Bernds, who worked for Columbia, Allied Artists, and American International Pictures in the 1950s, told of how he and his peers at Columbia "referred to Republic 'as the home of entrenched mediocrity' and felt that 'Yates made the Republic personnel so conservative that they didn't adapt' thus leading to the failure of Republic. Bernds felt that Yates was very loyal but stifled initiative in his staff."[46]

In February of 1954, Yates demonstrated his conservative nature by implementing a new strategy that was aesthetically questionable, although it may have made short-term financial sense at the time. In order to "meet the demands of the double feature market hit hard by a product shortage as studios continue to cut their production," Republic began selling "'re-edited' versions of their former 'deluxers.'" Films that had previously run from ninety to a hundred minutes were cut down to sixty or seventy minutes in length, with the newly edited version being retitled. Republic justified the practice by describing how "the attractions are mainly for smalltown situations which are accepting them 'willingly and hopefully.'"[47]

Such desperate measures were a symptom of Republic's steady decline. Beginning in 1955, the studio regularly threatened to suspend production and/or cease making films altogether. Yates even considered only producing films for television, claiming that the studio was not receiving adequate support from theater owners and demanding that exhibitors commit to higher rental fees and longer screening engagements. Any increased support that this threat might have brought the studio was a short-lived victory, since Republic canceled all production and laid off its staff in 1956. Multiple offers to buy out the studio were refused, with Yates still convinced of the studio's future viability. Republic would endure until 1959, largely as a distributor of a rapidly declining number of films. Whereas it had often released between fifty and sixty films annually, only twenty-seven films were released in 1957, seventeen in 1958, and a mere five in 1959. Toward the end, many of these films began to be turned over to independent distributors, making Republic a mere middleman.[48]

In December of 1958, a proposed three-way merger between Republic, RKO, and Allied Artists was reported: "Idea behind the move is to form one important motion picture company out of three whose prospects, individually, are not particularly bright." Republic's studio and laboratory facilities were considered a particularly enticing aspect of the deal to the other two studios, while "a joint production and financing program . . . [would] be put together by AA and RKO." Also of value was the fact that, despite having ceased production, Republic had "taken on distribution rights to the increasingly important pictures being turned out by American Broadcasting–Paramount Theatres." If fulfilled, the merger was not expected to meet with any legal adversities, since neither Republic nor Allied Artists was "party to the decrees in the industry antitrust action. Further, RKO, while having been a defendant in this case, has ceased as a major entity in the motion picture scheme of things."[49]

The proposed merger, which never came to fruition, represented the last chance to revive the dying studio. Yates quickly became aware of Republic's imminent demise: "We have one problem—getting out of the motion picture business," he said at the 1958 annual stockholders' meeting. Republic was sold in 1959, with the new owner choosing merely to rent its studio space to outside television and film producers and to maintain its laboratory, Consolidated Film Industries. The studio was soon sold to CBS, which transformed it into CBS Television City.[50]

Republic was one of the biggest casualties of the battle for the Bs in the 1950s, largely due to the fact that its films needed to evolve from their incarnations of earlier decades in order to fit in with the changing marketplace and audience demographics. The problem was not solely that Republic made B-films, but rather that the studio did not adapt to the fact that 1950s audiences would not pay to see the same types of films that they had in years past, which they could now see for free on television. B-films continued to be made in the late 1950s, but they no longer resembled those that had sustained Republic for so long.

Monogram Enlists Allies in the Battle for the Bs

While the proposed merger in 1958 between Republic, RKO, and Allied Artists signaled the extinction of the former two studios, the latter managed to endure well into the next decade by nature of the fact that its approach to the Bs evolved enough to keep pace with the changing B-film market itself. Allied Artists began as the Monogram Pictures Corporation in 1930, producing such notable films as *The Thirteenth Guest* (1932) starring Ginger Rogers, *Oliver Twist* (1933), and *Jane Eyre* (1934) starring Colin Clive and Virginia Bruce. Soon after merging with Herbert J. Yates to form Republic Pictures, Monogram reorganized itself as its own entity again in 1936, quickly reaching an output of approximately fifty films per year.[51] Former sales manager Steve Broidy was elected president in 1945 and would lead the studio in a new direction, forming Allied Artists Productions Inc. as a subsidiary of Monogram in November 1946.

Broidy made several moves to change the studio's reputation from that of a mere second-string B-film mill to a company that tried to compete in the A-picture market with the major studios. In 1950, he instituted a new category of films called "Gold Banner Productions," which would feature bigger stars and budgets than the studio's previous efforts. An increase in color cinematography was also implemented, with one-quarter of all releases shot in CineColor by the 1951–52 season.[52]

Such successes were built upon several years of financial loss. For the fiscal year ending July 2, 1949, Broidy estimated a loss of approximately $850,000, with the previous year's loss closer to a million dollars. The fact that 1949's loss was a sharply reduced one was seen as a positive factor, however, and operating costs and expenses were scheduled for a $300,000 reduction in the upcoming fiscal year. Despite the pervasive threat of financial ruin, Monogram's production schedule was ambitious at the end of the decade, as the studio spent $3 million on sixteen films in the final quarter of 1949. Forty-six films were scheduled for production in 1951, an increase over the twenty-nine produced in the 1950 season. Even with the upturn in production, however, Monogram was still recording losses by the end of 1950, with a $175,866 loss in a thirteen-week period as compared to the same period the year before.[53]

This downturn would only last a few months longer, as the studio's fortunes were helped considerably by the demise of Eagle-Lion Classics in April of 1951. Broidy quickly predicted that ELC's exit would propel Monogram to the forefront of the B-movie marketplace, particularly given Columbia's recent announcement that it would soon be cutting back on its production of Bs. As such, Monogram expected to increase its yearly output of B-films by 25 to 50 percent. "With one competitor dropping out of the market and another cutting down," said Broidy, "we naturally find ourselves in the strongest position we've been in since the formation of our company."

Broidy's confidence soon proved to be apt, as it was announced that the fiscal year ending in June of 1951 was the company's most successful to date, with a net profit of $1,061,648 reported in October of that year. The upturn allowed Monogram to become more ambitious in its production strategies, as Broidy guaranteed that at least one color film per month would be released from Monogram and/or Allied Artists during the 1951–1952 season. Forty-five films in total were scheduled therein, at a rate of four pictures per month.[54]

While the studio was producing more pictures than in past years, the move to color indicated that Monogram was also interested in making several films with relatively larger budgets in addition to its regular slate of Bs. Whereas Eagle-Lion and Republic both ultimately failed in attempting this strategy, the decision was an immediately successful one for Monogram, which reported a net profit of $600,000 for that fiscal year.[55] This figure was down significantly from the year prior, but it was still their second profitable year in a row after enduring many losing seasons. This success proved that B-movies could still be a viable entity in the 1950s, despite the industry's uncertainties and growing lack of faith in low-budget filmmaking.

By 1953, Monogram was releasing all of their productions under the Allied Artists banner, also beginning television production through a new division, the Interstate Television Corporation. On November 12, 1953, Monogram officially changed the studio's corporate name to the Allied Artists Picture Corporation. When asked whether, upon becoming president in 1945, Broidy had planned for Allied Artists to eventually phase out Monogram, he replied: "Oh, that was premeditated. We had trouble enough trying to run the one arm of the operation without trying to keep the other one going also. And we did. We successfully did that, to a point. We had a bad run of product for awhile. . . . We went from one picture to another and phased some of the smaller pictures into the Allied Artists program. We were trying to do the same thing as the major companies were doing, although on a more modified basis because we didn't have the capital structure or the fat."[56]

With the major studios moving away from B-movies in 1953, along with Republic's stated intent to follow suit, Allied Artists was seen within the industry as perhaps being the marketplace's primary source of B-movies—"most of [AA's] program consists of films in that class," declared *Variety*.[57] Allied Artists soon begin adding more A-pictures to its production schedule, however, as the new corporate name brought with it the opportunity for the studio to redefine its identity. Broidy announced in 1954, for instance, the production of two new A-films that would prove to be its most prestigious ventures to date, featuring major studio directing and acting talent: William Wyler's *Friendly Persuasion* (1956) and Billy Wilder's *Love in the Afternoon* (1957), both starring Gary Cooper.

It was a risky move given Republic's failure with A-productions, but Allied Artists broke even at the box office with the Cooper films. In essence, the strategy was similar to that of the majors during the studio-system era: use the profits from B-movies to help supplement A-productions. The difference was that Allied Artists did not have the luxury of employing this strategy in a vertically integrated, monopolistic system. Rather, it now operated in a horizontally organized system of distribution and exhibition that was inherently more risky than the former era of block booking. The studio's finances reflected this, with a loss of nearly $1.2 million on the books for 1957.[58]

Despite financial losses, Allied Artists maintained an aggressive release schedule, announcing in September of 1957 that it would release at least

three dozen features over the next twelve months, six more than the year
prior, to mark their biggest schedule in five years. Making bigger films was
still deemed important, as Broidy pledged that at least one film per month
would be both in CinemaScope and in color.[59] B-movies still remained a
major staple throughout the decade, as evidenced by such films as *Attack
of the 50 Ft. Woman* (1958), *Cole Younger, Gunfighter* (1958), *Cry Baby Killer*
(1958), *Daughter of Dr. Jekyll* (1957), *The Giant Behemoth* (1959), *Revolt in
the Big House* (1958), *Speed Crazy* (1958), *The Atomic Submarine* (1959), *The
Cyclops* (1957), *Undersea Girl* (1957), and *Unwed Mother* (1958). Republic had
generated a steady slate of westerns and serials, but Allied Artists recognized
the need to diversify its program by releasing films for teenage audiences
(1957's *Teenage Doll* and *Hot Rod Rumble*, 1958's *Hot Car Girl*) and in popular
new genres such as science fiction (1958's *Queen of Outer Space* and *War of
the Satellites*). It also recognized the need to make films similar to those
of such new competitors as American International Pictures, releasing
such films as *Attack of the Crab Monsters* (1957) and *Not of This Earth* (1957)
from producer-director Roger Corman (whose career is further analyzed in
subsequent chapters).

Invasion of the Body Snatchers (Walter Wanger Productions/Allied Artists Pictures,
1956)

One of Allied Artists' most notable films of this period was *Invasion of the Body Snatchers* (1956) from director Don Siegel, who had already found critical and commercial success with the studio in *Riot in Cell Block 11* (1954). Shot in twenty-three days on a budget of $382,000, the film's story of an alien force that replaces townspeople with unemotional, hive-minded replicas grown in giant pods has resonated in popular culture ever since its release—inspiring numerous remakes and having been chosen by the American Film Institute in 2008 as one of the ten best science fiction films ever made.[60] Much of the film's impact comes in the scope of how the story is told, with Siegel downplaying the number of special effects that are typically seen in science fiction films of this time. He noted that such effects work was "relatively unimportant" in the film: "We spent about $15,000 on special effects, a very small amount. Instead of doing what so many science fiction and horror films do—spend all their money on special effects and put poor actors on the screen—we concentrated on the performers."

Rather than attempt to show the interstellar travel of the pods' arrival on Earth or the way in which a person's original body turns to dust once it has been replaced (both plot points in Jack Finney's 1954 magazine serial *The Body Snatchers*, from which the film is adapted), the film's effects are generally limited to depicting the giant pods themselves and the mucus-like material within that covers the pod people as they gestate. By not making the special effects a central focus but rather having them intermittently establish and maintain the plot's central conflict, *Invasion of the Body Snatchers* becomes a genre film dealing in fantastical subject matter that is more interested in the psychology of its characters and the relevance of its social overtones than in spectacle-driven thrills. "The main thing about the picture," said Siegel, "was that it was about something, and that's rare," in reference to the story's implications for what many have seen as the conformity inherent in cold-war America and its McCarthy-era political and social climate.[61]

Another director whose B-movies were very successful for Allied Artists was William Castle, who made *Macabre* and *House on Haunted Hill* in 1958 for the studio. While the latter was one of the most successful Bs of the decade, it received mixed reviews from critics. The *Hollywood Reporter* declared it "a good spook story" in which "careful casting gives the picture more class than is usual in horror pictures," while *Newsweek* called it "more boo-boo than boo," adding that it "couldn't cure a child's hiccups." Regardless, the film earned $1.5 million at the box office, playing a major role in Allied Artists' turning a profit in the 1958 fiscal year.[62]

Castle was just one of many independent producers to whom Allied Artists increasingly turned in the late 1950s, leading *Variety* to predict in

House on Haunted Hill (William Castle Productions/Allied Artists Pictures, 1959)

November of 1957 that the studio might soon cease production altogether, relying exclusively on independents: "Allied Artists is moving toward a policy patterned after the United Artists type of operation—that is, tieing [*sic*] up with independent producers. AA is to provide the necessary bank guarantee and take distribution rights. Expectation is that AA will cease production itself and in the future will look to the indies as the sole source of product. Deals have been set with 11 film-makers who are to deliver 20 productions to AA. This is in addition to 12 films picked up from outsiders since last August."[63]

Independent producers typically had a larger degree of control at Allied Artists than at the major studios: "They couldn't have any more," said Broidy. "They had all of it. I mean, we had the final cut if we wanted to make changes, but I never exerted it. . . . But I think our approach to that was rather constructive, irrespective of what the contract might say. We gave them a lot of latitude."[64] Castle was particularly happy with the freedom that working with a smaller budget at an independent studio gave him. Talking about working "within the $150,000–$300,000 budgetary range," Castle said that directors "can get a lot of picture onto the screen for that kind of money, when you're free to do the job the way it ought to be done."[65]

In the late 1950s, the role of Allied Artists' B-movies within the film industry was becoming apparent to many, particularly with Republic's demise. Some exhibitors expressed concern that if Broidy's studio ever followed suit it would spell disaster for movie theaters: "It is vitally important to keep Allied Artists in business to assure us of their steady supply of pictures," Texas Interstate theater chain owner Robert O'Donnell announced in 1957.[66] Allied's sales manager Maurice Goldstein stated in December of 1958 that based on his meetings with theater owners, there was "an awakening among exhibitors about the necessity of keeping Allied Artists in business." B-movies were at the forefront of this awakening, with Goldstein describing how "bookings are beginning to come in" for "good exploitable product." The studio was currently in what he referred to as "a transition period" but was planning to produce more A-films in the near future. In order to achieve this goal, the need to book as many B-films as possible in the meantime was deemed critically important.[67]

January 1959 saw Allied Artists announce the scheduling of thirty-six films for its release slate that year, with six designated as high-budget A-pictures. *Variety* called it the studio's "most ambitious program to date."[68] This ambition proved to be warranted in the months ahead, with Broidy declaring in March that "the company figures to be in the black for the fiscal year 1959, ending June 30, after losses of $2,000,000 in 1957 and $1,100,000 in 1958." He stated that Allied Artists'"formula" for success was to "make potentially good grossing pictures," but specified that this did not mean a focus on A-pictures to the exclusion of all others: "Anyone who thinks blockbusters alone will carry the industry is crazy," he said.[69]

Thus, the B-movie was identified as still playing a key role in the strength of both Allied Artists and the industry as a whole at the end of the 1950s. *Variety* pointed in particular to Castle's horror films as "contributing largely" to the studio's improved fortunes at the end of the decade.[70] By November 1959, Allied Artists' finances improved even further, as its profits were up 134 percent during the first quarter of the 1959 fiscal year, with a net profit of $652,000.[71]

After enduring several lean years, Allied Artists was seen to be in a position of strength at the end of the decade, to the extent that *Variety* declared it to be one of the leading independents still remaining in the industry: "Roundup of important product coming from film companies . . . tends to show that the two companies which have passed out of the theatrical scheme of things have been more or less replaced. RKO and Republic bowed out and this, of course, was a blow to exhibitors. But since their passing, a help to theatremen is the fact that Allied Artists more and more is moving in on the big-time, production-wise."[72]

The studio continued production through the first half of the 1960s, until Broidy was replaced as president in 1965. Allied Artists became increasingly focused on television production, choosing to largely distribute foreign films and those acquired from independent producers rather than create its own cinematic product. While production resumed in 1968, and the studio was successful for most of the 1970s, Allied Artists was finally sold to Lorimar Productions in 1980.[73]

In the end, however, the studio enjoyed five decades in business after its formation as Monogram in 1930, making it one of the most successful independent studios in film history. That it was able to make the transition from the studio-system era of B-movie production into the modern era is a testament to its ability to successfully adapt its low-budget productions to a changing marketplace in the 1950s—something that its competitors Eagle-Lion and Republic ultimately failed to do. Indeed, many of Allied Artists' 1950s B-movies, such as *Attack of the 50 Ft. Woman*, *House on Haunted Hill*, and *Invasion of the Body Snatchers*, are among the company's best-remembered films, inspiring close attention from both critics and the public alike, along with numerous remakes.

If the cinematic marketplace was an unstable one in the 1950s, it was particularly so for the Poverty Row studios that struggled to maintain their niche in B-movie production amid changing audience tastes and exhibition patterns. The battle for the Bs saw numerous casualties throughout the decade, yet Allied Artists managed to endure. Its sustained presence came despite the frequent emergence of fresh opponents, in the form of new independent studios that appeared throughout the 1950s.

3

The Rebirth of the B-Movie in the 1950s

The rise of the new independent studios seeking to compete with Allied Artists and its Poverty Row peers became crucial to the survival of many exhibitors as a product shortage loomed. The 1950s was a period of changing exhibition patterns, as the film industry reacted to transitional forces. Smaller theaters, particularly those in rural areas or in neighborhoods and towns outside of major urban centers, were most affected by these changes. In turn, just as the operations of these theaters had consequences for the exhibition of B-films, the production of low-budget cinema was similarly affected by the prevailing volatility of the film industry.

As many of the older Poverty Row studios went out of business, and as Hollywood studios increasingly turned away from the B-movie in favor of new production strategies, many exhibitors began to complain of a growing shortage of available films. Many new independent production and distribution companies emerged to take advantage of this marketplace opportunity, providing low-budget product to exhibitors who were often desperate to fill screen time. Hence, the B-movie appeared to be becoming an increasingly marginalized product in the early 1950s, discarded by the dominant industry powers and adopted by a new breed of independent entrepreneurs. By the end of the decade, however, it was the independent B-filmmakers who would prove to be the industry's trendsetters, with the major studios frequently attempting to imitate their success.

In 1953, the year in which CinemaScope's widescreen debut cemented Hollywood's plan to concentrate on epic films at the expense of B-movies, there were approximately 17,500 theaters in America. Although many were part of large exhibition chains or circuits, more than half of the nation's theaters were either individually owned or else part of chains controlling fewer than five theaters each.[1] Neighborhood, small-town, and rural theaters accounted for the majority of these independent operators, which typically saw different booking patterns than those in major centers. While there were a few theaters in the downtown core of major cities that specialized in B-movies (such as the Times Square Rialto theater in New York), most theaters trafficking in the Bs were removed from the heart of the city.

B-theaters predominantly relied on a double-bill format, whereas many urban theaters had moved to single-film screenings by the start of the 1950s. By this point, 25 percent of all theaters nationwide programmed double bills regularly, and an additional 36 percent of theaters programmed them some of the time.[2] The need for B-movies to fill screen time was still a pressing concern for many smaller exhibitors as the 1950s began.

Smaller theaters not only needed to secure more film bookings than larger urban theaters but also faced unique challenges in satisfying their customer base. With populations often totaling fewer than five thousand residents within the surrounding area, most small towns were usually capable of supporting only one or perhaps two theaters. Film programs typically changed every two to three days to appeal to a variety of different tastes.

The specific films that audiences attending smaller independent theaters did get to see, however, were historically much different than those seen by audiences in larger urban theaters. Douglas Gomery describes how in previous decades, prior to the end of block booking, independent exhibitors not affiliated with the major Hollywood studios "had to conform and wait their turn as a third-, fourth-, or fifth-run house or risk that the Big Five corporations would not rent to them at all. Alternately, the independent exhibitor could turn only to Republic and Monogram for poor-quality features, knowing these films never made much money."[3]

As blockbuster films became more prevalent in 1950s Hollywood, many independent theaters faced another dilemma—with films playing longer first-run engagements than in years past, it took much longer in turn for these films to enter subsequent-run theaters. Many independent exhibitors began to complain of films that had "been milked dry" by the time they reached their theaters. One New Jersey exhibitor gave an example of a big-budget film that had gone "stale" by the time he was able to show it: "This particular blockbuster played for nearly a year on Broadway and did a smashing business," he said. "Then it moved into Newark for three months, and then into Elizabeth, N.J. for four weeks before I finally got my hands on it. I played it for one week and lost money. I played it because it was a prestige film and I had nothing else to play."[4]

Some smaller exhibitors were reasonably content with screening "poor-quality" films rather than "prestige" ones given that the Poverty Row studios produced a high proportion of westerns and adventure films—two genres that proved especially popular in small towns in the 1950s. A 1952 study of over

3,400 American exhibitors found that distinct genre preferences existed in relation to the population size of a given town: specific genres that did well in towns of 30,000 people or less did not find the same success in towns with larger populations. While "light musicals" led the study across all of its population categories ("Up to 7,5000," "7,5000–30,000," "30,000–100,000," "Over 100,000"), only the two smallest categories contained both the "Western Drama" and "Adventure" genres among the top five preferences. By comparison, such genres as the "Romantic Drama" and "Light Comedy" were preferred in the two largest population categories but were not popular in towns of less than 30,000 people.[5] The study suggested that small-town audiences frequently craved the type of faster-paced, more sensationalist product that B-studios specialized in, with exhibitors often catering to such preferences rather than automatically booking whatever films proved popular with big-city audiences. One B-film producer noted in 1950, for example, how "in small southern, western and midwestern towns audiences would rather sit and watch one of our little B's rather than most A's."[6]

Given the remote nature of most B-theaters, it is unsurprising that industry rhetoric regularly demeaned this unglamorous form of exhibition. *Variety* columnist Arthur Ungar, for example, referred to B movie theaters as "slough houses."[7] "Slough" is another word for swamp or backwater, the latter term being a derogatory one applied to rural areas. Furthermore, "slough" also refers to a state of moral or spiritual degradation, thus further demeaning the B-movie theater and its low-budget product.

While some trade publications like *Motion Picture Herald* frequently ran articles celebrating the importance and viability of small-town theaters in the 1950s (with such headlines as "There's Opportunity in Small Towns for Showmen"; "In Praise of Paramount's Small Town Premieres"; "What About Movies on Main Street?"; "The Small Town Manager Has Friends"; "Plight of the Small Exhibitor"; and "One Theatre Towns are the Soul of Show Business"), Hollywood executives were often far from supportive.[8] The *Wall Street Journal* even quoted one anonymous studio head's 1954 declaration that smaller theaters were essentially a nuisance and not worth his studio's time, given the relatively minor revenues generated. "You can play the first 5,000 theatres and get 90% of your costs," said the executive, but upon renting the same film to the next five thousand theaters—typically rural ones—the studio would only recoup 5 percent of the film's costs. Calling small-town exhibitors "the little guys," the anonymous studio head dismissed any complaints from such theater owners because they "get a $2 million picture for $20 or $30," and as such "were never worth the trouble."[9] In other words, first-run screenings in major city centers commanded the bulk of a studio's attention, while last-run screenings in rural towns were an unfortunate consequence of the distribution system: these small-town fourth- or fifth-run screenings generated relatively little profit, but were necessary in order to justify the higher prices charged for first-run films in the bigger cities.

As reactions to the effects of television intensified in the first half of the decade, some began to express concern for the ongoing viability of small-town exhibitors. *Motion Picture Herald* editor Martin Quigley Jr. declared in 1954 that the film industry "cannot survive in its present scope without keeping in operation the small town theatre. It is there that a very considerable part of the population of the country become acquainted, in their growing years, with motion picture entertainment. If these millions of customers are cut off from their local theatres, a chain reaction will set in and eventually do great harm to all theatres. The industry must not cut itself off from any segment of its audience, thereby turning them wholly over to television."

Quigley's argument was that many people who grew up in small towns eventually moved to larger cities, and if they were to become "deprived of the opportunity of regularly attending a theatre, the inclination to movie-going may die altogether." Small-town exhibitors therefore deserved "special consideration" from the Hollywood studios, he maintained, rather than an indifference toward what films the "little guys" played.[10]

Exhibition Patterns: Quality and Quantity

Despite the frequent condescension toward B-movies and the theaters screening them, the growing uncertainty within the film industry meant that the Bs were still a necessary factor for the success of many exhibitors. In many cases, B-movies meant the difference between profit and loss for certain theaters, with numerous small companies emerging to fill the growing marketplace void as the major studios began producing fewer but bigger pictures.

In 1950, a combined 423 films were released by all national distributors. By 1952, this number was down to 353, and by 1955, it had dropped to 283. While this reduced production benefited some within the industry (mostly the majors), others were negatively impacted. Neighborhood and rural theaters, with their habit of changing films several times per week, struggled to find enough product to meet audience demand. Some theaters became so desperate that they were forced to fill the holes in their programming schedule with less desirable foreign and reissued films, as well as to decrease how often their program was changed.[11]

Many exhibitors soon began calling the growing product shortage a "crisis," with Theatre Owners of America president Walter Read Jr. blaming the rise of "new processes" such as CinemaScope along with "an increased number of epic pictures" for the scarcity problem.[12] Exhibitors voiced their complaints to the United States Senate Select Committee on Small Business in 1956. Abram F. Myers of the Allied States Association of Motion Picture Exhibitors testified as to what the biggest concerns of exhibitors were:

1. The film companies have deliberately curtailed their respective outputs to the point where exhibitors must license all or nearly all the pictures released—especially the good ones—in order to operate.
2. The film rentals demanded for topnotch pictures are often so excessive that many independent exhibitors must forgo them altogether or else play them at a loss.
3. The film companies' current policy of fewer pictures to be played in fewer theaters at high admission prices has enabled them to attain a high degree of opulence while the independent exhibitors teeter on the brink of ruin.

Myers further estimated that there was "an annual deficiency of 150 feature pictures a year," primarily due to the fact that "film companies are obsessed with the idea that they can make more money by supplying a few pictures to the big key city theaters for exhibition on extended engagements at high admission prices than by producing a lot of pictures to play shorter runs in a larger number of theaters at normal admission prices."[13] One Texas theater chain owner surmised that the product shortage was costing the industry several million dollars in revenue in his state alone. Interstate executive R. J. O'Donnell foresaw the need for twenty-six more A-films for the 1954–1955 season than were available, calculating that without these films there would be "27,167 available playdates in Texas" that would go unfulfilled. O'Donnell figured that from June 1953 to March 1954, "45 top 'A' pictures released in Texas have averaged $143.55 each playdate. This can mean a total of $3,899,722.85 added revenue" that would be lost in the upcoming season from just one theater chain in a single state.[14]

Adding to the problem was the fact that some major studios did not truly believe there to be a product shortage. Charles J. Feldman, vice president of distribution at Universal, gave his position on the current marketplace in 1954: "It is stupid to say that any company limits its production only to cause a shortage. If I thought it profitable for Universal to produce two more pictures in 1955, wouldn't I do everything in my power to add the two films?" Acknowledging that the shortage was a definite problem for exhibitors with frequent program changes, he questioned whether it was financially feasible for Hollywood to produce films in greater numbers. "I don't think there are any stories not being made today that should or could be made profitably.

In this business . . . there are many, many people who know the market and every company knows the possibilities. Anytime there's a gambling chance to make a picture that will show a profit, there are people who will take that chance," argued Feldman.

An estimated 12,500 theaters relied on double bills in 1956. If each theater changed its program two or three times per week, this entailed a need for four to six new films weekly, totaling two hundred to three hundred films needed per year.[15] With only 283 films produced by all national distributors in 1955, an exhibitor could feasibly have to book nearly every single feature film produced in a given year in order to meet the desired quota. Even if logistically possible, this scenario would be generally undesirable to exhibitors given that not all films are attractive to all audiences.

With available product declining as the decade progressed, new independent companies emerged throughout the decade to capitalize on the growing need of exhibitors for a wider selection of programming. *Variety* picked up on the developing trend in 1954, noting that Hollywood's move toward fewer and bigger films "has had the result of bringing into the field new motion picture companies, complete with distribution organizations. While the plans of the new outfits are still mainly in the organizational stage, it nevertheless marks a new attempt to challenge the existing major film producer-distributors."[16] Most exhibitors welcomed the new companies, despite the fact that they made lower-budgeted films. "We buy all the companies," said Independent Theater Owners of America president Harry Brandt in 1956. "We need all of the product that is made. Particularly the small neighborhood theater," he said.[17]

While most major studios were abandoning B-movies, many exhibitors saw the Bs as their salvation. As one Massachusetts exhibitor told *Motion Picture Herald* in 1955, it was vitally "necessary to provide the exploitation type B pictures that many double feature and two change houses need." Simply put, without B-films many smaller theaters would have been driven out of business, with the sometimes-meager earnings of the Bs allowing many such venues to stay open and use their concession revenues to at least break even.[18]

Hence, smaller neighborhood theaters such as the Mode in Chicago, Illinois, survived the rest of the decade by regularly programming such B-movies as *Attack of the Crab Monsters* (1957), *Attack of the 50 Ft. Woman* (1958), *The Bride and the Beast* (1958), *I Was a Teenage Werewolf* (1957), *Machine Gun Kelly* (1958), *She Gods of Shark Reef* (1958), *20 Million Miles to Earth* (1957), and *Viking Women and the Sea Serpent* (1957). Many of these were shown in double and even triple bills and were targeted primarily toward youth and teenage audiences.[19] Similarly, the Regent theater in suburban Burnaby,

B.C., Canada, subsisted through the mid-1950s on programming B-movies for younger viewers. Saturday children's matinees consisted of such fare as the *Tarzan* and *Bomba* series, while evening shows were devoted largely to genre films for the teenage audiences who used the theater as a local gathering place.[20]

While some within the industry decried these "slough houses," such theaters also had their supporters—often highly prominent ones. David Sarnoff, chairman of the Radio Corporation of America, believed that smaller theaters were not necessarily inferior ones. Instead, he saw them as a potential asset to the industry. "Maybe the movie theatre of the future is not the multi-million-dollar cost structure," said Sarnoff: "Maybe it will be the smaller theatre whose flavor, aura and special appeal may come from a combination of circumstances, such as atmosphere, coziness, or the character of the clientele itself, or the special personal hospitality services of the management, much like one likes to patronize favored restaurants because one is treated 'importantly.' The big deluxers may be the 'problem' theatres, instead of the smaller houses, yet it's the bigger houses, as we now know them, which can support the top-rental film attractions, lavish stage-shows and the like."[21]

For those smaller theaters that sought a different "clientele," there were alternatives to programming B-movies. Edward L. Hyman, vice president of the American Broadcasting–Paramount Theatres chain, declared in 1955 that "art films, if properly used, can be employed to boost the box-office and prestige of 'B' theatres."[22] There were already separate art film theaters in the 1950s, described by Barbara Wilinsky in *Sure Seaters: The Emergence of Art House Cinema* as primarily being "small theaters in urban areas or university towns that screened 'offbeat' films such as independent Hollywood, foreign language, and documentary films."[23] Hyman's position, however, was that non-art-film theaters—particularly smaller, nonurban theaters, many of which specialized in B-movies—would benefit by incorporating art films into their programming schedule.

This strategy is an intriguing one because it indicates a blurring of the boundaries between art films and B-movies, which are traditionally considered to be very different cinematic products. Wilinsky points out the value in questioning

> how categories of cinema (such as classical Hollywood cinema, exploitation films, and art films) are created and why. These classifications, used by academics, industry insiders, and audiences, are interesting in that they provide information about the type of film under discussion and also suggest an entire context of production and reception. For example,

describing a film as a classical Hollywood movie not only provides information about the film's textual properties, but also allows presumptions
about the film's production, distribution, and exhibition. Formal and
industrial issues, therefore, tie into the categorization of films.

The screening of art films at B-movie theaters therefore challenges these
notions about how industrial presumptions affect the categorization of
cinematic product. B-movie exhibitors who incorporated art films into their
schedules subverted traditional classifications as per presumed contexts of
reception. Wilinsky further notes, for example, how "the ambiguities and
instabilities found within the categorization of art films necessitated the
support of an entire art cinema industry including institutions such as art
film distributors, theaters, and film societies to set boundaries around art
films and provide them with the desired meanings and values in the postwar
U.S. film market."[24] Yet B-movie theaters were a markedly different form
of institution; thus the exhibition of art films in such venues broke these
boundaries by using these films in a different industrial context.

Hyman described art films as "product, both foreign and domestic, which,
because of popular taste, will not reach its deserved potential if given regular
treatment."[25] Hyman's rhetoric is particularly interesting here since, as the
owner of a chain of mainstream film theaters, he sees art films as deserving
of a wider audience while acknowledging that both the tastes of the general
public frequenting his theaters and the exhibition and marketing strategies employed by these very theaters do not allow art films to reach their
full potential in the cinematic marketplace. Wilinsky states that art cinema
strove to create an "image of difference" from mainstream films such as those
typically screened in Hyman's theaters, doing so "for particular (and, often-
times, financial) reasons." Art films, she argues, were "in constant negotiation with the mainstream cinema, a process that has ultimately shaped both
cultures."

Yet as Hyman's comments illustrate, this process of negotiation was not
always an antagonistic one on the side of mainstream exhibitors, who often
recognized the value of art films. Wilinsky notes that in striving to create
"difference," art films potentially limited their ability to achieve optimum
market growth:

When profits rely on attracting as many people as possible, can an
industry afford to remain alternative, or does it feel the need to become
part of the mainstream in order to maximize profits? Although art film
audiences might be interested in keeping art films alternative and
exclusive, operators of the industry might constantly seek to expand
their audiences. Despite the apparent contradiction, would industry

participants attempt to "sell" the exclusivity of alternative culture to as large an audience as possible? Furthermore, how would the dominant culture, recognizing the potential profit from an alternative culture, try to integrate it into the mainstream?[26]

Hyman's proposal to integrate art films into B-movie theaters is one such example of how art films might have been incorporated into the mainstream. In 1956, only 226 theaters devoted themselves to the full-time exhibition of art films, along with another 400 part-time theaters. This represents only approximately 4 percent of the 15,029 indoor theaters in operation that year.[27] The incorporation of art films into B-movie theaters on a part-time basis would therefore have represented a substantial growth rate in total market share for art film distributors.

An impediment to this incorporation, however, was certain assumptions within the industry regarding the differences between art film theaters (or "sure-seaters") and B-movie theaters. "The sure-seater has a subtle snob appeal that helps at the box office," wrote Stanley Frank in 1952:

> You go into a theater that has a few tasteful paintings in the lobby and a maid serves you a demitasse of coffee. You've just paid top admission prices, but the coffee creates a pleasant aura. Then you're shown to a comfortable seat in a well mannered audience. The show lasts two hours; there is no Class C horror or murder mishmash to pad out a double-feature program. You see a picture that assumes you have average intelligence and it's such a refreshing switch that you are flattered to be among such perceptive folks who are sharing the experience.[28]

Here the implication is that B-movie theaters specialize in "mishmash" for unintelligent, poorly behaved audiences. The double-feature format of the B-theater is also indirectly chastised, as if resulting by its very nature in a lack of quality entertainment. Nevertheless, many art film distributors actively sought films that could transcend the limits of the art-house theater and find success in mainstream exhibition contexts among the general public.[29] For those distributors able to overcome their prejudices, B-theaters represented a viable opportunity for such a crossover into an often neglected segment of the mainstream market.

Hyman defined B theaters as "houses which get other than first choice on pictures and many suburban theatres," with "both groups now feeling the competition of television and drive-ins most acutely." He noted that art films could be used as supplements to regular programming but should not be considered "a program of 'salvation' and therefore must not be used to "completely fill the product gap." The Austin theater in Austin, Minnesota, for example, was able to increase revenues by running "a series of 12 'prestige pictures,' played single feature mid-week." Booking art films allowed theaters to bring in "a new element of patronage," which was of appeal to exhibitors who were looking for an alternative to the increasing trend toward youth audiences. Furthermore, "much of the profit potential" of booking art films came from "the fact that 'A' house admission prices in 'B' houses can be obtained." Of further appeal was that those theaters profiting from art films "devoted [their] least valuable playing time to these attractions—as the art film patrons will come as readily midweek as on weekends, if they will come at all."[30]

These films were marketed beyond just their regular patrons, however, and the advertising used therein highlights a compelling parallel between the promotion of B-movies and of art films. Commentators (both modern and those of the period) routinely use variations of the term "exploitation" when discussing how art films were marketed in the 1950s. Yet exploitation films had an entirely different connotation in the 1950s, being associated not with high art but with B-films and the lower end of popular culture.[31] Wilinsky notes, for example, that "people opposed to art cinema—those within Hollywood, censorship groups, and even the art film industry itself—pointed out the financial benefits gained by art film industry insiders who exploited sexual content to attract audiences." She also describes how "the art film producers, distributors, and particularly the exhibitors were the people charged with exploiting sex to sell films."[32] The rhetoric used here is similar to John E. Twomey's in a 1956 article for the *Quarterly Review of Film, Radio and Television* asserting that "these films have been advertised and exploited as 'exotic' motion pictures and that herein lies the clue to their popularity."[33]

The American marketing for several Italian neorealist films in the late 1940s, for instance, emphasized sexuality that was not prevalent in the films, such as *Open City* (1945) being "generally advertised with a misquotation from *Life* adjusted to read: 'Sexier than Hollywood ever dared to be,' together with a still of two young ladies deeply engrossed in a rapt embrace." Similarly, *The Bicycle Thief* (1948) "was completely devoid of any erotic embellishments, but the exhibitors sought to atone for this deficiency with a highly imaginative sketch of a young lady riding a bicycle."[34] Sexuality was similarly exploited in the marketing of many B-movies in the 1950s. Such provocatively titled films as *Girls in Prison* (1956) and *Diary of a High School Bride* (1959) were targeted toward the teenage male libido and featured marketing campaigns that attempted to capitalize on this demographic's sexual impulses.

This similarity in how both art films and B-movies exploited sexuality in their marketing suggests that while each is traditionally considered to be the cultural opposite of the other—the former being high art, the latter low art—the two were both highly successful in capitalizing on what Wilinsky describes as their perceived vulgarity. "On the one hand," she says, "art cinema was seen as 'noncommercial' and artistically motivated, offering an escape from the brash commercialism of Hollywood. On the other hand, though, critics depicted the art cinema industry as actually more vulgar in its commercialism than Hollywood, willing to take advantage of any sexual angle to attract an audience." Furthermore, she quotes *Variety*'s assessment that "art houses had to 'build an arty patronage of steady customers who come because of the theater rather than the billing.'"[35] This objective is one that also defines the B-theater as an institution, as exhibitors and audiences alike were largely unconcerned with the quality of individual films so long as a steady quantity was available. These patterns highlight the fact that while both art films and B-movies were marginalized products, typically existing on opposite fringes of the mainstream, they did share some remarkable similarities. With the exhibition of art films in B-theaters in the 1950s, these seemingly diverse cinematic entities became located in the same site of consumption.

Exhibition Patterns: Ozoners and Ballyhooing

While Hyman stopped short of calling art films the salvation of the B-movie theater, *Variety* applied religious rhetoric to a different form of exhibition in a 1956 article entitled "Drive-Ins Saviour for 'B' Features." The article draws a parallel between the distribution of foreign films and that of B-movies, using the city of Minneapolis as its case study. Although not receiving first-run exhibition in mainstream downtown theaters, it notes, many foreign films "have been yielding big rental payments to their distributors from initial and other arrangements in the city's few neighborhood 'fine arts' theatres." The article compares this market share not only to the drive-in industry in Minneapolis but also to distribution patterns of the B-movie in general:

> "B" pictures, which almost invariably nowadays experience tough box office standing if they're able to crash a first-run downtown theatre here, may be finding a profitable haven in the local drive-ins. At least, in several instances during the past two seasons such fare, after being rejected by the downtown conventional houses, has had its initial showings in the ozoners to healthy business. Latest example is Allied Artists' *Shack Out on 101* which recently finished a big grossing first-run

engagement at the local 101 drive-in theatre. The distributor had been unsuccessful in making a satisfactory loop deal for it.[36]

Identified in this article are two obvious but important trends affecting B-movies in the 1950s: they rarely received distribution in the premiere first-run theaters, and many Bs earned sufficient revenues despite being limited to drive-ins. Hence, both B-movies and art films were considered by executives and analysts alike as occupying a relatively marginal position within the industry because of the difficulty in attainting first-run distribution in major cities. Yet despite their routine allocation to what many would label the less desirable or fringe elements of the marketplace—neighborhood theaters and drive-ins—these films were often still able to provide strong returns.

This is not to say that drive-ins played B-movies to the exclusion of all other films. Rather, the overall decline in available cinematic product affected drive-ins particularly hard as compared to many indoor theaters. In determining release schedules of new films for any given period, the major studios generally did not consider the specific needs of fringe exhibitors such as drive-ins; such exhibitors complained of a need for more films because they were required to use double bills to be financially successful. This format requirement had little to do with box office admissions but was instead related to a rarely considered but crucial element of film exhibition. As reported in 1955 by the *Hollywood Reporter*, "Drive-in operators almost unanimously insist that they must run double-feature bills in order to draw and hold patrons for maximum concession business—which is of primary interest to a majority of the operators." Single-bill screenings, even if "a widescreen super running more than two hours," saw concession sales reduced by up to one-half.[37]

B-movies particularly benefited from the concession-stand concerns of drive-in theater owners given that exhibitors' booking habits were often swayed by a film's potential concession sales.[38] With B-movies typically drawing younger audiences than most other films in the 1950s, concession sales were aided by the avid demands of the teenager's distinctive metabolism. One drive-in manager even saw a correlation between low-quality films and concession-stand revenues: "'The worse the pictures are,' he reported, 'the more stuff we sell.'"[39]

The Bs were also aided by the fact that many drive-in exhibitors were more concerned with filling screen space than in securing top films. Many drive-in owners openly admitted that so long as they could get a certain quantity of films, they were not particularly concerned about quality: "Every type of picture, big or small, has a certain amount of drawing and 'pleasing' power, and . . . a season's program will average out satisfactorily so long as the quantity is there."[40]

This need for quantity over quality was a major reason why B-movies flourished in the mid- to late 1950s. Samuel Arkoff of American International Pictures stated, "We sometimes had to open our movies in drive-ins or, in some cities, they wouldn't play at all," and said that "the running gag about drive-ins was 'They play last-run movies, right after drug stores.' The major studios never really considered them reputable."[41]

The fact that drive-ins had such difficulty booking first-run films led to numerous lawsuits from exhibitors challenging what they deemed to be unfair distribution practices.[42] Writing in 1956, Frank J. Taylor pointed out that first-run films were typically rented to drive-ins "on a bid basis which may give the distributor up to 70 per cent of the gate take, plus a flat minimum guarantee." With the limited profit-margin involved in such a deal, many drive-in owners took "the attitude that they don't need first-run pictures to fill their ramps; second-run pictures will do just as well."[43]

It was under these conditions that B-movies were able to thrive at drive-in theaters, as exhibitors welcomed new sources of programming. Given that independent companies did not always secure distribution prior to a film's production, they were often limited to whatever segment of the market they could acquire. Despite such limitations, the appeal of many B-films could often be enhanced through the use of ballyhooing, a sensationalistic or gimmicky form of publicity used by both producers and exhibitors to attract audiences. Ballyhoo amounts to a variation on the "packaging" stage of media economics, occurring after the production stage, in which media content is created. Such content is then amassed or packaged together, turning it into a product for subsequent marketing and consumption.[44] Ballyhooing attempts to add an additional element of packaging to a film in order to make it more marketable, often in the form of a newly created exhibition process or interactive device given to audiences at each screening. Film studios typically package their films prior to the distribution stage, allowing individual exhibitors to implement their own respective marketing campaigns. Ballyhooed films, on the other hand, are just as likely to involve producer-controlled packaging aspects at the postdistribution level.

Ballyhoo has been a part of cinema since its inception, particularly with early versions of sound and color technologies. The definitive form of ballyhoo in the 1950s was 3-D, with no fewer than fifteen different systems for creating three-dimensional effects having been created by various companies, including those from the major studios along with others such as Depth-O-Vision, Natural Vision, and True Stereo 3-D.[45]

Numerous other gimmicks besides 3-D were attempted during the 1950s, particularly toward the end of the decade as increased competition led to a saturation of the B-movie market. Much of this competition was inspired by producer-director William Castle, whose horror films for Allied Artists are perhaps better remembered for their gimmickry than for their aesthetics. This isn't to say that Castle was not respected within the industry; on the contrary, the *Hollywood Reporter* declared that the film industry "might be better off if there were more producers like Bill Castle. Castle not only is a producer—he is a showman. When he gives the exhibitor a picture, he also gives them something to talk about." For his film *Macabre* (1958), Castle offered insurance policies with every ticket guaranteeing compensation to anyone who died of fright while watching the film. Ads were run in both the *Hollywood Reporter* and *Variety* promising

> $1,000 in case of DEATH BY FRIGHT* During the showing of *Macabre*
> *not valid for people with known heart conditions or for suicide.

In an instance of postdistribution packaging, *House on Haunted Hill* (1958) featured the gimmick of Emergo, whereby an illuminated skeleton was propelled over the heads of the audience. Castle incorporated this effect into the film itself, instructing exhibitors that this gimmick must be deployed at a specific moment in the film when a skeleton seemingly comes to life. In doing so, Castle was able to control how his film was packaged for audiences

Macabre (William Castle Productions/Allied Artists Pictures, 1958)

beyond the film's distribution stage. "The sophisticated may, rightly, consider this pretty corny," said the *Hollywood Reporter* of Emergo. "But as every house manager knows, sophisticates are a minority in movies audiences and Emergo, if properly ballyhooed, stands a chance to equal the success of the skeleton that, bathed in a green light, used to come gliding down on a wire from the balcony to the stage of the oldtime stock companies."[46]

Many such ballyhoo gimmicks were indeed old-fashioned in their approach, and not always as technologically developed as 3-D. Castle followed up Emergo with a new process called Percepto for *The Tingler* (1959), whereby theater seats were rigged, in a rather unique example of postdistribution packaging, to vibrate when the title creature appeared onscreen. By this point, Castle had many competitors in the ballyhoo area, no doubt inspired by his success. Independent companies continued to emerge toward the end of the 1950s to take advantage of the growth in the B-move market, as the ballyhoo cycle of films progressed. Gimmicks used in the late 1950s include Aroma-Rama, a system in which different odors were released through the theater to accompany particular scenes; Cinemagic, which promised to "take audiences into the fourth dimension" in *The Angry Red Planet* (1959); Dynamation, a stop-motion animation technique developed by Ray Harryhausen for *The 7th Voyage of Sinbad* (1958); Hypno-Magic, which involved inflating a "Hypnotic Eye Balloon" for use with the film *The Hypnotic Eye* (1959); the supposedly hypnotic Hypnovista technique used in *Horrors of the Black Museum* (1959); a method alternately advertised as both Mattascope and Amazoscope for *The 30 Foot Bride of Candy Rock* (1959) using process shots to achieve the film's title character; and PsychoRama, a subliminal process that has since been banned, used in *Terror in the Haunted House* (1959).[47]

The result of so many different ballyhoo gimmicks was an inevitable perplexity resulting from the fact that so many of them were similar in nature. "Horror pictures have become so commonplace recently that it is difficult for the public to distinguish one from the other," cautioned *Variety*. "As a consequence, producers and distributors are going all out to come up with a gimmick that will make one entry different from another. What is happening in effect, however, is that the gimmicks are being carbon-copied with slight variations and are becoming so numerous that the public is thought pretty confused," the magazine contends.[48]

If ballyhoo gimmicks were not enough to draw the public, B-movie producers and exhibitors could try a more grassroots approach to selling their films. In doing so, an attempt was frequently made to identify the particular demographics of, and audience response to, a film at the local level in various towns or regions in order to better tailor marketing approaches to target audiences. During preproduction for *Macabre*, Castle cited the need for a "barnstorming" approach to promoting the film, a term traditionally used for political campaigns or acting troupes that travel from town to town making brief stops, usually in rural areas. "First, we're going to revive the good old 'barnstorming' system," said Castle, "and go out with the picture under our arm, and play it in all kinds of territories, big cities and small towns, until we find out personally how good it is, or how bad, and learn how best to advertise it, exploit it, promote it in all the different kinds of media, working out a sales campaign that we then will know is right for the attraction. The time is right for this system."[49]

This approach was alternately referred to as "tub-thumping" by the *Hollywood Reporter*, which acknowledged that the strategy was indeed part of *Macabre*'s success at the box office.[50] Such rhetoric implies a carnival atmosphere in this approach to marketing, signifying that if all else failed, B-movies could be promoted using traditional methods of publicity popularized by sideshow barkers well before the birth of cinema itself. In fact, Castle even called his autobiography *Step Right Up! I'm Gonna Scare the Pants off America*, directly acknowledging this carnival connection and the way in which the hard-sell approach often used to promote carnival freak shows was so successful in getting audiences out to theaters for these ballyhooed B-movies throughout the decade.

Production Patterns in the Early 1950s: Lippert and the Independents

The evolving patterns of B-movie exhibition in the 1950s—from double-feature screenings reminiscent of those in previous decades to the nascent incorporation of art films in B-theater schedules to the proliferation of ballyhooing—are symptomatic of the fact that the B-movie itself changed as an entity during the decade. The industrial entity known as Poverty Row formed in the 1930s had all but collapsed by the early 1950s, signaling the end of a particular era of B-movie production. Eagle-Lion/Producers Releasing Corporation met its demise, Republic was heading toward its inevitable downfall, and Monogram evolved into Allied Artists.[51]

Yet just as the early days of Poverty Row in the 1930s saw a regular pattern of new companies forming to replace those that had folded, the 1950s also saw a relatively high degree of turnover among the smaller companies specializing in low-budget product. While Poverty Row's collapse ensued, increased competition was seen in the form of several new independent companies serving as either producers or distributors (or occasionally both). New opportunities for independent entrepreneurs were suddenly available, and many entered the industry in an attempt to acquire a small share of the B-movie marketplace despite the increased risk entailed in what was now a rapidly changing and uncertain cinematic marketplace.

The late 1940s saw the emergence of one company, for instance, called The Filmakers Inc., led by the husband-and-wife team of producer Collier Young and actor-director Ida Lupino. Far more than simply being typical Hollywood players going incorporated, Filmakers was established in 1949 in the hopes of creating a viable, ongoing independent company that could make films that were more socially relevant than most produced by the major studios. Upon their debut in 1949, the *New York Times*'s J. D. Spiro described Filmakers as "an off-beat company with some distinctive ideas about the what and the how of motion pictures."

Young's own stated mandate was to "produce movies based on vital subjects not likely to appeal to the great majority of producers."[52] "I suppose we were the New Wave at that time," Lupino reasoned. "We went along the line of doing films that had social significance and yet were entertainment. The pictures were based on true stories, things the public could understand because they had happened or been of news value," she said. The company was also committed to using new talent in its films: "Filmakers was an outlet specially for new people—actors, writers, young directors," said Lupino, who directed several films for the company herself.[53]

Rather than be content with distributing its projects via the major studios, Filmakers eventually established itself as a distribution organization in 1954, dealing in its own films as well as those of fellow independent producers. Specializing in low-budget thrillers and film noir that often had strong social themes, Filmakers lasted seven years and produced nine films: *Never Fear* (1949), *Outrage* (1950), *Hard, Fast and Beautiful* (1951), *On the Loose* (1951), *Beware, My Lovely* (1952), *The Hitch-Hiker* (1953), *The Bigamist* (1953), *Private Hell 36* (1954), and *Mad at the World* (1955). The company also served as a distributor for such films as *A Life at the Stake* (1954), *Crashout* (1955), and *Fury in Paradise* (1955). Although a relatively short-lived company, it was often a highly respected one, with Howard Thompson calling Filmakers "one of the West Coast's more ingenious independent film units" in 1954.[54]

Shortly before Filmakers' demise, Distributors Corporation of America (DCA) was formed as a distribution firm by Fred Schwartz, owner of the Century chain of theaters, along with former RKO sales executive Charles Boasberg.[55] DCA, which debuted in 1954, was of particular benefit to the B-movie market by serving as a venue for those smaller independent producers and companies lacking the means to distribute their own films. As such, organizations like DCA served as a vital source of product to those smaller theaters that were the most negatively affected by the industry's overall decline in the number of films produced. With its declared intent "to help increase the availability of films to theaters that have experienced the shortage of products in recent months because of the cutbacks in production of movies by the major Hollywood studios," DCA planned to release between ten and twelve films in its first two years of operation, and thereafter release the same number annually.[56]

DCA's initial strategy was largely to dub and reissue foreign films for the American market, such as *Il Bigamo* (1956) starring Marcello Mastroianni. Toward the end of the decade, the company moved into distributing independently produced science fiction films, including *The Strange World of Planet X* (1957) and *Monster from Green Hell* (1958). It went out of business in 1959 with (and perhaps due in part to) its final release, Ed Wood Jr.'s *Plan 9 from Outer Space* (1959). DCA was absorbed by Hal Roach Studios, which in turn formed Roach Distribution Corporation for the release of foreign films as well as Roach's own productions.[57]

DCA's competition in the B-movie distribution market included Howco International Pictures, formed in 1951 by theater chain owners J. Francis White and Joy Houck. Howco was essentially a states' rights distributor like those of previous decades and DCA. White and Houck's intent in forming the company was to secure films from independent companies and producers for initial exhibition in their theaters before offering them to theaters nationwide.[58] With obtaining a steady flow of new product becoming increasingly difficult for exhibitors as the decade progressed, the formation of distribution companies by theater owners was certainly one remedy to the problem. Howco would release such B-movies during the decade as *Jail Bait* (1954), *Mesa of Lost Women* (1956), *Carnival Rock* (1957), *The Naked Venus* (1958), *My World Dies Screaming* (1958), and *Lost, Lonely and Vicious* (1958). Howco enjoyed nearly three decades of success as a distributor, eventually shutting down in 1979.

One of the most successful independent companies emerging in the immediate wake of the 1948 antitrust ruling was Lippert Pictures Inc. Robert L. Lippert founded the company in 1949 after reorganizing the previous entity, Screen Guild Productions (SGP), for which he had served as executive vice president since 1945.[59] Having previously only operated in the film industry as a theater owner, Lippert produced his first film in 1948, *Jungle Goddess*, starring future Superman actor George Reeves and former Dick Tracy actor Ralph Byrd. Lippert made numerous westerns between 1949 and 1950, such as *I Shot Jesse James* (1949), *Treasure of Monte Cristo* (1949), *The Dalton Gang* (1949), *Marshal of Heldorado* (1950), and *I Shot Billy the Kid* (1950). These jungle adventures and low-budget westerns placed Lippert in direct competition with the remaining Poverty Row studios, making it appear likely that Lippert would suffer the same fate that soon befell those companies continuing to make B-movies that were more or less the same as those that had been produced since the early 1930s.

Lippert proved to be a savvy businessman, however, with *Variety* praising him for being able to take "low-budget filmmaking out of the shoestring category and put it on a big business basis": "He's turning out actioners for about $60,000 and showing a profit of somewhere around $15,000 each on them. That gives him a nice return, considering that he makes 10 or more a year, plus the fact that his own distributing company also makes a good fee for handling them."[60] While many businessmen formed unsuccessful Poverty Row studios in the 1930s, and many more formed short-lived independent companies in the 1950s, Lippert's success was due in part to the fact that he got his start as a theater owner before starting SGP. By 1949 he owned over sixty theaters in Oregon and California, giving him an experienced understanding not possessed by many of his competitors in the B-movie market of the dynamics of supply and demand based on his years of analyzing which kinds of films were successful at the level of exhibition. His well-rounded background in the film industry also extended to his service as a director for many of SGP's westerns, and he played bit parts in most of them as well. One reporter described him as "a man who looks the part of a western 'heavy'"; thus Lippert's roles gave him the opportunity not only to gain experience in yet another facet of filmmaking but also to save money on talent costs.[61]

Lippert is perhaps best known for finding early success in the science fiction genre before most of his competitors with the release of *Rocketship X-M* in 1950. Many film scholars have commented on how the science fiction genre in early 1950s America was an extension and updating of the horror genre, which had faded from popularity in the late 1940s.[62] While others continued to make genre films similar to those of prior decades, Lippert was savvy enough to recognize both the cyclical and evolutionary nature of genre films—capitalizing on the resultant potential of the science fiction genre as an untapped segment of the market.

Rocketship X-M was praised within the industry for holding a "payoff position in proportion of return to cost. It came in at $94,000 and has grossed over $600,000."[63] The *Los Angeles Times* noted that due largely to the film's success, "the scientific thriller probably will be a regular part of the program from now on. *Rocketship X-M* and *Destination Moon* have proved how successful that type of feature can be."[64] It is important to note that science fiction was not a viable genre in Hollywood at the start of the decade; the sci-fi cycle at the major studios did not begin until 1951 with Twentieth Century–Fox's *The Day the Earth Stood Still* and RKO's *The Thing (From Another World)*. Of these two films, *Variety* wrote, "Crystal ballers, eyeing grosses on the pair of men-from-Marsers, see them sure to hype an already existing 'cycle.'"

Also part of this science fiction cycle in 1951 was United Artist's *The Man from Planet X* and Paramount's *When Worlds Collide*: "Observer's guesses that this series of films will result in plenty more is based on normal Hollywood experience that success breeds cycles. These occur regularly despite squawks from exhibs, critics and the public and every effort by production execs to head them off."[65]

Together, *Rocketship X-M* and Eagle-Lion's *Destination Moon* prove that low-budget independent filmmakers can be trendsetters in the film industry, actively establishing film genre cycles rather than merely trying to capitalize upon them after they have already been initiated by the Hollywood majors. Whereas B-movies of previous decades typically imitated the trends and cycles of the major studios, 1950s B-movies were often themselves the innovators, spurring genre cycles and demographic trends that the majors could not help but take notice of and ultimately emulate.

Lippert's success attracted much attention in the film industry in 1950, particularly from his low-budget peers. On July 26 of that year, Monogram president Steve Broidy revealed that he was seeking a deal with Lippert surrounding the distribution of both companies' films. The two men had "discussed a possible arrangement under which physical handling of Monogram and Lippert product would be placed with the same exchanges." The tentative deal was reported as a possible merger in the trades, with negotiations supposedly already under way. Broidy was quick to emphasize, however, that "the arrangement would in no sense be a merger of the two companies," and that "so far the talks between the two have been exploratory."[66] While the deal never came to pass, it signifies the extent to which his rivals viewed Lippert as serious competition. Lippert Pictures Inc. was in effect one of the dominant players among the remaining independent companies, and viewed by many as essentially being the model by which B-movies should be produced during a period in which the fate of the Bs was increasingly uncertain.

Lippert followed *Rocketship X-M*'s success with similar science fiction efforts such as *Lost Continent* (1951), *Unknown World* (1951), and *Spaceways* (1953). He also reacted sooner than most Poverty Row and independent studios—and some major studios—in determining that his company should be diversifying into the A-film marketplace and making fewer but bigger films. In August of 1950, Lippert announced that the upcoming fiscal year would see twelve feature films made at a combined budget of over $2 million, released at a rate of one per month. This was the same amount that the company had spent on thirty-nine films the previous year, meaning that Lippert would produce fewer than a third as many in the new year. Six of the twelve films were expected to be A-pictures, although he acknowledged "the box-office will determine that." Three of the films were even slated to be in color, using a "new three-color process" by Cinecolor.

The change in policy was prompted not only by his recent box office successes but also by "the result of research conducted with big circuit and independent exhibitors."[67] As such, Lippert was actively trying to anticipate the needs of the marketplace while reacting to the emerging transitional era of filmmaking, as opposed to Republic's increasingly futile stay-the-course approach in making B-films that were practically identical to those of past decades. Lippert's decision to change his focus even attracted the attention of *Life* magazine, which noted that while Lippert began producing films "specifically to make low-budget 'B's,' [he] has now completely reversed his field and plans to cut the number of his productions in half, spend twice as much money and time on each, and—he hopes—make them at least twice as good. . . . From the public's point of view, of course," the article added, in a rather cynical reproach of B-movies, "this is the greatest news since sound."[68]

Lippert's company flourished in 1951, and like other studios at the time began offering financial aid to independent producers. Lippert declared that he was "opening the door to 'package deals' on terms more favorable than obtainable elsewhere," indicating that as independent production thrived in the early 1950s, there was increasing competition among the minor studios as to who could secure the strongest reputation as financier amid the ongoing collapse of Poverty Row.[69] Further to this, Lippert signed a deal in December that same year with the talent agency Famous Artists Corporation for the development of package deals with the latter's client list of actors, writers, directors, and producers. Along with profit participation on any films released through Lippert Distribution, the deal promised to offer those involved "a wider freedom in the selection of pictures," with the first such film released being the 1952 film noir *Loan Shark*. Lippert was so committed to the idea that he "was willing to give over as much as 75 percent of potential distribution profits to build up the plan of financial participation by talent in filmmaking."[70]

Despite his stated emphasis on making fewer pictures, Lippert was still able to increase production in 1951. It was announced that eight films would be released in an eight-week period, representing "a new high for any two-month period since the formation of his company three years ago."[71] The films themselves—including *Lost Continent*, *Unknown World*, *Savage Drums*, *FBI Girl*, and *Superman and the Mole Men*—were far from being the A-pictures Lippert had previously announced he was pursuing. Lippert may have left it up to the box office to determine their ranking, but with an average cost of well under $200,000 these films clearly fall under the B-range of production costs for feature films in the 1950s.

This fiscal trend toward larger budgets would continue in 1952 with Lippert's announcement at his company's first national convention in January that "the coming year should up the firm's shooting schedule from around a $2,000,000 production outlay of the past year to more than $4,000,000 in 1952." This new total budget was to be spread across twenty-two films, meaning that the average cost of each would be approximately $182,000.[72]

While this figure is higher than that allotted by many independent studios to their films in the 1950s, it is still nowhere near what was typically spent on an A-picture by any given studio, major or minor.

Yet Lippert's corporate agenda was clearly focused on the A-marketplace, as evidenced by his declaration in March of 1952 that he "wouldn't produce any more of the low-budgeters because 'there's no market left for them.'"[73] He did, however, come to embrace a key strategy that successful B-filmmakers increasingly employed in the 1950s—creative marketing in order to establish a distinctive product. Lippert stated that the "merchandising [of] film" was becoming increasingly important, as it "would add more profits to the company and is the only way to combat declining box office."[74] This strategy would find its eventual culmination in the ballyhoo trend near the end of the decade and in the innovative advertising strategies of American International Pictures.

This was not the only method that Lippert used to increase his profits. In 1955, Lippert Pictures Inc. was dissolved and an agreement made with Twentieth Century–Fox to serve as both producer and executive producer on various projects (described as "so-called 'program type' features") under the banner of Regal Films.[75] He was perhaps not entirely scrupulous in this new arrangement, as director Gene Fowler Jr. claimed that Lippert used to embezzle money from his new studio: "Lippert was releasing pictures through Twentieth Century–Fox; he had a deal whereby he'd make pictures for $125,000, and if the picture came in for less than that, he'd steal from the top," said Fowler.[76]

Despite his intention at the start of the decade to move away from low-budget production, Lippert was still involved with the Bs at the end of the 1950s with Twentieth Century–Fox. By the middle of the decade, Lippert's success as an independent producer had inspired the entry of multiple competitors into the B-movie market, in turn replacing the older Poverty Row studios that had flourished in previous decades. In some ways, Lippert's basic organizational model and his relationship with the dominant Hollywood system were comparable to that of Republic and its peers in the 1930s and 1940s. At the same time, Lippert was able to take more financial risks and anticipate marketplace demands more actively than his predecessors. Independent producer-director Herschell Gordon Lewis (1963's *Blood Feast*, 1964's *Two Thousand Maniacs!*) once declared that "the successful independent producer-distributor must produce and release pictures that the major studios either *could not* or *would not* make."[77] Lippert took such a risk in popularizing the science fiction genre with *Rocketship X-M*, the success of which forced Hollywood studios to reevaluate the kinds of genre films they were willing to produce. As such, Lippert's work established

the continued viability of the B-movie at the beginning of the 1950s—
an era in which the majority of the industry believed the Bs to be dead or dying.

Major Studios and B-Movies in the Mid-1950s

While smaller companies such as DCA emerged to capitalize on the growing
product shortage, many of the major Hollywood studios continued to dismiss
the potential of B-movies as the decade neared its midpoint and the trend
toward fewer and bigger pictures persisted. By 1954, some industry observers
even blamed the supposed demise of the Bs for virtually everything that
was wrong with the industry, with Barbara Berch Jamison describing how
"program pictures, the infamous 'B's,' are being snubbed and with their
demise hundreds of people in Hollywood are looking for other jobs, and
movie houses throughout the country are slowing down."[78]

At Universal, Feldman declared at year's end: "The possibility of making a
profit on low-budgeted pictures has been narrowed down in today's market."
He stressed, "The low-budgeted picture has diminished in quantity not
because of any studio policy, but because of the public's dictate and the
competitive situation." There was "no room for 'quickies,'" he went on. On
the contrary, he contended, "in the current market you must start out with
a story of substance and you can't purchase stories as you would groceries,
buying more as you need them. The public has set that policy, not the
studios," he declared.[79]

Not every major studio was against making low-budget quickies. Some in
Hollywood shared the same mentality as the emerging independent companies in seeing new opportunities in the recent dearth of B-movies, given that
there was now less competition. A January 1955 *Variety* headline declared
"3 Majors Thrive on 'B' Pix—Many Exceptions in All-Big Era," noting how
"lesser scale product seems still to have an economically important place
in today's market." Although "the majority of major studio administrators
insist they can get along with only 'quality' pictures," the article says, "the
fact is that filmmakers dealing with non-epic projects are making money,
too." While their studios officially declared an intent to eliminate all B-movie
production in 1951, executives at both Paramount and RKO—along with United
Artists—were reported as believing that "because 'B's' have been dropped
by several studios, pix in this class which continue to be made stand an
improved chance of wide playoff."[80] Paramount would be slow to act on this
notion, though, with executive Louis Phillips reaffirming the studio's position
in 1956 of "sparing no effort or expense to make pictures of outstanding
quality," and being content with the fact that it "eliminated to the greatest
extent possible all so-called B-pictures."[81]

If there was no room for the B-movie in 1951 as studios reacted to a newfound era of change, it would seem that Hollywood was beginning to come to terms with the transitional forces in the industry by the end of 1955, thereby opening up the possibility of reintroducing major studio Bs to the marketplace. Universal, despite Feldman's advice to the contrary, initiated a new program of relatively inexpensive science fiction films. The studio had found success in the genre in recent years with such films as *It Came from Outer Space* (1953) and *Creature from the Black Lagoon* (1954), yet their popularity can arguably be attributed to each being released in 3-D at the height of that trend's popularity. *Revenge of the Creature* and *Tarantula* were released by Universal in 1955, followed by *The Creature Walks Among Us* and *The Mole People* in 1956. This commercial focus on B-movies paid off for the studio, as both *Tarantula* and *Revenge of the Creature* were highly successful at the box office.

The science fiction cycle continued at Universal for several years with *The Deadly Mantis* (1957), *The Land Unknown* (1957), *The Monolith Monsters* (1957), and *Monster on the Campus* (1958). While these films are not as well remembered as those that began Universal's 1950s sci-fi cycle, most were still highly profitable for the studio. *The Deadly Mantis*, for example, cost $350,000, but industry estimates prior to its release anticipated a box office gross "of at least $1,000,000."[82]

As Hollywood began to understand the industry's changes, the function of the B-movie was becoming clearer in the decade's latter half. It became apparent after several years that the B-movie, initially abandoned by the major studios, was not obsolete but could instead play a vital role in strengthening the industry. *Variety*, recognizing Universal's success in making genre films on reduced budgets, championed the importance of the B-movie—and, notably, the B-theater—to the industry's ongoing viability in October 1956.

> The industry which is turning to blockbuster, long-running pictures is wondering if Universal can continue to compete successfully under the current market conditions facing the motion picture industry. U's program of slick, modest budget entries has made the company one of the most successful in the business during the past several years. If U can continue to operate profitably under this formula, it may succeed in revising the industry's thinking to some extent. U's program, of approximately 30 pictures annual, consists of action, science fiction, horror, and soap-opera type romantic films, all high in technical quality but low in budget in comparison to the big picture offerings of rival companies. . . .
>
> This policy has brought U hefty returns. It represents a marked differ-

ence from the era when U attempted to make high-budget intellectual films that almost placed the company in bankruptcy. Whether U can continue its present formula is a matter of speculation. . . .

However, if Universal can continue its present program successfully, it will prove to the industry that "bigness" is not the answer to the industry's ills and that the smalltown and neighborhood subsequent runs are still important to the industry's economy.[83]

Universal's success signifies that the Bs did not need to be subject to an industrial safeguard such as block booking in order to be profitable. The 1950s marketplace was therefore able to support a combination of both large and small films, despite the prognosis of many in the industry at the start of the decade. As was the case in years past, keeping costs down was the key to profitability. While *Tarantula* was a box office success, its $750,000 budget was still relatively high, as evidenced by a 1956 *Variety* headline proclaiming "Today's 'B' Returns $450,000: Economy a Must on L'il Films." The article states that while "big and costly productions are taking more of the spotlight, United Artists is continuing with its program of 48 releases a year, with a number of them obvious [sic] being of the modest-budget variety. Significantly, though, the cost of the smaller pictures must be trimmed more and

Tarantula! (Universal International Pictures, 1955)

more if the company, which finances and distributes its lineup, is to emerge fiscally okay."[84]

With both Universal and United Artists finding success with their low-budget productions, a viable economic model was in place for the rest of the major studios to emulate. Paramount formally declared its intention to resume making B-movies at the end of 1956, although—given the tentative rhetoric of one account in the *Hollywood Reporter*—perhaps begrudgingly: "Though Paramount's preoccupation will continue to be on high-budget productions, the company is not averse to taking on some low-cost projects provided the deals are sufficiently attractive. . . . Among stipulations by the studio are (1) story property of merit that can be made at a sufficiently low cost to assure a profit from their special market, and (2) vehicles offering opportunity to develop new talent."[85]

Indeed, by the beginning of 1957, the industry seemed in complete agreement that B-movies were once again a viable, cost-effective commodity. "'B's' Ride Again, Studios Busier," declared a January 16 *Variety* headline: "Increase in major studio production in 1957, after three years of slackened activity, is seen in the sudden resurgence of interest in 'B' product. Majors are eyeing the program market with more care than they've shown at any time since the widescreen processes were introduced," the article states.[86] Paramount soon after announced its plans for "turning to small-budget product to supplement regular release schedules." The studio was in talks with independent producers who could provide it with B-movies "budgeted at $150,000 and up."[87]

One of those independent producers was Roger Corman, who made many profitable Bs for American International Pictures in the mid- to late 1950s. Paramount was interested in securing "a full slate of programmers" from Corman, who had previously been in talks with Warner Bros. about a similar deal. Corman would instead sign with Allied Artists in 1957 to release *Attack of the Crab Monsters* and *Not of This Earth* that same year, but would go on to direct a major studio film with *I, Mobster* for Twentieth Century–Fox in 1959. Whereas in previous decades Hollywood studios used B-movie production as a training ground for cast and crew—often promoting talented actors and directors to A-pictures—the attempted deals with Corman in the 1950s represented a new strategy of recruiting the talent of independent producers and smaller independent studios. As these independents began finding success in the B-movie marketplace, Hollywood was in a position where it had to compete with the indies; before, it was the independents that sought to compete with the major studio Bs.

Warner Bros. responded by actively seeking producers "who could supply a slate of program material" in 1957, while Twentieth Century–Fox had recently signed an agreement with Lippert's Regal Films "for 25 'B's' to augment the studio's own top-drawer product."[88] Regal's efforts represented a number of different genres: westerns such as *Apache Warrior* (1957), *Copper Sky* (1957), and *Frontier Gun* (1958); the horror films *Back from the Dead* (1957), *She-Devil* (1957), and *The Unknown Terror* (1957); juvenile delinquent films like *Young and Dangerous* (1957) and *Rockabilly Baby* (1957); crime dramas such as *The Abductors* (1957), *Plunder Road* (1957), and *Gang War* (1958); and the science fiction efforts *Kronos* (1957) and *Space Master X-7* (1958). This slate of films is reminiscent of the something-for-everyone approach of prior decades, whereby studios made numerous films to appeal to various niche audiences with different tastes, a stark contrast to the growing trend in 1950s Hollywood toward making blockbuster films seeking to attract much larger audiences.

Furthermore, the return of major studio B-movies represented a turnaround in Hollywood distribution patterns and attitudes about exhibition, as the 1957 *Variety* article "Blockbusters vs. Mainstreet: 'B' (for Budget) Films Return" demonstrates:

> The "little" man in exhibition, and the low budget pictures he needs, are again drawing the sympathetic attention of the major companies. Attitude represents a drastic reversal in the business view of the film companies which, over the past couple of years, have drifted toward fewer releases and a concentration on keycity firstruns. Many predictions of the extinction of "little" exhibition were made by the leaders. There now appears to have evolved a return to the old concept of the "big" industry, with many theatres, and types thereof, plus a large product volume; this despite the obvious appeal of the blockbuster.

The article also points to a stronger relationship between distributors and exhibitors, whereby the long-standing concerns of B-theater owners were finally being addressed. Theatre Owners of America president Ernest G. Stellings noted that distributors have "recognized the need to keep the small theatres alive to insure their profit margin."

> There is speculation that changed distrib attitude vs. the small situations may be rooted in the realization that these small accounts can throw off a profit if:
>
> (1) The product isn't loaded down with a huge budget.
>
> (2) If distribution costs can be minimized.
>
> ... The sudden willingness on the part of the major companies to turn out more films is seen in the light of realization that the survival of the small house depends on the delivery of volume product that can be turned out at very low cost.

One counterargument raised by the article states that "the return to 'mass' production . . . ignores an expensive lesson learned in recent years." In response to this idea, it is noted that "the recent experience has been that the top budget and very low budget films have done well. The product that's been in trouble has been the in-between films."[89] Hence, as Hollywood B-movies regained a position in the industry, the adage put forth at the beginning of the decade that "medium-budgeters" were perhaps the most financially risky productions held true as the decade progressed.[90] The B-movie had finally found its niche in the 1950s marketplace after years of industry uncertainty over the fate of low-budget filmmaking.

Independent Studios, 1956–1959

Independent production of B-movies surged in the latter half of the decade. Many new companies were formed, and most existing companies thrived. As a result, the film shortages that had adversely affected many exhibitors in recent years were sufficiently quelled as the market absorbed this new product. The *Hollywood Reporter* also cited a massive upturn in what it called "hidden production" between 1956 and 1957:

> Production of unannounced, cheap exploitation films in the past year probably set an all-time record, with more than 75 such attractions placed on the market in an obvious attempt to cash in on the major studio curtailments and the consequent big exhibitor demand for any kind of pictures to fill out a double-feature program. In the last four-month period, according to a check-up of exhibition sources and theatre advertisements in newspapers, some 165 new pictures—including both major and independent releases—were shown in theatres covered by the principal film exchange centers. This would be at the rate of nearly 500 a year and is the highest total for any three-month period in the past decade. About 50 of the 165 pictures came from miscellaneous sources, with some foreign imports included, but not counting reissues.
>
> One large circuit disclosed that it had played between 80 and 90 small films last year that did not appear in regular trade release charts but were booked individually for states-rights distributors and other indies. Tracing the sources of the unheralded attractions, it develops that quite a number were made outside Hollywood and launched on the market via local or regional indie exchange outfits.[91]

Such films were often produced and distributed without the awareness of the dominant industry powers, as evidenced by the fact that they went regularly undisclosed on release charts and largely ignored by industry trade publications. As such, these independent B-movies were part of a cinematic subculture in the 1950s that served as a viable alternative for exhibitors to the mainstream Hollywood channels that many theater owners felt did not have their best interests at heart for much of the decade.[92]

Howco International Pictures, for example, served as a distributor for several small production companies that emerged to capitalize on the demand for "any kind of product," including Marquette Productions. The latter company was founded by Jacques Marquette, who produced all of its releases, directing one and serving as cinematographer on the rest. The films were so cheaply made that many of their special effects were deceptively simple. To create the effect of a falling meteor in *Teenage Monster* (1958), Marquette placed sparklers in front of a black background made of felt, then later superimposed the image onto shots of the landscape.[93] Marquette Productions made only two other films in addition to *Teenage Monster* in its short history—*Teenage Thunder* (1957) and *The Brain from Planet Arous* (1958). All three were released by Howco.

Making original films was not the only way to compete in the B-movie marketplace, since acquiring and modifying existing films could also yield quick profits. Producer Joseph H. Levine bought the rights to the Japanese film *Gojira* (1954) and crafted a dubbed version retitled *Godzilla: King of the Monsters* (1956), incorporating new footage with actor Raymond Burr. The changes cost approximately $100,000, and the film earned over $2 million from states' rights distribution on a city-by-city basis by TransWorld Releasing and Levine's own Embassy Pictures. The film's success led Levine to acquire the rights to the 1958 Italian film *The Labors of Hercules*, which was dubbed into English and retitled *Hercules* for a 1959 release. Levine used *Godzilla*'s success to secure distribution from Warner Bros., which gave *Hercules* a saturation release on six hundred screens and spent $1.5 million on advertising.[94] With the film earning close to $5 million domestically, Levine proved that low-budget product could earn several million dollars through more than just one form of distribution in the new exhibition landscape of the 1950s.

A less successful example of this process is also found with a group called Exploitation Productions Incorporated (EPI). This company name is, in a way, one of the most distinct of the decade even though it is also one of the most generic. Whereas a B-movie studio such as Monogram changed its name to Allied Artists in part because it sounded more prestigious, EPI seemingly chose its name for the opposite reason—because distributors and exhibitors would know that they were getting low-budget B-product. In 1957, EPI purchased the rights to *Dementia*, originally produced, written, and directed by John Parker under the company name J. J. Parker Productions in

1955 and receiving theatrical exhibition in that year. EPI changed the title to the more lurid and seemingly more marketable *Daughter of Horror*, releasing the film once more to theaters in 1957. New narration by actor-announcer Ed McMahon was added, while two minutes of footage apparently deemed too controversial by EPI was cut from the original version. The market for Bs was evidently so strong at the time that it could withstand the reuse of recent titles, even ones seemingly unsuccessful enough to have prompted their sale to a different company.

In a case of one B-film aiding the notoriety of another, *Daughter of Horror* is perhaps best known for its appearance in *The Blob* (1958). When the title creature of the latter film attacks a movie theater, *Daughter of Horror* is playing while the Blob breaks through the screen. There is even a shot of the marquee outside the theater featuring the title, with the phenomenal success of *The Blob* saving *Dementia/Daughter of Horror* from cinematic obscurity.

The Blob was produced by Jack Harris, who had previously worked as a regional distributor under the states' rights system. "I handled other people's mistakes for 21 years and always said, 'I could do better than that,'" said Harris on the film's origin.[95] Forming his own production company, Tonylyn Productions Inc., Harris produced the film as an independent project but was contacted by Paramount after its completion. A deal was made paying Harris three times the film's production costs, a small fraction of what it would eventually earn at the box office. This is a further example of a major studio recruiting an independent producer, with an emphasis on finding already completed films from external sources rather than developing new talent internally (as per the B-production units of previous decades).

With the industry's return to B-movie production came a renewed focus on particular genres such as horror and science fiction. "The road to riches is partly paved with gimmicks," *Variety* stated in November of 1957. "Inexpensive exploitation product, including the horroramas and outer-space entries, have done well in 1957," it noted. Hollywood simply could not afford to ignore the growing trend toward B-movies, forcing some studios to rethink their production schedules: "Last year Paramount dropped George Pal from its producer roster for the reason the company couldn't make money with the type of material ('When Worlds Collide,' etc.) in which he specialized. But aware of the current goings-on at the box office, this same company now has entered a deal with William Alland to make three science-fiction pictures. And, by way of hitching a ride on Sputnik, Par, like other outfits, is reissuing its back-number sci-fi epics."

The article surmises that "the public is buying freaks; pictures about normal people too often lack the offbeat excitement that sells tickets." Hence the major studios were often forced to imitate, or acquire outright, the films of independent studios formed in response to the very product shortage that Hollywood had created. The strongest example provided in the article is *The Curse of Frankenstein* (1957), which is described as a "shoe-string budgeter ($270,000) imported from England, and firmly rapped by the critics, [that] likely will gross over $2,000,000. This is spectacular, being well above the amount of coin racked up by many a Hollywood 'A' production."[96] *The Curse of Frankenstein* was the first in a cycle of profitable horror films from British studio Hammer Film Productions Limited. The studio, which was established in 1934, had found some success in the science fiction genre with *The Quatermass Experiment* (1955), which led to Warner Bros. picking up the distribution rights to its follow-up effort *X the Unknown* (1956) and in turn *The Curse of Frankenstein*.[97]

Warner Bros.' success with *The Curse of Frankenstein* led *Variety* to declare in November of 1957 that there was a "global boom" in horror films under way. Despite one review calling the film "corn on the macabre," it was acknowledged that "rarely has a motion picture stirred so much comment within the film trade itself as that of 'Curse of Frankenstein.'"[98] Hammer responded in the final months of 1957 by seeking deals with several of the major Hollywood studios, using the industry's trend toward obtaining independently made B-movie product to fullest advantage. Deals were made to produce three horror films for Columbia, one for Universal, and another for Paramount.[99]

This cycle of horror films and "freak" pictures would continue long enough to inspire more new companies to enter the marketplace with the hopes of capitalizing on the trend. Where there was once a product shortage, the late 1950s saw a tremendous growth rate in the number of films produced. While there were fewer than three hundred films released in 1955, the statistics projected regarding the increase in hidden production anticipated closer to five hundred films for 1957.[100] That year, for example, saw the formation of American Broadcasting–Paramount Theatres Pictures (AB-PT), a production company formed out of the American Broadcasting–Paramount Theatres exhibition chain, which itself resulted from the American Broadcasting Company's purchase of Paramount's theaters following the antitrust rulings. Like DCA before it, AB-PT Pictures saw creating its own films as one way of combating the product shortage. Once initially shown in its own theaters, the films could then be distributed elsewhere for additional revenue.[101]

In May of 1957 AB-PT president Irving H. Levin announced a schedule of seven films to be produced with an initial total budget of $3 million, with all seven to "meet the exhibitor's call for 'highly gimmicked and exploitable' product." The first two films, *The Unearthly* (1957) and *The Beginning of the End* (1957), would initially be booked as a double bill at eighty of the chain's theaters in Illinois and Indiana.[102] The second double bill that emerged was *Eighteen and Anxious* (1958) and *Girl in the Woods* (1958). While distribution plans beyond their own theaters had not yet been finalized at the time of this announcement, a deal was reached the following month with Republic (which had since ceased production itself) to distribute AB-PT's films after their initial run at the chain's theaters.[103] *Variety* saw this strategy as being potentially successful, noting of *The Beginning of the End* that, "based on its cost, its protected haven in the AB-PT houses, and its susceptibility to exploitation, the film can conceivably wind up as a modest money-maker."[104]

Yet AB-PT quickly succumbed to the temptation that was the undoing of other, larger B-movie studios during the decade. The company announced on September 24, 1957, that it would "move into production of 'major' quality features next year with approximately 5 of its scheduled 15 films to fall into this category." The company's plan for these new films was an ambitious one, whereby "budgets will run between $500,000–$1,000,000 as compared with average $300,000 budget for firm's 'modest' productions so far."[105]

These major films would never emerge, as ABPT would ultimately produce only the above four films. Yet as was the case in the 1930s with the original Poverty Row studios, there was a relatively high degree of turnover among the independent production companies that specialized in B-movies in the late 1950s. Both circumstances were the result of a large influx of competition due to exceptionally good commercial opportunities created by marketplace demands—the introduction of double bills in one era, and the growing product shortages of another.

Screencraft Enterprises was another such short-lived company that began production in 1957, although it had been creating both television programs and industrial films since 1952. It obtained a distribution deal with Astor Pictures to release what would be the company's only two feature films, *Giant from the Unknown* and *She-Demons*, both released in 1958. Both received highly negative reviews, with the *Hollywood Reporter* calling *She-Demons* an "unbelievable and sophomoric drama," a "tale for the customers to laugh at—rather than with," featuring direction that "does nothing to enhance the values of the film" and a "cast [that] walks through in ordinary style."[106] *Giant from the Unknown* fared no better, being described as a film that "plods along with boring dialogue" and that had "no imagination to the storyline." It was labeled as "strictly a filler for the secondary houses," although for many of the new production companies this may have been exactly their ambition—to simply generate as much short-term profit as possible while the market was still strong.[107]

While Screencraft ceased production in 1958, any gap in the market-place created by its departure would soon be filled by the newly emergent Associated Producers Inc. (API), which announced a slate of five films in December of that year. The company had arranged a distribution deal with Twentieth Century–Fox for the release of five films, including *The Alligator People* (1959) and *Return of the Fly* (1959), both of which were described as "Better than Average Horror Dualers" by a *Hollywood Reporter* headline.[108] *Return of the Fly* marks what is perhaps the first time an official sequel to a major studio film—Twentieth Century–Fox's *The Fly* (1958)—was made by an independent company. API enjoyed more longevity in the industry than most of the newly formed companies of the late 1950s, producing a total of thirty-two films between 1959 and its demise in 1965. Its ability to acquire major studio distribution was surely a large factor in this achievement, as it ensured that API's films would get widespread exposure and not remain "hidden" among the growing number of low-budget independent films that had become so prevalent within the industry by the end of the decade.

Major Studios and B-Movies in the Late 1950s

As more independent studios continued to make low-budget product, a few within the industry were becoming disenchanted with B-movies altogether in the decade's final years. For some this feeling was economically motivated, fueled by the belief that the current cycle could not be sustained for much longer. Others felt a growing dissatisfaction with the content of these B-movies itself.

British critic Frederick Woods turned his attention to the Bs in a 1959 issue of *Films and Filming*, also addressing the double-bill format that still persisted. His venomous comments are directed at a specific cycle of low-budget British crime films, but they could easily apply to the surge of American B-movies that appeared in the late 1950s and were routinely savaged by American critics:

These films—it's safe to generalise—are inept, stupid, badly written and acted, ludicrous and worthless. The only entertainment one gets is from unintentional laughs. For the rest—boredom, impatience and a ruining of one's appreciation of the main feature. They are a cheat. We, the public, do not pay only to see the main feature; we pay for the whole programme, and if half the programme stinks, then we should get up and throw the seats at the screen. It isn't as if low-budget films have to be bad. *Time Out of War*—not a crime film but certainly low-budget—is a minor classic. The American thriller *The Killing* is a first-rate piece of writing and direction, and it was only a second feature. An Edmond O'Brien film called *D.O.A.* was, again, a striking support film. . . . A job—any job, be it film-making or designing a poster—can be done well or badly for the same money. Quality is not synonymous with expense. These films don't need to be bad, they could form an equally gripping part of the programme as the main film.[109]

Even producer Sam Katzman, who had worked on over two hundred Bs since the mid-1930s, expressed lack of interest in low-budget filmmaking. "Columbia has given Sam Katzman an okay to produce top-budgeted product after he wraps up a pair of low-budgets already in the works," reported *Variety* on April 2, 1958. Katzman was cited as being in agreement with Columbia president Abe Schneider and vice president Leo Jaffe "that there is no market for 'B' pix today": "'The B pictures are passé today, there just isn't enough market anymore. With blockbusters such as 'The Bridge on the River Kwai,' 'Peyton Place' and 'The Long Hot Summer' playing, they have no need for B's, so this type of picture suffers. But the situation will adjust itself and there will again be a market for the B—but not today,' said Katzman."[110]

Katzman's comments highlight the cyclical nature of B-movie production at the major studios in the 1950s. Dismissed at the start of the decade in the move toward higher-budgeted production, and slowly reintroduced by mid-decade, B-movies became subject to the cyclical trends in production that are an inherent part of filmmaking. Whereas block booking insured a guaranteed marketplace for the Bs of the 1930s and 1940s, B-movies became subject to the demands of a more competitive marketplace in the 1950s. As such, they went in and out of favor at most of the major studios on a periodic basis according to cyclical trends.

While Katzman and Columbia may have stated their aversion to the Bs in 1958, B-movies would not disappear entirely from Hollywood production schedules by the end of the decade. A December 9, 1959, *Variety* headline noted that there was still a "Quiet Buzz of Persisting B's" in Hollywood that would be carried over into the start of the 1960s:

> With all the big talk about epic-sized productions due in 1960, the fact remains that "B's" are continuing very much in the scheme of things. Exploitation specials, westerns and just plain inexpensive features are included—and numerously—in everybody's line-up.
>
> Lesser-scale films are being scheduled for a variety of reasons. There's always a chance of making a profit with them; they round out release schedules so that a distribution company can be kept busy 12 months of the year; they fill exhib programming needs; foreign market execs like them (many do far better abroad than domestically); some can be

picked up cheaply from non-Hollywood producers; they can be used to introduce new talent, and so on.[111]

With this myriad of reasons why B-movies were still economically viable, the majority of major Hollywood studios produced a wide range of Bs in 1959 and 1960. Columbia's release schedules for these years contained a number of films that were both relatively low budget and of genres traditionally associated with the Bs, such as the crime thriller *City of Fear* (1959) and the science fiction effort *12 to the Moon* (1960). Columbia also recruited William Castle, who would produce eight horror films for the studio between 1959 and 1964, including *The Tingler* (1959), *13 Ghosts* (1960), and *Homicidal* (1961).

Warner Bros. was still attempting to capitalize on the teenage demographic as late as 1959, when it acquired *Teenagers from Outer Space* (1959) from independent producer Tom Graeff's short-lived Topaz Film Corporation. It was not the only major studio still attempting to reach the youth market at the end of the decade, as MGM—which had steadfastly denied making B-movies in earlier decades—released the juvenile-delinquency-themed films *The Beat Generation* (1959), *Girls Town* (1959), *The Big Operator* (1960), and *Platinum High School* (1960).

Universal continued its program of making films that were high in technical quality but low in budget that had already been successful throughout the decade, releasing such horror and science fiction films as *The 4-D Man* (1959), *Dinosaurus!* (1960), and *The Leech Woman* (1960). It also continued in partnership with Hammer, distributing *The Mummy* (1959) and *Brides of Dracula* (1960). Twentieth Century–Fox also retained an interest in low-cost genre films in 1960, such as the crime drama *Twelve Hours to Kill* and especially westerns like *Desire in the Dust*, *Oklahoma Territory*, and *Young Jesse James*. United Artists featured a range of genres such as the horror films *The Four Skulls of Jonathan Drake* (1959) and *Invisible Invaders* (1959), crime films such as *Riot in Juvenile Prison* (1959), *Cage of Evil* (1960), *The Walking Target* (1960), *Vice Raid* (1960), and *Three Came to Kill* (1960), and such 1960 westerns as *Gunfighters of Abilene*, *Noose for a Gunman*, and *Oklahoma Territory*.

The industry even continued to regularly use the A/B dichotomy in its production terminology. One 1958 headline in the *Hollywood Reporter*, for example, reads "20th to Make 30 'A' Pics in 1959," in reference to Twentieth Century–Fox's upcoming production schedule.[112] The article contains references to "Grade 'A' films," " 'A's,' " and " 'A' product,' " symptomatic of how—despite the fact that many film historians see the demise of the B-movie arriving with the end of block booking—the A/B divide between lower- and higher-budgeted films was still prominent in the industry's lexicon at the end of the decade.

The Bs would continue their quiet buzz in Hollywood as the 1960s began, indicating that the tradition of low-budget filmmaking that began with the B-movie's rise in the early 1930s had to some degree survived the highly volatile, transitional era of 1950s filmmaking. But the B-movies of the 1950s had changed substantially from those in prior decades, spurred by an inundation of new independent companies in the wake of both the antitrust rulings and the eventual product shortages. This new breed of Bs was typically aimed at demographics that Hollywood had either abandoned or not yet considered, resulting in the need for the major studios to compete with these independents by the end of the decade.

4

Attack of the Independent

American International Pictures and the B-Movie

Of all of the new independent companies to emerge in the 1950s, none was more successful than American International Pictures, largely because it proved the most skilled in reaching the increasingly important teenage audience. Its mid-decade debut signified that a distinct era of B movie filmmaking was fully under way: if the films of Lippert Pictures Inc. and its competitors at the beginning of the decade could be seen as similar in any way to their Poverty Row predecessors, AIP's entrance signaled a definite shift in the B-movie marketplace. AIP was conspicuously different in many regards from both the major studios and independents alike. It established unique patterns of production, especially in its inventive preproduction methods and cost-effective shooting techniques, that ensured it a financially successful end product. It was also an innovator in its approaches to distribution and exhibition, particularly through its strategic use of marketing and in embracing younger audience demographics.

AIP was perhaps the biggest success story in independent filmmaking in the 1950s, despite the fact that its origin was a precarious one. Founder Samuel Arkoff used a gambling metaphor in describing the studio's creation: "The 1950s were just about the worst time to launch a new film company. But [we] found rolling the dice an irresistible temptation."[1] Co-founder James H. Nicholson told of how when they were first organizing their new film company, "two major companies went out of business. We started with no capital. Basically, our success has to be in the fact that a majority of our pictures are financial winners," a fact that stands in sharp contrast to the typical 80 percent failure rate.[2] Producer-director Roger Corman, whose career flourished as a result of his years at AIP, has boasted of how only fifteen films out of four hundred in his entire career ever lost money—a phenomenal 96 percent success rate.[3]

AIP's films constituted a new cinematic entity in the 1950s—a low-budget approach to filmmaking that departed from previous methods of B-movie production. The company was successful not only in forging a new way of creating B-films, but more importantly in devising a radically new business model that saw it become a serious contender in the film industry for over two decades. AIP quickly became an industry leader in the B-movie market, causing both the major studios and rival independents alike to imitate many of its creative and economic strategies. AIP's entry into the market in 1954 was a deciding factor in the industry-wide rebirth of the B-movie in the latter half of the decade. Furthermore, AIP's mode of production anticipates that of modern Hollywood in many regards, further signaling that the company was creating a product that was remarkably different from its low-budget predecessors.

Origins and Audiences

In his autobiography, *Flying Through Hollywood by the Seat of My Pants*, Arkoff told of how the creation of AIP was fueled by the industry's growing product shortages. He and Nicholson rationalized that independent films faced better odds than in years past of getting shown in theaters that had previously been controlled by the major studios. Their eventual success is especially remarkable given that the company was initially formed with a minuscule investment of only $3,000—split equally among Arkoff, Nicholson, and investor Joseph Moritz, an exhibitor for whom Nicholson had previously worked.[4]

Nicholson, a former theater owner himself and sales manager for the small film distributor Realart Pictures, had sought a partner for the creation of a new film distribution company. Arkoff was a lawyer dealing with a copyright infringement case against Realart, where he met Nicholson and discussed the new distribution venture. According to producer Herman Cohen, Arkoff and Nicholson forged a deal whereby "if [Arkoff] got a piece of the company, he would do the contracts for 'em."[5] Their combined business savvy and industry experience allowed them to quickly move beyond the company's humble origins, with Nicholson serving as president and often taking a more directly creative role while preferring to leave vice president Arkoff in charge of most of the company's commercial and legal dealings (although such roles were sometimes blurred).

AIP was initially formed as the American Releasing Corporation (ARC) in 1954. Arkoff noted how they wanted the AIP name from the very beginning, but an existing company in California was already named American Pictures.[6] While searching for their first film to distribute, Nicholson and Arkoff were introduced to a young producer who would soon play a prominent role in the company's future—Corman, who had recently completed his first feature, *The Monster from the Ocean Floor* (1954):

> Each had something the other wanted, and several distribution deals were discussed. There was a bottom line from which ARC was unwilling to budge, however: the company could not offer Corman any money up front for *Monster from the Ocean Floor*. Nicholson suggested they release the picture on a regional basis, which meant there would be a long wait before Corman would see any substantial return on his OPM (Other People's Money) investment.
>
> Roger didn't want to wait, so he sold the film outright to Lippert Pictures. That deal made him enough money to reimburse his investors and reap a decent profit besides.[7]

While the deal allowed Corman to fund his next film, the sale of a single film produced with independently raised funds to an outside agency represented a business model that both the fledgling producer and AIP's founders would quickly progress beyond. Later deals would involve using a completed film as leverage to raise capital for the production of future films. In short, Corman, Nicholson, and Arkoff were clever businessmen who recognized how to move beyond short-term profit to create long-term revenue.

Corman took $50,000 of the $60,000 advance from the sale of *The Monster from the Ocean Floor* to Lippert and produced the car-race drama *The Fast and the Furious* (1954), shot in nine days. Republic and Columbia were both interested in distributing the film, but in either case Corman would not have seen any payment for at least six to eight months, leaving him with no immediate capital to fund his next project.[8] Instead he turned to AIP, with Arkoff describing how their first deal together was born: "'I already have these other distribution offers from established companies,' Roger told us. 'But I can see myself falling into the pattern of most independent producers, which is putting out your money, making the film, sending it into distribution, and getting your money back a year later, hopefully along with a profit. I'm looking for a quicker return than that so I can have some cash to start my next movie. What can you offer me?'"

Arkoff and Nicholson proposed that they would contact the various states' rights distributors in the attempt to both find distribution for *The Fast and the Furious* and secure financing for future films. A four-picture deal was offered to Corman, a risk on their part because it entailed convincing the states' rights distributors to book his film (and fund others) sight unseen. Nicholson used his contacts cultivated from his time at Realart to arrange meetings in New York, Chicago, Atlanta, and New Orleans. "Here was our proposal to the twenty-eight franchise holders that covered the country," said Arkoff:

"'We have *The Fast and the Furious* in the can, and we'd like to lease you the rights to release it in your territory. Also, we're going to deliver three additional movies from Roger Corman. We'll relinquish an extra five percent fee if you agree to put up the money when each picture is delivered to you. But if you come up with the money at the *start* of principal photography, we'll give you an extra ten percent.'"9

The offer of an increased percentage secured the deal, proving that despite the quality of its product a new independent company could find success in the film industry if it was run by skilled entrepreneurs. Once the film was released, ARC wasted no time in capitalizing upon the momentum created by the deal, announcing plans for eight releases in 1955, including four color films and another in a widescreen process called Vistarama.10 This proposed schedule ultimately proved to be somewhat ambitious, as seven films were actually released in 1955 (including *The Beast with 1,000,000 Eyes*), only two of them in color. This initial release plan signifies how the company quickly projected an image of success (despite the fact that these were actually "lean years," in Arkoff's words) in order to establish itself as a leader within the B-movie marketplace. ARC was finally able to change its corporate name in March of 1956, the preexisting American Pictures company

The Beast with 1,000,000 Eyes (San Mateo Productions/American Releasing Corporation, 1955)

having gone out of business.[11] The transformation was announced in the *Hollywood Reporter* on March 26, with AIP using the opportunity to publicize a new release schedule of fourteen films over twelve months beginning in June.[12] From its initial $3,000 investment, AIP had quickly established itself as a dominant player among the new independent companies formed in recent years.

Much of this success can be attributed to the way in which the company understood its audience. The period between 1946 and 1960 saw the number of American teenagers more than double from 5.6 million to 11.8 million.[13] This change in population growth was ultimately reflected in audience demographics during the 1950s, and AIP quickly positioned itself to take advantage. "I began to see the value of aiming pictures at this teenage market," said Arkoff, "which also contained the dating crowd into their mid-twenties. I often marveled at how the studio chiefs were ignoring them. The studio chiefs apparently didn't understand that their primary audience had changed, that movies were no longer the major form of entertainment for adult Americans. To the big studios, the youth culture was an unknown entity. But I could see who was going to the movies, and it was young people."[14]

AIP's approach to audiences went against prevailing industry notions at the time, whereby the major studios made blockbuster films in the hopes of attracting a wider range of viewers. The idea of making films that had something for everyone was an old one in Hollywood; producer Walter Wanger announced in 1938, for instance, that "the Hollywood system required attractions of equal appeal to all classes, races and ages, 'from 8 to 80.'"[15] AIP's stance was just the opposite: "You don't make a picture for everybody and then hope that out of that group, two or four or six million people will come,"[16] Arkoff rationalized. Instead, "you aim the picture to a specific audience," and in the 1950s the demographic with the most potential was that of youth audiences. "TV might have been keeping parents at home," said Arkoff,

> but teenagers needed to get out of the house and be with kids their own age—and the parents couldn't wait for them to leave. There's some primeval, tribal thing, where boys want to be with boys, girls want to be with girls, and eventually they want to be with each other. They need a place to go with their friends and their dates. They also had a lot more spending money than kids did in the Depression era, thanks to allowances from their parents or their own jobs in fast-food restaurants. We [at AIP] eventually realized that if we concentrated on movies aimed at the youth market, we might be able to create a lucrative niche for ourselves.[17]

AIP determined that "younger children would watch anything older children would watch, and girls would watch anything boys would watch, but not
vice versa; therefore, 'to catch your greatest audience you zero in on the 19
year old male.'"[18] This strategy was in opposition to the majority of existing
youth-oriented films produced in the 1950s, such as those of Walt Disney.
Arkoff argued that to Disney,

> whether you were 8 or 18, you were a kid. What he didn't realize, and
> what a lot of people didn't realize when they kept talking about family
> pictures, was that, if you're 8 years old, the worst thing that can happen
> to you is when your dog is lost. When you're 18, there are a hell of a lot
> of other things more important than your lost dog. You've got to worry
> about your parents, you've got to worry about your teachers, you've got
> to worry about the other sex, you've got to worry about your own sex.
> You've got a hundred different things that are far more important. And
> everybody was ignoring them.[19]

Variety noted how AIP was successfully drawing teenage audiences in a
1957 article entitled "Action-and-Horror Staple Stuff; 20,000,000 Thrill-Seekers
(12 to 25) Backbone of Exploitation Pix," commenting that the company "relies
upon action and horror yarns to pull audiences in the 12 to 25 age bracket."
The article pointed out that this was not necessarily a new phenomenon,
with Arkoff describing how "it was used by the oldtime serials. It's the same
basic formula that gets 'em in . . . but you have to freshen it on exploitation
pictures. Stereotyped gangster films, of course, are obsolete." At the same
time, Nicholson believed that while certain audience tastes never change,
they could always be updated "by use of modern expressions such as 'Hot
Rod,' 'Drag Strip' and 'Rock 'n' Roll,' etc."[20]

With the last of the serials appearing in the mid-1950s, AIP can arguably
be seen as filling a void left in the market by the decline of these obsolete
chapter plays that no longer drew youth audiences. Director Joe Dante has
described how the appeal of AIP's films was due in large part to their being
"movies your parents wouldn't want you to see."[21] To a certain extent there is
a generational effect at work in the popularity of different types of B-movies:
serials represented an outdated form of filmmaking associated with previous
decades and older generations, whereas the films of AIP and their competitors were a distinctly new kind of B-movie entity appealing to the modern
sensibilities of 1950s teenagers.

But not all films targeted toward teenagers were successful. Arkoff and
Nicholson cautioned that youth films "must not ever, under any circumstances, seem to have been especially chosen for them, conditioned to their
years, or equipped with special messages."[22] That major studios often ignored

this warning was a large factor in why AIP was able to dominate the teenage market. In 1959, for example, Twentieth Century–Fox released *Blue Denim*, a film about teenage pregnancy aimed largely at youth audiences, spending an extraordinary amount of money to advertise it in trade publications. A full-page ad for the film appeared in *Motion Picture Daily* on July 8, 1959, using rhetoric that was clearly aimed at teenagers: "Ask yourself . . . how could it happen to Janet . . . so shy, so young, so very much like yourself! Where did she go wrong . . . and why . . . WHY . . . W H Y? And what about the boy . . . he was a really decent kid . . . ask his mother, his father, his friends! 'Blue Denim' goes into the solutions teen-agers are forced to find for themselves!"[23]

The ad also boasts that it is the "first of a series of national magazine advertisements" and "will be seen in the August issue of SEVENTEEN by a readership of four million." *Seventeen* magazine actively courted the film industry for advertising money in the immediate postwar years by reminding filmmakers that "the movie Teena wants to see is the movie her boyfriend takes her to see."[24]

This was followed by a full-sized, four-page advertisement for the film in *Motion Picture Daily* on July 16, 1959, one of the largest trade ads of any film for the entire decade. Yet the creators of *Blue Denim* failed to heed Arkoff and Nicholson's advice that youth films not be perceived as being chosen for, or conditioned to, teenage spectators. In a move that most teenagers would likely find highly patronizing, the ad describes the film as "the motion picture which talks 'heart to heart' with Young America." Unlike Twentieth Century–Fox, AIP understood that teenage audiences did not want to talk heart to heart with their elders. "I have always felt," said AIP producer Herman Cohen, "that most teenagers think that adults—their parents or their teachers, anyone that was older and that had authority—were the culprits in their lives . . . and in talking to many teenagers, I found out that that was how they felt."[25]

Rather than try to fold teenagers into the establishment itself by talking with them heart to heart, many of AIP's films directly incorporate an anti-establishment theme. Arkoff believed that the major studios had essentially been approaching youth films as "a moral lesson, a lecture. But by the late '50s the kids were beyond lecturing." As a result, he said, "fundamentally what we were doing" at AIP "was making pictures for teenagers who didn't want to have a lecture crammed down their throats."[26]

Corporate Organization and Preproduction

Although AIP has often been referred to as being primarily a distribution company in its early years, its mode of production was radically different from that of similar groups such as Distributors Corporation of America and Howco International Pictures. While the *Hollywood Reporter* announced in

1956 that AIP would "function primarily as a distributing organization," the company typically played a far more active role in the creation of the product it distributed than did its peers.[27] Gary Morris notes that AIP "acted primarily as a distributor for films either produced independently and given to them, or funded and then distributed by them."[28] In fact, AIP's mode of production was not so simple; it had a far more complex relationship with its production companies than did other independents of the decade, such as DCA or Lippert Pictures Inc.

The 1956 announcement stated that "five independent production units have been signed": Golden State Productions, Sunset Productions, Nacirema, Angel Productions, and Roger Corman's eponymous production company.[29] Balboa Productions and Carmel Productions would join these later in the year. Rather than allow all of these companies to make films autonomously, AIP made a deal to use the production facilities of American National Studios in California (which was also shared by Ziv Television). The "entire production staff of [AIP's] subsidiary companies" was "transferred to the AN lot" in November 1956, allowing AIP to exercise close control over the production of each film.[30]

These multiple companies were employed essentially so that AIP would receive larger tax breaks than if it had formed a single production unit of its own. Arkoff explained:

> We would determine what production company we would use by the state of the profit and loss division. . . . In other words, whenever a picture would get into a certain kind of profit, or it would begin to pay off profits, then you'd have to pay taxes above the minimum level of taxes. Then we'd dump another picture to be made in that corporation. So we'd get a new write-off coming very quickly because we made the picture so fast and got 'em out so fast. This is how the thing would work, in essence, like revolving companies.[31]

Corman, for instance, despite having his own production company, was signed by Sunset Productions to direct *It Conquered the World* (1956).[32] The ownership and administration of many of these subsidiary companies were highly familiar—Nicholson was president of Sunset and served as executive producer on *It Conquered the World*. Arkoff and Nicholson served as executive producers on the majority of AIP's films in the 1950s, while each was credited as producer on several as well. Industry trade publications soon came to regard AIP as effectively being a production company as well as a distributor. An article in the *Hollywood Reporter* from November 1958 about the search for new production facilities noted the "fact that AIP plans production of 30 films in the next year has cued Nicholson to seek out space on a regular basis for the filming of the bloc of pics."[33] Another article in that month similarly stated that AIP, which had only been renting studio space over its four-year history, now "felt it could effect an economy in taking over a whole studio where AIP could centralize production and distribution operations."[34]

Arkoff and Nicholson maintained tight financial control of AIP's productions from the beginning, and their devotion to the bottom line was notorious. If a film began to go over budget during production, Arkoff was not above cutting parts of the script in order to speed up completion. Such ruthlessness was deemed necessary due to the fragmented nature of AIP's financing; for any given film, said Arkoff,

> we didn't start with any money—we put bits and pieces of things together. For example, I'd go to the franchise holders in the U.S. and I'd get maybe $40,000 in advance for a picture to be delivered. And then I would go and get maybe $14,000 for the U.K., half of it in advance. And then I'd get a little money out of foreign—not much. Then I'd get $25,000 from the laboratory in cash, plus a deferment, and then I'd get actors and others to defer their salaries for a time. And we'd put together fifty, sixty, seventy thousand dollars toward a $100,000 picture—that's how we made our pictures. And we kept expanding, so even if we *had* been successful, we wouldn't have had any money. Probably the best thing that ever happened to us was the fact that we never had any room to breathe.[35]

To ensure its products' success and maintain this diverse network of financing, AIP took several steps prior to starting a film. The company subverted the traditional mode of production by not beginning the filmmaking process at the script level. Instead, AIP's films usually began with an idea or a title and developed marketing strategies before ever beginning the script. It was common practice in the 1940s for B-movie producers to pretest film titles with audiences before scripts were conceived, such as Producers Releasing Corporation's *Girls in Chains*, *Isle of Forgotten Sins*, and *Jive Junction*.[36] AIP took this rationale one step further, however, by devising extensive advertising campaigns complete with posters and artwork to be pretested with both exhibitors and their target demographic before scripts were commissioned.

AIP operated much like a marketing firm, "analyzing the market, dissecting the social and political trends, and reflecting on where the motion picture industry was headed" in the attempt to minimize risk before starting production. Throughout the company's history, Arkoff contended, "before raw film was ever loaded into the camera for a new movie," he and Nicholson "knew precisely who our audience for that picture would be."[37] He professed surprise "that so many of the pictures in our business are made without the sales department or the merchandising department being consulted. We didn't take a script and shoot it, and then, when the picture was done, send it to the advertising department and say, 'Now figure out how the hell you're gonna sell it.' That's putting the cart before the horse."[38]

In keeping with this audience-based focus, preproduction at AIP would routinely begin by devising a catchy title. "Exhibitors were not going to hold onto our movies and wait for word of mouth to build an audience," argued Arkoff. "We needed to get people to buy tickets immediately, on that very first weekend." Without well-known actors, directors, or source material, the films' titles and the advertising alone would have to be strong enough to attract audiences. AIP "had to work differently from the studios" with its advertising strategies. The studios "would simply use the portraits of the stars of their pictures in the ads; we had no stars, so Jim had to rely on strong titles and catchy lines," said Arkoff.[39]

Nicholson himself was often instrumental in the development of a new film's title—indeed, Nicholson may perhaps be seen as the key creative force at AIP. While Arkoff's legal experience benefited the company's financial maneuvers, Nicholson's creative background played an invaluable role in AIP's success. His time spent in Realart's advertising department saw him devise new ads and titles for its reissued films, and he had a youthful passion for genre films, having worked on a science fiction fanzine in high school with Forrest Ackerman, the editor of *Famous Monsters of Filmland* magazine.[40] In turn, Nicholson would create such memorable titles as *Day the World Ended* and *Invasion of the Saucer Men*. "He was a great title man," recalled Arkoff in describing his partner's creative ability during preproduction. "We had titles and we had artwork. And that's what we sold. So Jim Nicholson was the guy who used to be able to make that work."[41]

Once he had his title, Nicholson would start by designing the central concept for the film's advertising campaign, as well as creating various tag lines and a rough artwork description or layouts. Artist Al Kallis would then create potential artwork for the film's posters and advertising, which was followed by publicity manager Milt Moritz developing specific ad campaigns. "Once the artwork was done," Arkoff explained, "and before investing any more time and money, we took steps to reduce our risks in a very risky business. For the pictures we aimed at young audiences, we would test Milt's ad campaigns with some high school and college kids, as well as a few advertising executives. We also showed it to some handpicked exhibitors whose judgment we trusted. . . . If the reaction was positive, we moved ahead, creating the story line, commissioning the script, and preparing for the actual shooting."[42]

This mode of production stands in sharp contrast to that employed by the majority of studios in the 1950s, both major and minor. "We do our planning backwards," said Nicholson of this inverted approach to marketing. The major studios, Arkoff said, believed that AIP was working "backassward," but from his point of view AIP was simply "doing it the way American industry works. They find out whether there is a public that will buy their product."[43] In an industry where only 20 percent of films earned a profit, AIP applied the business model of product testing to ensure that its films achieved much higher rates of success. Whereas B-movie studios in decades past typically made films in a number of different genres in the hopes of attracting a wide range of viewers (with a film's content determining its audience), AIP's films were specifically tailored in advance to defined audience demographics—with audiences therefore determining the content of a film.

AIP's relatively quick success drew significant attention among journalists, including the *New York Times*'s Irving Rubine. He devoted an entire article to the company on March 16, 1958, entitled "Boys Meets Ghouls, Make Money," declaring that an AIP film "makes no pretension of size or quality." The article was a highly positive assessment, seeking to provoke what Rubine calls the "Hollywood pundits" who advocated making fewer but bigger pictures throughout the decade. These pundits, he wrote, "have watched with perplexity the growth of a brash young company that has succeeded handsomely with a program of horror pictures that are definitely neither bigger nor better." Rubine noted that "$150,000 was established [by AIP] as the maximum budget for each of their offerings," and that this figure "has never been exceeded," according to Nicholson.[44]

Keeping their budgets to a minimum was crucial to AIP's success and entailed that salaries be kept extremely low by industry standards. For *Day the World Ended* (1956), writer Lou Rusoff received approximately $3,000 for his screenplay, a meager amount even in the 1950s. The film's total budget was $96,234.49;[45] to contextualize this figure, Universal's 1941 B-movie *Horror Island* was one of the cheapest horror films ever produced by that studio at $93,000.[46] That AIP's budget was little more than that of one of the smallest Hollywood studio B-films produced fifteen years prior denotes just how impoverished the mode of production was for independent companies in relation to the Bs that previously came out of the studio system.

Since AIP could not rely on the strength of its production values to sell tickets, other strategies were adopted to ensure financial success. One approach was to capitalize on trends and subjects that were currently popular, a practice that many B-movie producers followed in the 1950s. In addition to films about various aspects of teenage subcultures such as *Hot Rod Girl* and *Dragstrip Girl*, AIP sought to take advantage of current news issues, as with its film *The She-Creature* (1956). "Like many AIP pictures," said Arkoff, "the concept for *The She-Creature* came off the front pages of the newspapers. It grew out of news stories about Bridey Murphy and the claims of a woman reliving her past lives while hypnotized." Author Morey Bernstein's book

The She-Creature (Golden State Productions/American International Pictures, 1956)

The Search for Bridey Murphy was a best seller at the time. When interest in the story peaked, Nicholson sought to develop a film about the topic before the public's curiosity faded.

While the film hoped to capitalize on the book's popularity, it was crucial that any copyright fees be avoided. Nicholson "began pondering the details of an advertising campaign that would help tie in AIP's new monster movie to the Bridey Murphy case without naming specific names (and having to pay any associated fees)." The solution to the problem was demonstrative of AIP's gift for exploitative marketing, settling on "a line of copy on the posters and print ads that proclaimed, 'It can and did happen! Based on authentic FACTS you've been reading about!'"[47]

With a strong advertising strategy in place, scripts were then written to incorporate the studio's marketing vision for each film. AIP's primary screenwriter was Lou Rusoff—Arkoff's brother-in-law—who wrote nearly thirty films for the company. Having previously written scripts for television, such as the children's program *Terry and the Pirates*, Rusoff was accustomed to a fast-paced, budget-conscious, and often collaborative creative process. "More than any other writer, Lou had a real appreciation for what we were trying to do," said Arkoff: "He understood how to keep costs down by limiting the number of sets and locations. He framed his scripts beautifully into our titles and artwork."[48] In order to reduce a given film's budget, scripts were written to facilitate the shortest possible production schedule.

Once scripts were completed, they were also subject to further revision by producers. With *Invasion of the Saucer Men* (1957), inessential scenes (such as military vehicles driving down a highway) were cut in order to keep costs down.[49] A scene like this one would likely require the use of expensive props, vehicle rentals, and/or miniature model work. Typically used to establish narrative context rather than serve as the site of primary action or character development, such scenes were deemed extraneous. A further budgetary measure employed by AIP when scripts were finished was requiring directors to storyboard the film prior to production—"before the actual shooting," said Arkoff, "when it doesn't cost money." He firmly believed that the lack of organization created when directors failed to plan their shots in advance was why films "cost so much and take so long to finish."[50]

Production Methods

With all of its films, AIP "did everything possible—and impossible—to cut costs." Arkoff professed that he and Nicholson were "merciless" in their cost-cutting measures: "We cut down production schedules by using the same sets for different pictures. We combined locations to save physical moves during productions. We even tore pages out of scripts if the director didn't pick up the pace of shooting. When we filmed *Girls in Prison* in 1956, and violent winds created chaos on the set, we instantly wrote a storm into the script rather than lose a day of shooting."

AIP often took such cost-effective techniques to extreme lengths, commonly inventing new methods of reducing costs as it went along. One of the first decisions AIP made in order to reduce the cost of filmmaking was to produce films with relatively short running times. That meant fewer total scenes were needed, requiring less production time, labor, and resources, and even less film stock used. AIP's films were "approximately eighty minutes long, shorter than many features [in the 1950s], but that was by design," said Arkoff, who also believed that shorter films were consequently better paced than longer ones. Bemoaning the fact that most directors are hesitant to make any cuts to their films, he refused to give any of his directors final cut at AIP.[51]

In fact, directors at AIP were often not involved with a film until just prior to the start of shooting, affording them little opportunity for creative input. For instance, the preproduction on *Hot Rod Girl* was detailed in the *Hollywood Reporter* on March 2, 1956, in an article describing how the film's production manager was currently preparing the set for the first day of shooting on March 10—and stating that the film's producer, Norman Herman, "will sign a director early next week."[52]

As AIP's most prolific director, Corman was occasionally given slightly more preparation time before shooting. His track record in the 1950s is unparalleled, with his first twenty-seven films financially successful before finally losing money on the twenty-eighth.[53] This success rate is partially attributable to the consistency of his techniques as both director and producer, which came to typify the AIP style of filmmaking. Corman's production methods serve as a key case study of AIP's mode of production, as his work is the most representative of the studio in the 1950s.

On March 21, 1956, the *Hollywood Reporter* announced that Corman had been signed to produce and direct *It Conquered the World* (1956), which began production on the fifth of April. This amounted to a period of just two weeks of possible preproduction for Corman, during which time Rusoff was still completing the film's screenplay. In contrast, Allied Artists also signed Corman that year to produce and direct *The Hypnosis of Diana Love*, set to begin production more than two months later.[54] While the project would eventually be filmed as *The Undead* (1957) for AIP, the announcement is indicative of the differences in how the two B-movie companies approached the scheduling of their productions.

Contributing to this often harried style of preparation was the fact that Corman frequently undertook a busy production schedule. It was announced, for example, that he would be doubling his slate of films from five in 1955 to an expected ten productions in 1956.[55] Actress Betsy Jones-Moreland described Corman's typical schedule, somewhat hyperbolically: "Roger was going along making a movie every *month*—two weeks pre-production, two weeks shooting, two weeks pre-production, two weeks shooting."[56] Corman argued that he simply worked better under these conditions. "I can key myself up emotionally to work very hard for a brief period of time," he said. "Maybe some people are distance runners and others are sprinters."[57]

While directors and producers were hired on a film-by-film basis at AIP, Corman received the same basic deal for each film: "Upon delivering a completed film, he would receive $50,000 . . . plus a $15,000 advance on the projected foreign sale. Though he was also guaranteed a percentage of the movie's eventual profits, Corman never counted on this potential income. His strategy was to come in under $65,000 per film, so as to have enough capital for his next project. The fact that he would plan every third or fourth feature to be ultralow-budget below the $30,000 range) would ensure a healthy profit in the long run."[58]

Corman was therefore able to implement a relatively longer-term business model for his AIP films than for his first, *The Monster from the Ocean*

Floor, ensuring a steady flow of capital for future productions. "I realised that with independent backing," said Corman of how he made that film, "you raise the money, you take a certain length of time to make the picture, and then you take more time to get your money back, so you can only make one picture every year or year and a half." With AIP alternatively offering him advance money for future projects, Corman was instead able to "make a series of pictures and get at least a portion of the negative costs back, and not have to go through this wait" associated with making films with independent financing.[59]

With this deal in place, Corman soon began investing some of these profits in a number of the films he made for AIP "in order to get better terms as far as profit percentages."[60] With his own money often involved, Corman had direct incentive to adhere to AIP's budget-conscious mandate. Corman excelled in frugality, perhaps often taking it to extremes. "Anything that costs a penny over his minuscule budget turns Roger Corman into a monster," said actor Richard Devon. When a speech was left out of the script given to Devon on the set of *The Undead*, Roger "was not just upset, he was *maniacal . . .* He is a dual personality," said Devon. "You meet him in his office and he's absolutely charming. . . . You get him on the set, and he's Attila the Hun. With Roger, if anything costs more than what he has figured, it's a disaster for everybody that's around him."[61]

If Corman was ever unprofessional on the set, it can perhaps be ascribed to how he chose to become a director: not necessarily for the love of the job, but because as a producer he could maintain more fiscal control over his films if he directed them himself. Corman said that his directorial debut, *Five Guns West* (1956) was "a breakthrough," because with "almost no training or preparation whatsoever, I was literally learning how to direct motion pictures on the job. It took me four or five of these 'training films' to learn what a film school student knows when he graduates."[62]

Yet according to several actors who worked with Corman, even after this "training" period ended, his skills as a director were still lacking at times, particularly in how he instructed his talent while filming. "It was pretty much 'Do it quick,'" said Mike Connors. "There wasn't a lot of acting direction going on. For him, it was where to set the camera and how to make the most of the time he had. You were pretty much on your own" as an actor while on set.[63] Dick Miller added: "To be honest, [Corman] never really directed much. He set up the shots. . . . He seemed to know where the next shot was going to be, because he'd be yelling, 'Cut!' while he was walking, and everybody would grab a reflector or something and follow him to the next setup."[64] Corman rarely took the time to praise the efforts of his cast and crew while on set, always preferring to move ahead with the next shot. He once advised first-time director Allan Arkush never to "stand around and congratulate the crew" after any given take, "because that'll take up a minute of your time. You'll do maybe thirty to forty set-ups a day, and you'll lose thirty to forty minutes."[65]

Similarly, when asked if he received much direction from Corman on set, Antony Carbone replied: "No. He would set it up and then we would just *go*. If it worked for him, then it was fine, and if not, we'd do it again."[66] As such, Corman approached his role on set more as that of a producer than as a director, concerned more with keeping the film from going over budget than with the aesthetics of the finished product. His films for AIP differ greatly from the B-movies of previous decades, in that the latter often served as training grounds for the artistic development of such celebrated directors as Jacques Tourneur, Edward Dmytryk, Joseph H. Lewis, and Robert Wise.[67] While Dmytryk and Wise would both go on to make Academy Award–nominated and/or–winning films, Corman had no aspirations of artistry but was instead predominantly concerned with creating a financially successful product. Corman ended his directorial career in 1971, choosing instead to work as a producer on over three hundred films in subsequent decades.[68]

Corman's strategy relied heavily on reusing resources, occasionally to severe extents. Costumes were routinely borrowed from previous films, with little opportunity for repair should they be damaged during filming. Betsy Jones-Moreland described one such occurrence while filming *Viking Women and the Sea Serpent*:

> We had on leather costumes that were left over from some John Derek movie. They were leather. We are now in salt water, so the leather shrank. We were in the hot sun; we were in already abbreviated costumes; and they were abbreviated even more. There were no doubles [duplicate costumes]; forget doubles! On a Roger Corman picture, you're lucky to have anything single, let alone double. We didn't have anything else to put on, so for the rest of the picture we were sort of shrunk. We also lost our shoes so they stayed lost—that was the end of the shoes![69]

Corman also reused his acting talent to bring down labor costs. Rather than paying for numerous extras to round out the cast of a given film, he routinely used actors in multiple roles. Dick Miller, who played both a cowboy and an Indian in *Apache Woman*, remembered that "[I] just about shot myself in the end because I was part of the posse that was sent out to shoot my Indian." Such discontinuity was fairly common in Corman's films: "Everybody doubled for Roger's pictures," said Miller.[70] This type of economic prudence was apparently sometimes too extreme even for Arkoff, who once famously exclaimed, "Roger, for fuck's sake, hire a couple more extras and put a little more furniture on the sets!"[71]

Corman's reuse of sets—from his own films or other AIP productions—was similarly frugal, often with little attempt to alter their appearance. To reduce the cost of filming *A Bucket of Blood* (1959), Corman used some of the existing sets from *Diary of a High School Bride* (1959) that hadn't yet been dismantled.[72] He also took this rationale one step further, often shooting two films in rapid succession at the same location: one for AIP or a similar company, the other produced with his own funds. The latter would then usually be sold back to AIP, which was largely unconcerned about Corman's atypical production methods.[73] *Variety* described this trend as being Corman's new permanent mode of production in 1957, noting he "will henceforth shoot pix in pairs as a means of reducing production costs." This "'back to back' policy" would allow him to "hold production crews together as well as lowering such fixed costs as equipment rentals, transportation, etc."[74] The same method is often practiced by modern Hollywood producers to save money when filming franchise pictures. The second and third entries of the respective series *Back to the Future*, *The Matrix*, and *Pirates of the Caribbean* were all shot back to back in order to reduce production expenses, as was the entire *Lord of the Rings* trilogy.

While the producers of those films often sought to save money on the cost of expensive set pieces and filming in exotic locales, AIP's films typically had neither of these problems. Many films, especially those toward the end of the 1950s, were shot almost entirely on location. "It was almost always less expensive to use real houses, buildings, and streets," Arkoff recalled. "At the same time, lights, cameras, and sound equipment had become so lightweight, mobile, and high-quality that we could shoot virtually everything on location. It became so much more economical than supporting acres of real estate and sound stages."[75]

Location shooting had another distinct economic advantage to low-budget producers—the ability to avoid union involvement if so desired. Corman was "always running one step ahead of the unions," said Jones-Moreland, which "were always trying to come and shut him down" for not adhering to union labor standards, which required, among other things, hiring union members for all crew positions and using them for only one job.[76]

The issue of what role the unions should play in independent filmmaking was a prominent one during this era, leading the journal *Film Culture* to publish an article entitled "Film Unions and the Low-Budget Independent Film Production—An Exploratory Discussion" in 1961. Here, a group of independent directors and union executives discussed the matter, debating the notion that "a general feeling [exists] among independent film-makers that the unions stand between them and their art," as director Lew Clyde Stoumen put it. Director Shirley Clarke described, for example, how during the filming of *The Connection* (1961), she "didn't get a single concession [from the unions] on a film costing $150,000 compared to the films that cost $3,000,000. They expected from us exactly the same." As in that case, independent films were typically required to employ additional crew members that their creators deemed to be highly unnecessary given the reduced scale of the production. This added cost in turn forced many independent filmmakers to make their films surreptitiously without any union involvement at all. Director Jonas Mekas stated, for instance, that when making a film with a mere $6,000 budget, "I wanted to use some union people, to have more 'craft' in some areas, but how could I even dream about the unions with this budget? With my 200 locations and six-months shooting schedule, it would have cost me a million, to work with unions. And most of the independent low-budget productions are made with $30,000–$60,000."[77]

With Corman's definition of what constitutes a minimum crew being vastly different from that of the unions, he devised a shrewd method of ensuring that union labor requirements could not be enforced during production—they had to catch him first. "Each day we were shooting at a totally different place," recalled Jones-Moreland, "and I didn't realize until later that we were shooting at each location for only one day for a very good reason!"[78]

While certain professional liberties were often taken in AIP's films in order to minimize labor costs, its production methods were not entirely unprofessional. In fact, the company regularly screened the dailies, that is, looked at the first prints of each day's footage during shooting. AIP's adoption of the standard Hollywood quality-control practice differentiates the company from most other low-budget studios, whose methods were not quite as institutionalized, and ultimately not as successful. AIP's dailies were screened at the Pathé Lab—which did all of AIP's developing—with select crew members watching the previous day's footage at the end of each production day. Producer Alex Gordon recalled that he would screen the dailies with his cameraman and production manager but notes that actors were never invited "because they would want to re-do their scenes! We never re-shot anything unless there was something in the frame that *shouldn't* be in the frame."[79]

Arkoff usually visited the set of each film three or four times during production, and he would take what the major studios would consider to be drastic measures if filming fell behind schedule. He would begin by asking whether the ending had been shot yet, rationalizing that AIP "couldn't sell a film that had no ending, though we could fill in other parts by running blank leader if we had to make up the running time." Arkoff might then say to the director, "If we don't have time for everything, let's re-arrange the shooting schedule and shoot the ending the day-after-tomorrow. . . . Then we'd work to see what we could eliminate from the script," he said, "how we could speed up shooting by combining sets, and work other things to meet the deadline."[80]

Distribution and Promotion

While theater owners were grateful for the extra films that smaller companies provided in an era of decreased major studio product, independents like AIP did not receive the same rental agreements from exhibitors that the majors did.[81] Instead of getting a percentage of the total box office receipts, B-movies were commonly sold for a flat rate throughout much of the 1950s, as were their predecessors in previous decades.

AIP's early films consequently earned the studio a standard weekly rental rate of one, two, or (in rare circumstances) three hundred dollars per print. In some small-town theaters the rate could even be as low as fifteen dollars per week.[82] Such arrangements were made through various states' rights distributors, with AIP's films initially being handled by twenty-nine such companies. "As cooperative as the franchise holders were in the early days, however," said Arkoff, "they and the exhibitors treated us like a 'comfort station'—someone to call and support when nothing else was available to play in their theaters." AIP soon realized the need to control the distribution of its own films in order to progress beyond flat rental sales. Over a four-year period in the late 1950s the company began to take over these franchise contracts itself, "waiting for them to expire so we could have our own national distribution organization," as Arkoff described it.[83]

In order to achieve a percentage basis for the sale of their films, AIP used what Corman describes as a "double bill experiment," selling two films together on a dual program so that exhibitors would pay "the same rental figure as they paid major studios."[84] "If we're always at the bottom of the bill," Arkoff reasoned, "we're never going to grow, and maybe not even make our investment back." He described the double-bill solution that he and Nicholson arrived at:

> "What do you think about creating our own combinations?" Jim asked me. "We'll combine two pictures of the same genre—two science fiction films or two horror features—and we'll sell them to theater owners for what they're paying the major studios for just one feature. It's the same concept I was using at Realart." The studios had been approaching double bills differently. They'd play a big picture at the top of the bill—perhaps a musical—and then book it with a second, less-expensive feature from a completely different genre—maybe a Western or action movie. They thought they'd draw a more diversified audience that way.

But at about this time, I was becoming convinced of the potential of the teenage market. And I felt that to get the youth audiences into the theaters, we'd have to grab them with two features on the same subject, selling them "a night of science fiction" or "a night of fast cars."[85]

Rather than practice diversification, AIP instead sought to consolidate its audiences by targeting specific demographics with combination double bills, a profitable enough move to become standard practice for the company throughout the 1950s. Much of this strategy's success was due to what the *Hollywood Reporter* headlined as a "New Uptrend" in double-bill programming in the mid-1950s; the accompanying article described how "long-time strong-holds of the single bill," such as those in southern territories, were "swinging to double features" as they realized the profit potential in the dual format. Nicholson is quoted as stating that AIP's "whole-show package" approach of two similarly themed films was being adopted by theaters that had never shown double bills before. "The demand for exploitation packages is now coming from not only the drive-ins and established double bill territories but from the hold out single bill areas," said Nicholson.[86]

AIP's double-bill format did meet with initial resistance from exhibitors, however. "Exhibitors everywhere told us, 'we want to split up the movies and turn them both into second features,'" said Arkoff. The company remained steadfast, demanding a percentage basis for the dual programs, finally achieving a booking under these terms in a Detroit theater in December of 1955, only because the exhibitor expected smaller audiences due to both a blizzard and newspaper strike.[87] The combination of *Day the World Ended* and *The Phantom from 10,000 Leagues* proved so successful in this initial run that the package gained widespread distribution the following month in such cities as New York, Los Angeles, Chicago, Boston, and Dallas. In two Boston theaters alone the combination earned a total of $45,000 in a single week and was held over for a second. *Variety* noted, "Reports from all around the circuits" where the films were playing in 250 New England theaters "were the same—sock biz."[88] In Los Angeles, the combination played six indoor theaters and eight drive-ins, grossing $140,000.

With this new distribution strategy in place, AIP began to release all of its films as combinations, offering eleven double bills in 1957 that were all financially successful.[89] The format's distinctive nature was further exploited when a "novel program package" was announced in 1958, whereby the second feature of a proposed double bill would be the sequel to the first feature: "'Last Woman on Earth,' which will be a sequel to 'End of the World,' will carry over to its cast one of the women in the preceding feature, who will survive the end with seven men. Each picture will be complete in itself."[90] Although these films were ultimately not produced by AIP, the announcement illustrates how the company strove to be innovative with its distribution schedule by devising creative programming combinations.

AIP's success was also due in part to how its distribution policies capitalized on the industry's traditionally unsuccessful seasons. The summer months had been previously deemed a slow season by the major studios until AIP demonstrated their profit potential.[91] Arkoff explained, "The studios were overlooking the summers as a time to target audiences with new pictures. Because many theaters weren't air-conditioned, the studios believed that people just wouldn't go to the movies in the summer. But teenagers would."[92] In particular, AIP saw the potential in distributing its films to drive-ins during the summer months. The year 1956 saw a weekly summer attendance of 83 million viewers, accounting for the highest summer box office receipts to date. The *Hollywood Reporter* surmised that drive-ins accounted for the majority of that money: "Better than 60 percent of the increase went into the big open-air theaters that flourish during the summer months, with more of them open and each getting a greater attendance during the days of no school, poor TV and warmer nights."[93]

"Until the late fifties," said Arkoff, the major studios

shied away from releasing their big pictures in the summer, convinced that people were just too busy vacationing or having backyard barbecues to go to the movies. They just didn't realize that some drive-ins were capable of grossing $50,000 or better a week during the summer, which was far better than most hardtops. Once the studios had heard about some of AIP's summer box office successes, however, they began rethinking. In the summer of 1958, the majors started releasing some of their biggest movies of the year in the summer, making it increasingly harder for us to get into the theaters, even the drive-ins.[94]

Prior to this increased competition, AIP's films were viewed as the salvation of many drive-in owners. One outdoor exhibitor in the San Fernando Valley stated that before AIP joined the marketplace he had been "thinking of shutting down to three nights a week. [AIP] saved us."[95] The benefit was often immediate to exhibitors, as the company's strategy was to maximize the first weekend's box-office receipts for its releases. Most B-movies "don't last," Arkoff rationalized. "They play one, two, three weeks, depending on how big the area is. . . . You go in, you get your money, and you get out."[96] Known as "first-weekend syndrome" in modern Hollywood, this phenomenon has the added benefit of reducing long-term advertising expenses. AIP frequently used such a saturation-booking distribution process, a relatively rare practice in the 1950s, as well as advertising on television:

Unlike the majors, who at that time would open their movies in just one flagship theater downtown and then slowly move them into outlying theaters and surrounding communities, we would book our pictures into as many neighborhood theaters and drive-ins in a single city as possible, transforming these theaters into our "first run" houses. We rarely played in single flagship theaters in Beverly Hills or on Broadway, but we'd cover a city with multiple screenings in thirty, forty or more theaters. The reason: to get as much mileage as possible out of our TV advertising.[97]

Variety noted as early as January 1956 how the fact that the company's films were "hypoed [*sic*] by strong exploitation on tv" contributed strongly to its financial success. Arrangements were made with local stations in cities where AIP's films were opening to acquire all unsold late-night advertising time, often spending a thousand dollars for a block of thirty to forty ads run over the course of a week.[98] Using a late-night time slot for these ads was not only less expensive, it also reached the company's target audience of moviegoers. Television stations routinely aired movies later in the evening in the mid- to late 1950s, via such packages as *The Million Dollar Movie* and *The Late, Late Show*. Children and teenagers often stayed up late to watch these broadcasts, which allowed AIP to effectively reach its desired demographics without paying for more expensive advertisements during the day.

These ads were often supplemented by live publicity appearances on popular daytime programs, usually featuring a title creature from one of the films. For the release of *The She-Creature*, the film's costume was worn on two Los Angeles daytime talk shows in 1956, *Quinn's Corner* and *Campus Club*. The latter appearance became what, in retrospect, was deemed a "wildly successful publicity stunt," as the *Campus Club* broadcast "nearly turned into a riot as the show's college-age live audience stampeded the stage" to inspect the monster more closely.[99] While the shortcoming of such an event is the damage that the costume might have sustained (it would be reused in multiple films), the word-of-mouth promotion created by the television appearance was invaluable.

Thomas E. LaVezzi, president of the Theatre Equipment and Supply Manufacturers Association, declared in 1958 that the film industry "needs to adapt a 'hard sell' advertising approach" in order to revitalize itself. He lamented what he saw as a general curtailment of ads in trade publications, noting that with a few exceptions "there is a complete lack of enthusiastic 'sales pitch' for the great majority of product. Contrarily, those that are advertised and otherwise extensively promoted are doing excellent box office business."[100]

AIP may be considered one such exception, with its sales pitches being some of the industry's "hardest" and consequently its films being relatively lucrative. Its trade advertisements employ both provocative rhetoric and tantalizing promises—the ad for one double bill describes *I Was a Teenage Frankenstein* as depicting the "Body of a Boy! Mind of a Monster! Soul of an Unearthly Thing!" while also vowing *"Blood of Dracula* Will Give You Nightmares Forever."[101] Despite LaVezzi's position that this hard-sell approach would benefit the industry, AIP's advertisements were often criticized for their garishness. Hy Hollinger's November 5, 1958, article "Is Carny Come-On Necessary?" documented the criticism:

> Executives of American International Pictures, faced with attacks from both within and outside the industry for their exploitation pictures and their advertising policy, frankly admitted in N.Y. last week that their ads "are obviously overdrawn for the deliberate and calculated purpose of bringing people into theatres."
>
> They acknowledged that the promises made in the advertising are not always fulfilled in the actual pictures, but they defended this policy on the ground that the film industry is essentially a carnival business and that it must therefore deal in carnival terms. Just as books should not be judged by their covers, they contended that their pix should not be condemned because of the advertising.[102]

I Was a Teenage Frankenstein (Santa Rosa Productions/American International Pictures, 1957)

This carnival approach, in keeping with the general nature of ballyhoo techniques, was indeed a "necessary" aspect of the 1950s B-movie and one of the most celebrated. Due in large part to AIP's "calculated" efforts, in 1958 the company "provided over 10% of the total product available to exhibitors," proving that it had not only cornered the B-movie market but also carved out an impressive segment of the overall cinematic marketplace.[103]

The Late 1950s: From Whole Shows to Big Singles

By the late 1950s, AIP faced competition from smaller companies seeking to duplicate the low-budget formula created by Arkoff and Nicholson, a sign of just how widespread the B-movie marketplace had become as the decade progressed. By 1959, the popularity of AIP's drive-in double bills that had connected so well with teenage audiences just the year before was in decline, due to the inundation of numerous imitators. While AIP's market share had been growing steadily up until this point, there were soon signs that changes in its mode of production lay ahead. It announced the release of twelve films from May through July 1958, a schedule described as "the largest in the company's history."[104] By the third quarter of 1958, however, theater bookings became more difficult to acquire due to increased competition from other independent companies such as those detailed in the previous chapter. As Arkoff notes, most of these films "had very little originality to them, and could have been AIP clones," such as Clover Productions' *Life Begins at Seventeen* (1958) and *Teenage Crime Wave* (1958).[105]

Nicholson spoke out to *Variety* in 1958 about the glut of competing B-movies, warning of how "the exploitation market will die if program pictures don't maintain some semblance of quality." Of films made by other low-budget companies for $50,000, he said that "the difference shows. When a moviegoer sees one, he's not anxious to go back to see another exploitation picture," said Nicholson, explaining how "exhibitors who play 'the cheap imitations' are aiding the demise of the market and eventually their own doom." Younger audiences "want thrills rather than involved plots," he said, "but they can tell the difference between a quickie and a well conceived film. "[106]

Part of this competition came from Corman himself, who founded the new distribution company Filmgroup in 1959 in order to achieve more creative autonomy, although he would continue to direct films for AIP as well. Ten films were announced in February 1959 as being scheduled for release, most of them also AIP clones such as *High School Big Shot, T-Bird Gang*, and *The Wasp Woman*.[107] To distinguish themselves, Arkoff and Nicholson recognized the need to differentiate their product, budgeting $15 million to be spread over thirty films in 1959, a record amount for the company. Nicholson cautioned that these higher budgeted films were "no indication that American is interested in crashing the 'A' market," but rather served as "recognition that gimmick pix can no longer be filmed on short purse and be successful."[108] Unlike older Poverty Row studios such as Republic that attempted in vain to diversify their product line by releasing a handful of A-films (while largely failing to change the way in which they approached B-filmmaking), AIP instead saw the need to augment its existing approach toward B-movie production in order to differentiate itself from its low-budget competitors.

With this change in production strategies came an evolution of distribution policies. After three years of only producing combination double bills, AIP also began to produce films intended for single-bill distribution.[109] Arkoff and Nicholson announced to delegates at the company's first international convention in April of 1958 that "quality single bill features, increase in the use of color and CinemaScope and a full diversification of product" were part of AIP's "new change of policy." The "standard double bill package by which the company has made its name will not be ignored," but instead "there will be fewer such bills and they will be designed to meet the changed tastes of the public."[110]

The first such film was *Horrors of the Black Museum* (1959), budgeted at $500,000, making it the "costliest ever authorized" by the company at approximately five times the budget of many of its earlier films.[111] The film's producer, Herman Cohen, who had also produced *I Was a Teenage Werewolf*, believed that what had worked just two years earlier would no longer sell at the end of the decade. Audiences "just won't go for something that is cheap. Today you must give them color, 'scope, spectacle; you've got to give them more than just a crazy horror story."[112] An acerbic *Variety* headline summed up this sentiment: "Is It Becoming 'I Was a Teenage Bore?'"[113]

Filmed in Eastman Color and in CinemaScope, *Horrors of the Black Museum* was praised by critics for having "the highest production standard yet offered by American International."[114] The film was a success with audiences as well, setting a record first-day gross in the Los Angeles area for an AIP film and also breaking records internationally in Naples, Brussels, and Tokyo. With its bigger budget and higher production values, the film even received bookings in "some better theatres than AIP films formerly played" and ultimately earned close to $3 million worldwide.[115]

As a result of this success, Arkoff and Nicholson began to change their corporate strategy, essentially trying the bigger-but-fewer approach used by the major studios at the start of the 1950s. "We can't go on any longer with these combinations and hope to survive. We've got to change," Arkoff told Nicholson. "We can take the money that we would have otherwise spent on two movies and channel those funds into just one. . . . Rather than making two $150,000 black-and-white features, we can produce one $300,000 color motion picture." The *Hollywood Reporter* announced on June 3, 1959, that AIP had "sharply changed course" and was "heading for a higher plateau of production." In doing so, it was now abandoning its former policy of not diversifying its audiences. Arkoff explained the new direction:

> The future of this industry and theaters which support it depends on a supply of new and different product. Product must be tailor-made for theaters of different types. There are different audiences, different markets. Specializing in one while neglecting the others is a crime which this industry has been guilty. A producer's "line" must be comprehensive to reach all the markets—high, low and medium. American International will shoot now to serve all theatres, A, B, C or D. Our budgets and subject matter will be gaited to take care of varying types of exhibitors. If there are 3000 houses which can play a certain type of product profitably for both of us, we will make it for them. Too much production has been only at one level.[116]

AIP therefore began to branch out beyond the teenage demographic that had defined the company since its inception. It would continue to make films for this audience, of course, but no longer to the exclusion of all others. Arkoff noted that the new policy was not immediately popular with many exhibitors, who wanted AIP to continue producing low-budget combinations for the marketplace: "'What are you guys trying to prove?' one [exhibitor] bluntly asked." The unspoken concern among such theater owners was that if AIP began making bigger-budget films, they might be sold at the same percentages as major studio releases. "They wanted us to keep delivering pictures on cheap terms. . . . It's like they'd prefer to keep us barefoot and pregnant," Arkoff complained.[117]

For its first high-profile film under the new policy, AIP turned to the stories of Edgar Allan Poe. This marked the company's first attempt to adapt literary source material, and Poe's selection was aided by the fact that his work was in the public domain—"where else could you get a better writer that was cheaper?" said Arkoff.[118] AIP released *House of Usher* in color and CinemaScope in 1960 at a cost of $300,000. It also marked the first time that the studio used an actor with marquee value in star Vincent Price, who had already headlined major studio horror films for two decades in *The Invisible Man Returns* (1940), *House of Wax* (1953), and *The Fly* (1958).

House of Usher was a success with critics, who recognized that the film's appeal extended far beyond the usual teenage demographic. "It is a film that should attract mature tastes," wrote *Variety*, "as well as those who come to the cinema for sheer thrills. . . . All things considered, pro and con, the fall of the

'House of Usher' seems to herald the rise of the House of AIP." The *New York Tribune* praised its "restoration of finesse and craftsmanship to the genre of the dread," while the *Los Angeles Examiner* called it "a film that kids will love that never once insults adult intelligence." The film was a financial success as well, earning "nearly $1 million in domestic rentals in its first six months of release."[119] This led to a cycle of seven more Poe adaptations between 1960 and 1964, all directed by Corman for AIP in the "big singles" format of color and CinemaScope.

Despite the higher budgets, many of the company's traditional cost-effective production methods, which had helped establish it in the first place, remained. Corman reused all of the sets and props for each of the Poe films. "If we had the same art department budget on our second picture," he said, "we had, say, $20,000 of sets stored from the first, so it became a $40,000 design. For the third set, we had, say, $40,000 in stock and spent another $20,000 on new design," which explained how the cycle "looked increasingly more elaborate without stretching the production budgets or shooting schedules."[120]

With these traditional production methods at work under its new overall mode of production, AIP reinvented itself as a leading independent studio. Its films were still relatively low budget compared to major studio releases and therefore still considered B-movies by most, yet they were remarkably different from the black-and-white double-bill product that had been released throughout the 1950s. New companies would emerge to make the latter type of films in the early 1960s, but none would ever be as successful as AIP. Arkoff and Nicholson took various economic risks throughout the company's history, but never foolish ones. "This is a gambling business, but like the Las Vegas casinos, we tried to take only calculated chances," said Arkoff.[121]

The year 1979 marked AIP's twenty-fifth in business, and the Museum of Modern Art in New York hosted a retrospective tribute in celebration. Thirty-nine of the company's films were shown at MoMA, an accomplishment that Arkoff said he "would have been startled" to have been told was coming had he known during AIP's inception. "We did not deliberately make art," he told the MoMA audience on opening night of the retrospective. "We were making economical pictures for our youthful market, but at the same time," he speculated, "I guess we were also unconsciously doing something unique and extraordinary."[122] In 1980, AIP merged with Filmways with the intention of making bigger-budget productions. Arkoff would sell his stock in the company within the year, however, subsequently forming the awkwardly named Arkoff International Pictures to make several films throughout the decade.

While it was the end of an era for the original company, AIP left behind a strong legacy in the film industry. It may have begun as just another small company seeking to cash in on the growing product shortage, but AIP quickly became an industry trendsetter, and not only among the ranks of its independent peers. Its success would also lead most other Hollywood studios to reexamine their approach toward both low-budget films and younger audience demographics in the late 1950s and throughout the 1960s. The major studios ultimately adopted many aspects of AIP's production methods in subsequent decades, demonstrating just how truly innovative 1950s B-film-making often was.

5

Small Screen, Smaller Pictures

New Perspectives on 1950s Television and B-Movies

While companies such as American International Pictures allowed B-movies to thrive at the box office in the 1950s, the Bs also had a substantial presence on television in this decade, and, even though scholars often cite television's growing popularity as a primary cause for the demise of such Poverty Row studios as Republic and PRC/Eagle-Lion, B-filmmaking simultaneously influenced certain patterns within the television industry. B-movies played a unique and at times integral role in the development of the television medium in the 1950s, yet few detailed accounts of this interplay exist despite the wealth of scholarly literature comparing the two media in this period.

Two case studies will help to illustrate the complex role that B-movies played in television's early history. The first demonstrates how the sale of B-movies to various stations in the early 1950s established programming patterns that became well entrenched by the time the major studios began offering their films for television broadcast by mid-decade. The second examines how episodes of numerous programs were turned into B-movies for cinematic release, an example of collaboration between the two media that predates most instances of major studio development for the small screen.

Media historians frequently describe a significant tension between the film and television industries when chronicling the origins of the latter, with each medium seeking to dominate the entertainment landscape in the early 1950s.[1] Despite this seemingly bitter rivalry, various efforts to unite the two industries occurred throughout the decade. Such ventures as "theater television" (whereby viewers could see special small-screen broadcasts such as sporting events on the big screen at movie theaters) were launched, along with "subscription television" (an early pay-per-view movie service).[2] Given that this intermedia rivalry often saw significant cooperation, scholarship in media history such as Christopher Anderson's *Hollywood TV*, William Boddy's

Fifties Television, Tino Balio's *Hollywood in the Age of Television*, Michelle Hilmes's *Hollywood and Broadcasting*, and Kerry Segrave's *Movies at Home: How Hollywood Came to Television* has sought to trace the dynamics of this relationship, as well as to explore the holes in the grand narrative of television's origins. It does not account, however, for some of the more overlooked and unusual parallels between the film and television industries—those in which the B-movie plays a central role.

Segrave notes, for example, that in the early years of television programming, the only films available to the small screen "consisted of westerns, B films produced by 'Poverty Row' studios such as Republic and Monogram, a few A pictures from independents and some foreign fare, virtually all from the U.K."[3] Part one of this chapter provides nuance to this general overview of film programming patterns by assessing specific films and stations as illustrations of just how significant the Bs were to television's development as a medium.

Part two examines the phenomenon of the made-from-TV movie, a collaborative effort between the two industries arising in the early to mid-1950s. Such films transported television content to the arena of B-movie distribution. The films and programs discussed herein are therefore an unexamined area of negotiation and crossover between the film and television industries in an era in which the two were frequently at odds with one another.

Many of the patterns established by the crossover between the Bs and television helped to establish practices that became ingrained in the latter's programming structure long after such experimental ventures as theater television were abandoned. While B-movies were often considered a mere stepping-stone for television as it awaited Hollywood's eventual presence, the role of the Bs in television's early history is far more complex and important than many realize.

Part One: Television Broadcasting and B-Movies in the Early 1950s

While the major Hollywood studios began selling their films to television in 1955, there was certainly no dearth of films on television in the first half of the decade. Films were shown on the small screen in mass quantities during this period, the majority (but, as will be demonstrated, not all) of them being B-movies. Movies appeared on television almost from the very beginning of the latter medium's postwar debut. In 1948, British producer Alexander Korda sold twenty-four films to New York television station WPIX, while CBS negotiated with Monogram.[4] The J. Arthur Rank organization soon followed, selling a package of seventy films in 1949.[5] American studios also followed within the next year, with the B studios first offering their films for sale to the new medium.

By the end of 1950, Poverty Row studios such as Monogram, Eagle-Lion (formerly Producers Releasing Corporation), and Republic Pictures had already offered approximately four thousand of their films to television.[6] Monogram's films were particularly abundant, with at least one of the studio's films airing nearly every day in the spring and summer months of 1950, often during prime-time viewing hours. While Segrave describes how "generally throughout the 1950s, films were programmed outside primetime hours by network-affiliated stations,"[7] and *Business Week* declared in 1956 that feature films "haven't cracked the pattern" of the "domination of programming" by television networks, this was not the case at the start of the decade.[8] CBS often ran films at least once a week starting anywhere from 8 to 9:30 P.M. throughout much of 1950, including many Monogram films.

Whereas Republic's film sales concentrated heavily on westerns, the Monogram films sold to television were of a wide array of genres. Audiences in 1950 saw horror films (*The Corpse Vanishes*, 1942, starring Bela Lugosi), mysteries (Charlie Chan entries such as *The Jade Mask*, 1945), comedies (Bowery Boys films such as *Boys of the City* and *That Gang of Mine*, both 1940), action-adventure films (such as *Navy Secrets*, 1939, and *Federal Bullets*, 1937), and war films (including *Wings over the Pacific*, 1943). Even though complaints about the steady repetition of the same films on television emerged as the decade progressed, a high degree of turnover existed throughout 1950 and 1951—with many films sold under the provision that they could be shown on television only twice each year.[9]

The increasing number of films sold to television was an alarming trend to the California Theatre Owners Association (CTOA), whose television committee reported on December 12, 1950, that the "use of old films on telecasts to homes has just about struck the reissue and 'B' feature market for theatres a death blow . . . [that could] eventually put every independent producer and small company out of business."[10] Radio Corporation of America chairman David Sarnoff also expressed concern about the role of B-movies in the matter of what he called "Hollywood versus home TV." Noting how there "will always be a lush market for first class pictures," namely bigger-budget A-films, Sarnoff speculated as to how television would affect the Bs. "[It is] a question in my mind," he said, "about the B's in relation to the movies one can see and will continue to be able to see on home TV. The question then follows as to whether Hollywood can live on A's alone, at least in the manner to which it has grown accustomed."[11] If B-movies were to play a vital role in Hollywood's future, as Sarnoff seems to imply here, then television would significantly impact the viability of the Bs as more films began to appear on the small screen.

As the decade began, films were quickly becoming the desired type of programming for more than a third of all television viewers, with the

CTOA revealing that as early as 1950 approximately "38 per cent of set owners preferred films to all other TV programs."[12] Films were programmed throughout stations' daily schedules; viewers could usually find a film on at least one channel from midday onward. In the New York area alone, stations such as WABD, WATV, WCBS, WJZ, WNBT, WOR, and WPIX regularly programmed feature films. Two of these stations adopted ornithological monikers in 1950 for some of their film programming, with WATV running an *Early Bird Matinee* weekdays at noon and WPIX hosting *Night Owl Theatre* in the late evening. Some television stations actively sought to offer audiences as many similarities as the new medium was capable of delivering with what had heretofore been the dominant visual medium of entertainment, so as to lure more viewers into watching films at home. In May of 1950, for instance, WPIX introduced *Double Feature Theatre* on Sunday nights, in which viewers saw two films back-to-back in a two-hour block, attempting to re-create a theatrical double-bill format.

In June of 1950, 70 percent of WATV's seventy-seven-hour programming week was reportedly devoted to films, proving that they were therefore far more than just a supplement to regular television programs.[13] The CTOA's concern that selling films to television would put independent producers out of business did not appear to be an immediate threat to many of them. Producers Sol Lesser and Edward Small, for example, formed Peerless Television Productions Inc. in 1951 in order to distribute many of their films, announcing that they would offer a package of twenty-seven films "with name casts and good values." Los Angeles station KTTV acquired broadcast rights for an eighteen-month period, and a Chicago group for twelve months, with multiple runs of each picture allowed.[14] Such films included *Kit Carson* (1940), *International Lady* (1941), *The Red House* (1947), *T-Men* (1947), and *Raw Deal* (1948).

Even if independent producers released their films to theaters through a major film studio, there were still opportunities to profit from sales to television. The *New York Times* noted in 1950: "Although an independent producer usually releases his product for theaters through one of the major companies, after so many years all rights revert back to him. Then he is free to try and peddle it for further gains, a case of trying to milk the cow after it's gone dry. Today one of his best bets for a run-down product is television. He contacts a distributor, the middle man who will do the selling to video stations. If a producer is hard up for cash, he may sell his product outright to the distributor."[15] The independents often saw the opportunity to sell their old films as a welcome relief in the face of the marketplace uncertainty created by both television's debut and the demise of the block-booking system that had fed the demand for product for so many years. Republic particularly welcomed the chance to supplement its typically meager earnings, as evidenced by its selling 125 pictures to television in August of 1951 and 174 more in October.[16] Studio founder Herbert J. Yates would later declare that the reason for the sale was "to make up for a loss in revenues from the sale of [the studio's] films to theatres." Yates was of the opinion "that it is better 'to live with television' and 'get your share of the business' than fight it."[17] This policy would ultimately serve to bring about the end of Republic, as television programming eventually rendered the studio's films obsolete given how they failed to adapt to changing marketplace demands.

The major studios would not begin selling their own films to television until mid-decade, when RKO's films were programmed on New York station WOR's *Million Dollar Movie* broadcasts in 1955.[18] Still, many of the films initially offered by the majors were B-movies, with Twentieth Century–Fox selling a package of Charlie Chan films, for example.[19] The year 1956 saw an even wider sale of major studio films to television, with Columbia renting a package of 104 films to its subsidiary company Screen Gems in January of that year for $5 million, while in March Warner Bros. sold the broadcast rights to 850 features and 1,500 short subjects to Associated Artists. Twentieth Century–Fox and MGM each made similar arrangements by the end of the year.

Films offered to television in the early 1950s were almost always pre-1948 titles, since these were exempt from requiring residuals to be paid to various performer and craft unions, while more recent films were not.[20] There were exceptions to this rule, as a few films released after 1948 were occasionally shown on television. March of 1950 saw WPIX show the 1949 comedy *Bride for Sale*, starring Claudette Colbert, while WCBS aired both the Marx Brothers film *Love Happy* (1949) in April of 1950 and the 1949 film noir *The Crooked Way* in February of 1952. While residuals might conceivably have been paid for each title, it is more likely a case of a few independent producers being unconcerned with the consequences of union retaliation to the sale of their films, particularly given that the production companies for the first two films (Crest Productions and Artists Alliance) had already gone out of business by 1950.

These newer films were still anomalies, however, with the vast majority of films shown on television being what trade publications in 1951 started calling "old" films, as most were B-movies from the previous two decades. Debate soon arose over how outdated such films might be for the new medium of television:

> Whether old films will continue to exert viewer appeal on TV is a topic fraught with sharply divided opinion. Producer-distributor-exhibitor Robert L. Lippert feels that ancient Hollywood pictures will only see another year or two on video screens. In contrast, a CBS TV spokesman this week cited a big pickup in viewer response to its "early" and "late"

film shows as an indication that "old movies" are here to stay. TV calls for an integrated series, Lippert maintains, rather than the use of old films with different faces and themes each night. The public, he avers, gets accustomed to the Phil Harrises, Jack Bennys, Eddie Cantors, et al., and wants to see more of the personalities it's familiar with. Dated pix can't do this, since they have no continuity and the talent is continually changing.[21]

Whereas previous concerns about whether films were "old" and "dated" had been limited to decisions about re-releasing titles to theaters in subsequent years, television's debut meant that producers now had to weigh multiple factors in how best to profit from their films in the years following a given title's initial release. The Independent Motion Picture Producers Association even advised its members in 1950 that their primary concern "must be to find a way to sell their pictures to television 'shortly after their exhibition in theatres.'"[22] For the major studios, however, it would not have been in their best interests to offer films that were too recent, so as to ensure that the public had to visit their local theater to experience the bigger, more spectacular brand of cinema that was unavailable on television.

The film industry eventually realized that the minor studios would soon have few films left to sell: "TV Dries Up Old Pix Sources," declared *Variety* in November of 1951. "Unless the majors suddenly open their vaults," it noted, "there are few more old features in prospect for television. It has pretty much chewed up the independent U.S. and British product." As a result, Poverty Row studios began charging even more for their B-movies, even though many of their top titles had already been sold: "Feature-length product is in more demand and fetching higher prices than ever," noted *Variety*. "But the telepix distribs who have been bidding for it have pretty much encouraged the indies to scrape the bottom of the barrel. There are just very few additional pictures of any merit left—even on TV standards.[23]

A-Pictures on Television in the Early 1950s

Yet at least one major Hollywood producer actively pursued the sale of his films to television in the early 1950s. David O. Selznick visited New York for several months in late 1951 with the intent to "further explore income potential from his pix on TV," having already sent a representative some months earlier for the purpose of "studying various ways in which the pix could be sold." Despite anticipating protests from exhibitors, Selznick described feeling "obliged to investigate the potential of the TV market for top quality pictures," such as Alfred Hitchcock's *Rebecca* (1940), *Spellbound* (1945), and *The Paradine Case* (1948), along with *Little Lord Fauntleroy* (1936), *Since You Went Away* (1944), and *Portrait of Jenny* (1948). One of the more interesting options explored was "the possibility of chopping them into parts for a sort of serialization."[24] *Duel in the Sun* (1946), for example, was offered up in five half-hour segments at a cost of $30,000 each.[25] In this case, Selznick's strategy was to use the developing thirty-minute programming format to his advantage, modifying the content of one medium to fit the form of another. This approach was ultimately rejected, with stations unreceptive to the idea of serialization. Selznick would instead sell his films in their entirety, earning over $3 million for the sale of twenty-two films between 1951 and 1952.

What trade reports of this period do not mention is that several of Selznick's films had already appeared on television more than a year before his reported intent to explore this form of "income potential." Hilmes describes how Selznick "broke the A picture barrier in 1951" by selling his films to television, implying that A-films did not have a presence on the small screen before this year.[26] Three of Selznick's films actually aired between March and June of 1950—WNBT ran *Nothing Sacred* (1937), and WPIX ran *The Young in Heart* (1938) and *A Star Is Born* (1937). This raises the issue that, despite the claims of most contemporary historians and even many journalists of the time, not all films shown during television's early years were B-movies, and that the appearance of an A-picture on the small screen was not an extremely rare occasion. Boddy states, for example: "Few feature films of any vintage from the major studios were available to television before 1955, and the available American theatrical feature films tended to be low-budget and from minor studios."[27]

There is a general tendency to believe that films shown on television in its earliest years were of uniformly poor quality (that, aside from the British films, they were all B-movies, in other words). *Business Week* noted in 1956, for example, "Although a trickle of slightly better films had been flowing out of Hollywood earlier, the dam didn't burst until late last year."[28] But in examining the television listings of the early 1950s, several hidden patterns emerge. Not all of the American films shown on television at the start of the decade were low budget; many instead featured famous stars and were made by eminent directors. Each of the aforementioned Selznick films is an A-picture starring such well-known actors as Douglas Fairbanks Jr., Paulette Goddard, Carole Lombard, and Fredric March. Independent producer Hal Roach also sold many of his films to television, with the following titles broadcast in 1950 alone: *Of Mice and Men* (1939) with Lon Chaney Jr. and Burgess Meredith; *One Million B.C.* (1940), starring Victor Mature and Carol Landis; and the Laurel and Hardy films *Sons of the Desert* (1933), *Way Out West* (1937), *Swiss Miss* (1938), *Zenobia* (1939), and *Saps at Sea* (1940).

There were actually so many films sold to television in this period starring well-known actors that stations began to designate specific programming blocks for the showing of these star-laden films during the prime-time evening hours, with most films starting between 8 and 10 P.M. WPIX hosted both *All-Star Theatre* and *Premiere Theatre*, showcasing films with recognizable stars: the former included *A Star Is Born*, for example, while the latter featured Edward G. Robinson in *Thunder in the City* (1937). Similarly, WCBS created *Premiere Playhouse*, showing René Clair's *I Married a Witch* (1942), starring Veronica Lake, Fredric March, and Susan Hayward. In this way, film-programming patterns came to be established that were maintained throughout the history of television. Films with all-star casts and those having their network premiere were typically shown in prime time so as to garner the best ratings. Subsequent screenings as well as films with lesser-known actors were shown predominantly in the afternoon or late evening, under such generic programming banners as *Film Theatre* and *The Late Show* (the latter soon followed by *The Late Late Show*).

While *Thunder in the City* is one of many British features that were among the first films to be sold to television, it is also notable for having been distributed by Columbia Pictures in its North American theatrical release. Given that the rights to independently made films eventually reverted back to their producers, many films that were distributed by major Hollywood studios in the 1930s and 1940s became available for sale to television. Thus, while the majors did not begin selling their films to television until the middle of the decade, many A-pictures still aired in the early 1950s because of the nature of the majors' distribution patterns in prior decades. Through acquiring independent films for theatrical distribution, the major studios often elevated the status of films that might not otherwise have been deemed A-pictures—lending to them a sort of "cultural distinction" that resulted in better press coverage for such films as well as distribution in more prestigious theaters than they would likely have otherwise received.[29]

Such distinction allowed many films produced by independent studios to be seen and read about by a wider audience than if they were distributed independently. A form of cultural currency was subsequently transferred to these films during their network broadcasts despite the fact that the majors no longer held their legal rights. This process allowed television audiences in 1950 to see such famous actors as James Stewart in *Pot o' Gold* (1941, Globe Productions, distributed by United Artists); William Holden and Susan Hayward in *Young and Willing* (1943, Cinema Guild Productions, distributed by United Artists); Raymond Massey and Conrad Veidt in *Under the Red Robe* (1937, New World Pictures Ltd., distributed by Twentieth Century–Fox); and even Orson Welles providing the uncredited narration for *Swiss Family Robinson* (1940, The Play's the Thing Productions, distributed by RKO).

Similarly, television audiences were also able to see films by celebrated directors who had made features for independent producers, or who had formed their own production companies. Such films airing in 1950 alone include Alfred Hitchcock's *Foreign Correspondent* (1940), starring Joel McCrea and George Sanders; Fritz Lang's *Hangmen Also Die!* (1943), starring Brian Donlevy, Walter Brennan, and Gene Lockhart; Joseph von Sternberg's *Shanghai Gesture* (1941), starring Gene Tierney, Walter Huston, and Victor Mature; Ernst Lubitsch's *To Be or Not to Be* (1942), starring Jack Benny and Carole Lombard; René Clair's *It Happened Tomorrow* (1944), starring Dick Powell; and Frank Capra's *Meet John Doe* (1941), starring Gary Cooper and Barbara Stanwyck.

Another method by which A-pictures were shown on television was practiced by Astor Pictures, a small Poverty Row distributing company. Astor often purchased films from a wide range of studios—major and minor—for theatrical re-release. These reissues were handled via the states' right distribution system, playing mostly smaller theaters in rural communities that were often neglected by mainstream Hollywood distribution channels. The films that Astor acquired for re-release were typically around five or six years old, but it also handled films that were anywhere from three to ten or more years past their initial theatrical release. One such film it acquired was *Second Chorus* (1940), starring Fred Astaire and Paulette Goddard, which had originally been produced and distributed by Paramount. Hilmes states, "Not until the 1953–54 season did pre-1948 film from any of the major studios find its way to TV."[30] The appearance of *Second Chorus* on television on WPIX in March of 1951 is evidence that major studio films did occasionally find a way onto the small screen as a result of the major studios having done business with smaller companies prior to 1948.

Tailored for Television

Just as there were many ways in which films were sold to television, Selznick's tentative plan to serialize his films demonstrates that there were also ways of distributing films to television that were deemed unsuitable to the formal characteristics of the new medium. Where Selznick's plan failed, many Poverty Row producers were more successful in recognizing how the differences between the media might affect the sale of their films to television. In a case of trying to obtain revenues by any means necessary, several Poverty Row studios and independent producers specifically customized their films for television as early as 1951. While the major studios continued making films in the 1950s without any thought for how they might later play on television, the smaller studios were very much aware of this factor. If stations were not willing to cut the running time of movies after the fact, as per Selznick's films, then B-movie producers determined that they would have to cut the running time of their own films during production itself in order to accommodate the programming requirements of television.

It was simply in the best interests of the minors to consider the rival medium of television, since they had been the primary source of films shown on the small screen. In short, even though the new medium has been cited as a major factor in the decline of the B-movie in the 1950s, the smaller studios could not afford to view television as a source of competition as the majors did—instead the minors often decided to work *with* television, rather than fight against it. *Variety* described how "B productions tailored for television" was "the new trend among independent film producers and sub-major studios." Such B-movies were produced "with an eye on the TV market after their product has made the rounds of the theatre circuits." In a case of one medium determining the mode of production of another, B-movie directors "on some lots have been ordered to whittle the running time down to 54 minutes, which will leave six minutes for the insertion of commercials when the films are sold to video. A cut of six minutes not only makes it more convenient for the television sponsors but saves money for the producers. In the ordinary 'B' pictures it will eliminate the expense of a day's shooting."[31]

As the demand for programming grew, some Poverty Row studios began to be revamped as television studios. Eagle-Lion saw all six of its studio stages filming television shows—sometimes called "vidpix" or "telepix productions"—in November of 1951, which was the most activity the studio had seen in three years.[32] Republic announced a $1 million "remodeling program of its studio facilities" on November 5, 1951, in order to develop its own programs for television and rent studio space to independent producers with the same intent.[33] Monogram, not wanting to be outdone, announced the next day that it was developing its own subsidiary company, Interstate Television Corporation. It began by producing thirteen half-hour programs, filmed at the Monogram studio.[34] The mode of production for many early television programs was perhaps closer to that of the B-movie than of a major studio film, given that B-movie studios were designed to enable an accelerated shooting process—sets, for instance, were kept relatively indistinct so that they could be used multiple times in different films with minimal adjustments.

This parallel between the aesthetics of early television programs and B-movie production methods is particularly applicable to half-hour programs, which regularly featured those genres specialized in by the Bs, such as westerns or jungle adventure films. Since each of these genres is mythic or exotic in nature, producers could apply a more neutral approach to set design. Rather than be re-created in precise detail, settings such as "the savage jungle and "the Old West" merely had to be suggested, allowing the (typically juvenile) audience's imagination to fill in the rest. Most of the television productions shot at Eagle-Lion, for example, were westerns such as the Range Rider series produced by Gene Autry's Flying A Productions.[35]

The adventure program *Ramar of the Jungle* was also filmed at Eagle-Lion between 1952 and 1954, at the rate of three episodes per week.[36] The *New York*

Times described the show as an "obviously hurried, budget-wise production" but praised it overall.[37] At thirty minutes per episode, the weekly mode of production on *Ramar* is comparable to that of the innumerable feature-length B-movies made in approximately seven days. This was certainly the case with the show *Adventures of Superman*, which began employing more cost-effective production methods in 1953. Scripts for the entire second season were written in advance of initial production, so that every scene at a particular location could be shot simultaneously. Hence, every scene at Clark Kent's apartment for the entire season was shot all at once, as were scenes at the *Daily Planet* office and other such locations.[38]

The success of these programs had an obviously negative effect on the box office popularity of certain kinds of B-movies in the 1950s, especially those that still resembled the Bs of decades past. Most notably, as the television western flourished, Poverty Row studios such as Republic Pictures soon found that the western genre would be hit the hardest by the sale of their films to television—or, as *Variety* put it, " 'B' Gallopers Slow Thataway as TV Cues Boneyard Exit of Hoss Opry." Describing them as both "oaters" and "low-budget hoss operas," the article declared that while B-westerns were "once a prosperous type of film, responsible for the rise of many a star and many a production executive," they were now "facing extinction" in 1953: "Decline of the low-budget western is attributed to mounting production costs and tele. Nowadays, kids can see their western stars for nothing in old pictures or films made especially for TV."[39]

Western films featured prominently on television as the decade began, with WPIX regularly showing titles under the banner of *Six Gun Playhouse*. Late-afternoon programming, as children returned home from school, was especially common, as were weekend slots. In 1950, WABD ran a series of western films on Sundays at 6 P.M., many starring Bob Steele: *Western Justice* (1934), *Alias John Law* (1935), *Sundown Saunders* (1935), *Big Calibre* (1935), *The Law Rides* (1936). Even though many of the westerns shown on television were from the mid-1930s or even older, audiences did not necessarily find these films to be dated. While *Variety* stated that "only a small portion of the films made and released prior to 1935 are suitable for TV release," it also pointed out in 1951 that "westerns and action dramas of that era would hold possibilities of potential grosses [in television sales] due to being undated by the styles of the era."[40]

In turn, the ultimate downfall of many minor studios like Republic was due in large part to the fact that audiences could see the kind of lower-quality films these studios continued to make in the 1950s at home on television for free. *Variety* summed up the situation in 1953 with a terse, daunting headline: "No Profit Anymore in B (for Bad) Pictures." "Instead of producing 42 pictures in a year," said Warner Bros. head Jack L. Warner, "shoot 16, but throw the budget for those 42 into 16. Producers can no longer turn out a cheapo film and expect even a small profit. The public can see mediocre pictures on television for free."[41]

AIP and the Bs on Television in the Late 1950s

Whereas Republic's business practices saw the company's downfall, at the same time American International Pictures was growing highly successful. While AIP's films are often associated with lack of professionalism, its corporate strategies were far from amateur. In order to avoid the fate of the original Poverty Row studios, AIP took an opposing stance to that of its predecessors in a key area of distribution—it refused to sell its films to television in the 1950s so as to protect the image of its product as being distinct from that which audiences could see at home. In 1957, James Nicholson and Samuel Arkoff wrote a letter to Ernest Stellings and Julius Gordon, heads of the Theatre Owners of America and the Allied States Association of Motion Picture Exhibitors respectively, pledging that AIP would not sell any of its films to television for a minimum of ten years after their theatrical release.[42]

Nicholson reiterated this promise in a September 1958 speech at the Allied Theatres of Michigan convention,[43] while Roger Corman sought to make it an industry-wide policy. Corman displayed a surprisingly pro-union sentiment (given the regular attempts to avoid detection of his nonunion production methods) as he argued,

> Hollywood unions and guilds should make such high demands for participation in TV revenue of post-1948 features that the aggregate payoff to talent would make it unprofitable for companies to make the product available for telecasting. . . . The thousands of pre-1948 major studio pictures now available to TV stations are seriously affecting theatre boxoffices throughout the country, and the addition of post-'48 films would mean the end of the motion picture industry as we know it. . . . only an adamant stand by the Hollywood unions and guilds can prevent sale of the newer pictures to TV . . . [but] for the protection of their members and the preservation of the motion picture industry they must do so.
>
> . . . "The most important factor concerning the future is the disposition of the major studio backlogs of post-1948 features," Corman declared.[44]

Rather than shortsightedly offer its films to television, AIP instead mounted plans to create its own series directly for the small screen. The *Hollywood Reporter* announced on March 18, 1959, that AIP was "entering telefilm production" with a series entitled *Terror House*. Nicholson and

Arkoff negotiated with National Telefilm Associates for the distribution of the series through syndication, with AIP using its own writers, producers, and directors.[45] The series never emerged; still, the company's progressive attitude toward the television medium further differentiates it from the Poverty Row companies that eagerly sold their films to the small screen for short-term profit.

AIP succeeded in part by crafting a different relationship with television than its predecessors. As the trend toward youth-oriented films replaced the old model of B-filmmaking, the appearance of the Bs on television simultaneously decreased in the latter half of the decade. With the major studios selling thousands of feature-length and short films to television, an influx of A-pictures quickly halted the demand for the Poverty Row Bs that had previously been a staple of programming patterns for more than half a decade. Most B-movies, particularly those of minor studios and independent producers, would rarely be shown on network television as the decades progressed. For several years during the infancy of the medium, however, B-movies played a dominant role in the establishment of programming patterns for films on television. "The opening of Hollywood's flood gates turned feature film distribution into a big business," declared *Business Week* in 1956.[46] Yet it had already been big business to the Poverty Row companies for many years—they initially staked their financial livelihood on these television sales, the eventual impact of which ultimately sealed their demise.

Part Two: Made-from-TV Movies

While movies were routinely sold to television throughout the 1950s, this process was occasionally inverted during this period. Although such instances are little known, television content was sometimes packaged and sold for theatrical exhibition in what is therefore termed the made-from-TV movie (MFTVM). Such films represent a key moment in the history of film and television as an early instance in which the two media converged. With the emergence of the MFTVM in the early 1950s, B-films served as a forerunner of the eventual cooperation between the major studios and the television industry that took place by mid-decade.

To define what MFTVMs are, it is first necessary to start with what they are not. The term is an obvious takeoff on the made-*for*-TV movie, feature-length films produced solely for television broadcast rather than theatrical distribution. The idea of movies that are made *from* television programs has already been used on occasion, as Richard Corliss does in a 1994 *Time* article, to describe the phenomenon of Hollywood remakes of what are often fondly remembered shows from decades past (such as 1993's *The Fugitive* and 1994's *The Flintstones*).[47] Yet these cinematic remakes should instead be labeled *inspired*-by-TV movies, since they are easily compared to other films that loosely adapt a novel, comic book, play, etc., often keeping only the basic plot structure and characters while creating a new story line. Whereas films that are inspired by television programs generally follow the same production process as films adapted from any other kind of source material, films that are made *from* television programs retain large portions of the actual episodes themselves.

Films inspired by television shows are often criticized as stemming from a lack of creativity and a desire to capitalize on recognizable brand names on the part of modern Hollywood producers, yet the act of using shows as the basis for feature films is almost as old as the medium of television itself. Perhaps the most distinguished examples of films adapted from television programs come from such celebrated *Playhouse 90* episodes as *Requiem for a Heavyweight* and *The Days of Wine and Roses*—along with *The Philco Television Playhouse* episodes *The Bachelor Party* and *Marty*. Preceding these films by several years is a little-known B-film based on a children's genre show. The 1949–1955 science fiction program *Captain Video and His Video Rangers* was one of the first television shows to be adapted into a film, the Columbia serial *Captain Video, Master of the Stratosphere* (1951).[48] Hence, B-movies can presage trends that are later seen in the A-picture marketplace, a phenomenon that is remarkably common yet not always recognized.

As the decade progressed, many other studios began to see the appeal of adapting television series to film. MGM brought Lucille Ball and Desi Arnaz together for the 1953 film *The Long, Long Trailer*, in which (despite a change in character names) they took their domestic sitcom personas on a road trip. Warner Bros. released feature film versions of *Dragnet* to theaters in 1954 and both *The Lone Ranger* and *Our Miss Brooks* in 1956. Each featured new stories and starred the original actors from the television series—all of which were still producing new episodes in the year that they made their cinematic debut. *Variety* picked up on the growing trend in 1955, attributing the success of such films to "the 'pre-sell' of television personages." The article described the major film studios as "increasingly prone to exploit a pre-sold audience presumably willing to pay to see their favorite tv shows and stars in feature-length films" and saw this Hollywood enthusiasm for television product as an "alliance" between the two rival media.[49]

This adaptation process was actually reversed in 1955, as Warner Bros. developed television programs that year out of its earlier films *Cheyenne* (1947), *Kings Row* (1942), and *Casablanca* (1942). MGM followed in 1957 with a series based on *The Thin Man* (1934), as well as the 1958 series *Northwest Passage*, based on the 1940 film. Such cooperative efforts between the film and television industries are predated, however, by the rise of the made-from-TV movie in the early 1950s, whereby independent producers who shot a particular series on film rather than as a live broadcast would select several episodes (usually two or three) and combine them together into a length resembling that of a feature film. Sometimes these individual episodes would be part of a longer serialized narrative, but more often they were largely unrelated except for their recurring characters and settings. The end product was then typically retitled and sold through cinematic distribution networks dealing primarily in B-movies for smaller neighborhood and/or rural theaters.

The profits involved in creating such films were certainly minimal, but they were a welcome supplement to the revenues already generated by the television series itself. Many independent television producers in the early 1950s, especially those creating genre-based programs, had previously produced low-budget films. With demand for B-movies steadily declining in the late 1940s, many producers sought fresh opportunities in the new medium of television. In December of 1950, I. E. Chadwick, head of the Independent Motion Picture Producers Association (IMPPA), announced that those producers who had regularly made B-films in the past decade were being "forced out of business and must find additional revenue from the television market if they are to survive." IMPPA members only released forty films in 1950, down significantly from ninety films in 1949 (which was itself a then-record low number for the association).[50]

This search for new forms of revenue brought many low-budget producers to television, and in turn led some to consider how to turn their small-screen efforts back into cinematic product. In an era marked by competition between film and television, those producers willing to serve the tiny niche market for MFTVMs demonstrated a distinct flexibility in how they approached the two rival industries. Since many such producers had worked with minuscule budgets at such Poverty Row studios as Monogram and Producers Releasing Corporation in the 1940s, B-movie production techniques made a relatively easy transition to the small screen because B-films and television programs typically shared far more similarities in the early 1950s than did the latter and Hollywood movies: reduced budgets and production values, faster shooting schedules, less recognizable actors, and more limited settings and locations, among other factors. Furthermore, independent producers regularly had to consider new and different forms of distribution and exhibition, often turning to such alternatives as states' rights distribution, exhibition practices such as four-walling (running a film in a theater rented for the purpose, and retaining 100 percent of the box office), and drive-ins in order to reach viewers and earn a meager profit.

It might be something of an exaggeration to declare those 1950s producers turning programs into films to be pioneers of the cross-media collaboration between film and television that began to fully take hold in

1955. Nevertheless, MFTVMs are a significant and unheralded part of the history of television's development as a medium. Stokes describes how "each cultural technology defines itself through its relationship with other cultural technologies."[51] MFTVMs are therefore seen as contributing to the way in which television defined itself in the 1950s as it cultivated its relationship with the film industry.

Conditions Leading Up to MFTVMs

As television progressed in the early 1950s, a central question began to emerge—would the future of the medium consist primarily of live or filmed broadcasts? The number of programs shot on film grew larger with each passing year, tripling between 1952 and 1953 before finally breaking the 50 percent mark in 1955.[52] Many television critics were quick to attack this trend, such as the *New York Times*'s Jack Gould, who chastised filmed programming in a December 1952 article entitled "A Plea for Live Video," calling the decrease in live programs "the colossal boner [mistake] of the year." His criticisms ranged from the technical inadequacies of filmed shows (a "grainy overcast" to the screen image, "diffuse and fuzzy" lighting, "tinny and artificial" sound) to the "qualitatively" superior aesthetic of live broadcasts ("The unforeseen occurrence or the occasional mishap on stage are the best possible testament of television's power to transmit actuality"). "To regard television merely as an extension of the neighborhood motion picture house is to misunderstand the medium," stated Gould.[53]

Although his plea went mostly unheard, it resurfaced again in 1957 in writer-producer (and *The Twilight Zone* narrator) Rod Serling's article "TV in the Can vs. TV in the Flesh." Both Gould and Serling negatively compared filmed television programs to B-movies: Gould saw the bulk of "canned" programs in 1952 as "grade B productions" that had been "turned out" for the small screen, while Serling described filmed programs as being mostly "uninspired, formulated, hackneyed, assembly-line products that could boast fast production and fast profit, but little strain on the creative process," rhetoric that is commonly directed at B-films.[54]

Granted, a higher proportion of filmed shows were genre based (such as action/adventure, sci-fi, and westerns), as these often proved somewhat more difficult to shoot live in a studio given such factors as special effects, outdoor settings, animal unpredictability, etc.[55] Live programs such as *Four Star Playhouse* and *Kraft Television Theatre* predominantly aired dramas, rarely straying into the aforementioned genres and thus arguably appearing to be more serious to television critics. The pedigree of live programming therefore stems from the fact that the often generic nature of filmed shows made them appear too similar to the B-films that were quickly falling out of favor in Hollywood. The fact that filmed programs could be so easily combined together into feature-length films for the B-movie marketplace would likely only infuriate critics of canned television.

While the argument may have been made for live television's aesthetic superiority, the economic incentive to produce filmed programming proved unavoidable and soon led to the virtual demise of shooting "in the flesh." Serling even conceded the economic logic of shooting on film as "inarguable," citing the fact that filmed programs can be aired multiple times. Such reruns bring in more money not only to producers but also to writers and actors in the form of residual payments, resulting "ultimately in five to ten times what single-shot salaries bring in live television."[56] Filmed programs could also make further profits through syndication, allowing shows to be sold to multiple markets at different times and often to stations not affiliated with a major network.

Syndication also allowed a program to make continuing profits in the years following its initial broadcast run, with producers occasionally using syndicated rerun performance in subsequent years as an indicator for whether to make new episodes. *Ramar of the Jungle* originally ran from 1952 to 1954, although syndicated reruns continued through 1957. Producer Leon Fromkess announced his (ultimately unfulfilled) intentions in March of 1955 to resume production on the show later that year, rationalizing the yearlong hiatus by stating that he "want[ed] to recoup his investment" with his existing episodes currently being rerun "before making additional firstruns."[57]

Had his plans for new episodes of *Ramar* come to fruition, Fromkess would have faced stiffer competition in 1955 than in years past. Warner Bros., MGM, Twentieth Century–Fox, and Paramount all began producing programs in that year, joining such smaller studios as Columbia, Universal, and Republic, which had been creating television programming since 1952 through various subsidiary companies. With many of the major studios also starting to sell their catalogues of pre-1948 films to television in 1955, journalists such as Thomas Pryor began announcing the "marriage of the motion picture and television industries."[58] In so doing, they reminded readers of the supposedly long-standing animosity between the film and television industries. One 1955 article described how the major studios were overcoming their former "antagonism" toward television, whereby in years prior they would "flatly reject even the idea of dealing with tv."[59] Another article began: "Hollywood, once so fearful of television, today is riding the crest of a video-inspired boom. The prosperity of the nation's glamour town surpasses the heyday of the film capital in 1945. By this autumn, the West Coast center of the show business will provide at least ten times as much entertainment for national television audiences as for motion picture theatre audiences."[60]

If television and the movies were indeed finally married in 1955, they had certainly fooled around together for years before officially tying the knot.

To cast this nuptials metaphor in a less flattering light, the proliferation of MFTVMs in the early to mid-1950s represents a brood of bastard offspring that, claimed by neither parent, quickly became orphaned. Independent producers were the predominant creators of television programs prior to the 1955 major studio production boom, with as many as one hundred independents existing in the six years prior to 1954.[61] The majority of these independents produced only a single show, which meant that the financial rewards were often minimal—and much less certain—when compared to those eventually reaped by the majors (whose larger production slate could subsidize losses on any one particular program).

Independent producers favored shooting programs on film rather than recording live for several fiscal reasons, the first being that their costs could be amortized over more markets than with live programming. *Business Week* explained that "a filmed show costs less to put on than a live show of comparable quality. The producer or sponsor can peddle the program in a variety of markets to as many as 50 different sponsors . . . [and] can begin on different dates in different cities."[62] Along with the potential to sell filmed programming to foreign markets, as well as the potential for additional income provided by reruns, the reasons to shoot on film were typically too great for independent producers to ignore.

A few enterprising producers in the early 1950s soon got the idea to use the same filmed content for both television episodes and cinematic release. Hal Roach Jr.'s production of *The Three Musketeers* for CBS's Magnavox Theater in 1950 was soon released as the theatrical film *The Sword of D'Artagnan* in areas of the country that did not yet have television stations. Directed by B-movie veteran Budd Boetticher, the film stands as one of the earliest MFTVMs on record. It was hailed in the press as "the first full-length television feature film on television"—with the awkward repetition of the word "television" perhaps signaling the novelty of such intermedia collaborations at the time.[63]

June of 1951 saw the announcement that independent producer Rene Williams had completed numerous fifteen-minute television programs that he hoped to not only sell as a series but also compile together for theatrical release. The series was to be called *Bits of Life*, while five narrative segments would be united into a feature entitled *Quintet*. Williams considered the film to be something of an experiment that would test the industry's desire for such a unique product and planned to screen it initially in only a single theater in order to gauge public response: "He is going to book it into a standard theatre," reported *Motion Picture Herald*, "exploit it appropriately, and see what happens. On the basis of what happens, or doesn't, he'll make a deal with a distributor, or he won't."[64] Such cautious rhetoric—neither Williams nor the *Herald* seems fully confident that the same material could be sold in each medium—is indicative of the uncertain relationship between the film and television industries in the early 1950s. In July of that same year, Robert L. Lippert rearranged his existing plans to sell two projects as both television episodes and theatrical films. Initially planning to release up to sixteen such ventures in association with Roach, Lippert balked at the extra compensation required by various film unions for the television screenings of theatrically released material. Claiming that it would be virtually impossible to achieve a profit under such conditions, Lippert released his only two completed projects, *Tales of Robin Hood* and *As You Were*, to theaters later in the year.[65]

November of 1951 saw the release of a film with a far more deliberate plan for its relationship with television, as audiences first saw George Reeves play the title role in *Superman and the Mole Men*. Distributed in theaters by Lippert Pictures, the film was essentially made as a pilot to attract a sponsor for the subsequent *Adventures of Superman* series and was split into a two-part episode during the first season.

The following year brought the films *The Yellow Haired Kid*, *The Ghost of Crossbones Canyon*, and *Trail of the Arrow* by distributor Allied Artists, each combining two episodes of the first season of *Adventures of Wild Bill Hickok* from 1951, starring Guy Madison. These proved successful enough to encourage the release of four more *Hickok* films in 1953 (*Border City Rustlers*, *Secret of Outlaw Flats*, *Six Gun Decision*, and *Two Gun Marshal*), along with eight more such films between 1954 and 1955.

Each *Hickok* film ran fifty-two to fifty-four minutes, making them convenient programmers for the largely rural theaters that continued to run B-western double bills in the 1950s. With the Federal Communications Commission implementing a freeze on station licensing between September 1948 and April 1952, television viewership did not expand as rapidly as it might have in the early 1950s.[66] Little more than a third of American households had a television set in 1952, and it wasn't until 1954 that televisions were in more than half of the country's homes. Major urban centers typically had more stations and better reception than rural areas during this period. Under these circumstances, rural audiences—a substantial portion of the country—were not only still eager for the entertainment provided by their local theater, which regularly included B-films, but more receptive than urbanites to MFTVMs, given that the TV programs themselves were frequently unavailable.

In 1953, a joint venture was announced between the distributor Vitapix and the production company Princess Pictures for a different kind of television-cinema hybrid. The two companies planned to produce twenty-six films that would first air on television before later seeing theatrical release. The product that each medium received varied, however, with the running time of each film being shorter for television than it was for cinematic release. Each film would be edited in advance to fit a one-hour television time slot, with theatrical audiences getting just over a one-hour running time.[67] One such production, *Phantom Caravan* (1954), aired on WCBS in New York on October 29, 1955, from 6:15 to 7:10 P.M., just enough time to hold the film's edited length of fifty-four minutes. Theatrical audiences, on the other hand, enjoyed a running time of sixty-one minutes for the same film. Other films were closer to seventy minutes long for theatrical release, with Vitapix promising that its edited television versions were "accomplished without cutting any of the bone." Initially distributing them to second-run theaters in those areas not already showing the films on television, Vitapix planned to eventually release the films in theatrical markets where the film had already been seen on the small screen.[68]

Production Strategies

With all of these various parallels between cinema and television in play by 1953, the MFTVM phenomenon soon seemed like a legitimate venture, at least for those independent producers willing to try something new. Such budding entrepreneurship is symptomatic of the debate that occurred in the early years of television surrounding the nature and potential of the medium itself. William Boddy surmises:

> The most basic questions about television—the formats and aesthetic forms of programs, the responsibility for program production, the structures of distribution and sponsorship—were subject to both aesthetic speculation and commercial conflict in the first half-decade of the medium. . . . The early years of television witnessed considerable speculation about the appropriate forms and sources of television programming, speculation informed by wider social and cultural attitudes toward contemporary culture and business life.[69]

Made-from-TV movies therefore represent a key case study of such speculation and conflict because they entail a format wherein the boundaries between media become blurred. The content and aesthetics of MFTVMs typically originate in the production methods of the television industry, and the distribution of these films involves a sort of redistribution given that their origins lie outside of the cinematic medium.

When made-*for*-TV films debuted in the 1960s, television networks actively sought programming alternatives to Hollywood films, leading to the creation of films directly for the small screen. They quickly proved to be so successful that 70 percent of feature-length films shown on television were made-fors by the end of the 1970s. Furthermore, these made-for-TV films "could earn additional revenue for their producers and the networks through foreign theatrical and television release, and, by the 1980s, through cable television and videocassette release."[70] Similarly, MFTVMs can be seen as an alternative enterprise for television producers, a way of creating additional revenue from existing product by selling their shows in a new format for theatrical release in both foreign and domestic markets.

By far the most famous MFTVMs are Disney's *Davy Crockett, King of the Wild Frontier* (1955) and *Davy Crockett and the River Pirates* (1956). Each was compiled from multiple episodes of the *Disneyland* weekly television series between 1954 and 1955, and both were highly successful, with the first film earning approximately $2.5 million over 1,300 theaters despite the original episodes having already been seen at home by 90 million people.[71] Anderson suggests that much of the success of the *Disneyland* program lies in how it presented serialized stories rather than just narratives that resolve themselves in a single episode: "Before Disney, prime-time series were episodic; narrative conflicts were introduced and resolved in the course of a single episode. Open-ended serials were confined to daytime's soap opera genre. Disney certainly wasn't concerned about issues of TV narrative, but the *Disneyland* series demonstrated an incipient understanding of the appeal of serial narrative for network television. The success of the three-part 'Davy Crockett' serial was attributable at least in part to its ability to engage viewers in an ongoing narrative."[72]

Yet *Disneyland* was not always a true serial: different parts of the same story were often shown weeks apart. For instance, the first three *Davy Crockett* episodes were shown on December 15, 1954, and January 26 and February 23, 1955. Viewers might have to wait a month or more for the next installment, a format that more closely resembles a B-movie series such as the Hopalong Cassidy films from William Sherman Productions with multiple releases in the same year (eleven films in 1941 alone) than it does the weekly chapter serials made famous by Republic, Columbia, and Universal. Furthermore, the three episodes that make up *Davy Crockett, King of the Wild Frontier* are indeed episodic in the way that each introduces new characters and conflicts and resolves those conflicts at the end. The first episode chronicles Crockett's early years as an "Indian fighter," the second depicts his time in Congress, and the third portrays his efforts at the Alamo.

In contrast to this more episodic narrative approach, another program that debuted in 1954 serves as a much stronger example of how viewers could be engaged in an ongoing narrative. In January of 1954—nine months before *Disneyland*'s television premiere—*Rocky Jones, Space Ranger* made its syndicated debut with a format that regularly saw three-part narratives air on a weekly basis.[73] Much like the cinema's chapter-play serials, each narrative typically involves a single main villain or conflict and features unresolved cliffhanger endings to individual episodes (something that *Davy Crockett* lacks). Each three-episode *Rocky Jones* arc contains a single story title, identified both visually in the opening credits and verbally by the show's announcer as either the first, second, or third chapter of the story. Viewers are therefore alerted to the serialized nature of the program (and the need to watch regularly to get the entire story). Each three-part story line was then compiled into a feature-length film format, often with a new title, for release in subsequent years.

The *Rocky Jones* films are not quite MFTVMs in the strictest sense, however, given that they were distributed to television rather than in theaters. While they aired as feature-length films and featured new opening credits to distinguish them from the show itself, the *Rocky Jones* films only appeared on television. Perhaps a case of the show's production company, Roland Reed Productions, being unable to secure theatrical distribution, the *Rocky Jones* films still demonstrate a desire to turn filmed televisions episodes into an alternative format for redistribution after their initial syndication. A more definitive example of the MFTVM is found in the films created from episodes of *Ramar of the Jungle*, which will serve here as a central case study.

In his book *Disney TV*, J. P. Telotte suggests that the *Davy Crockett* films demonstrate how "product created for television could, if it was good enough and had high production values, be recycled for theatrical exhibition."[74] While this might be true for companies seeking to achieve substantial profits from first-run theaters, strong production values were certainly not a requirement for transporting television episodes to the cinema. *Ramar*, like most of the shows that spawned MFTVMs, was shot on a low budget and utilized a mode of production comparable to those of B-films and serials.[75] Each episode of *Ramar* cost approximately $13,000, with three installments typically filmed per week. Scenes requiring animals were usually accomplished through the use of stock footage, and the series' music was leased from the MUTEL Music Service and consisted of excerpts that had originally been used in such serials as *Radar Men from the Moon* (1952) and *Jungle Drums of Africa* (1953).[76]

Ramar began its syndicated release in October of 1952, with its first MFTVM, *White Goddess*, distributed in early 1953 by Lippert Pictures. With several domestic markets not picking up the show until April 1953, and with episodes not always being syndicated in the same order on each station, some audiences would have seen *Ramar* in cinematic form before they could find it on their local television stations. A second film, *Eyes of the Jungle*, was released later that year, and two more in 1955 (*Phantom of the Jungle*, *Thunder over Sangoland*). To create these films, producers Fromkess and Rudolph Flothow selected three episodes from the first season that could be combined to form a feature-length narrative. Fifty-two episodes of the show were produced in total, organized into four thirteen-episode shooting schedules. While most episodes are set in Africa, some take place in the jungles of India (although all were filmed at Eagle-Lion studios in Hollywood). Episodes chosen for inclusion in each *Ramar* MFTVM were therefore always either set entirely in India or entirely in Africa, maintaining a certain unity in each film's setting despite the show's nonserialized narrative format.

Each of the 1950s *Ramar* films consists of three episodes presented almost in their entirety, although the films vary slightly as to how much they retain of the original episodes' content. The only major alteration of the episodes used to create *Eyes of the Jungle*, for example, is in the opening credits and establishing stock-footage shots. The film begins with shots of the Taj Mahal; the television episode that begins the film—"The Mark of Shaitan"—opens with shots of various crowds, architecture, and public sites in India. While the Taj Mahal footage was actually used in a different *Ramar* episode, the producers presumably wanted to use their most recognizable establishing shots of India rather than the less distinct waterfront and marketplace imagery that begins "Shaitan." All of the *Ramar* films eliminate the various epilogues from each episode that are unrelated to the narrative, whereby star Jon Hall addressed the audience directly while both explaining key

Eyes of the Jungle (Arrow Productions Inc./Lippert Pictures, 1953)

facts related to the show (such as the differences between various jungle animals, the history of the different languages used, etc.) and promoting Good 'n' Plenty candy bars.

Aside from the missing epilogues and stock-footage substitutions, each episode used to create *Eyes of the Jungle* remains virtually unchanged. Other *Ramar* films such as *Phantom of the Jungle*, however, cut short certain shots or eliminate them altogether. This strategy is often applied to the opening stock-footage shots of jungle terrain and wild animals, such as in the second episode used for *Phantom*—"The Golden Tablet." While "Tablet" begins with five shots—the jungle terrain; grazing animals; a lion; a gazelle; a group of animals at a watering hole—*Phantom* retains only the first two shots. In addition, each of these two sequences features different music, with the film using a slow, tranquil melody in place of the faster-paced, more adventurous music that opens the episode. Through divergent musical cues and editing choices, even though many of the visuals are the same, each creates a different narrative mood and pace. Using slower music and fewer establishing shots in *Phantom* creates an easy transition for viewers between the episodes that construct the film, whereas pairing the faster music with more establishing shots of wild animals is intended to create a sense of excitement for television audiences as the episode begins.

Further stock-footage shots are removed throughout *Phantom*, in addition to cutting short some scenes involving actors. This is often done for the highly practical reason of eliminating the fade-out/fade-in transitions around commercials that interrupt an extended action sequence. While television viewers in this situation would ordinarily have no difficulty in reorienting themselves to the episode's setting and narrative after the commercials, film-goers would more likely read a fade-out/fade-in as a signal of time passing, and indeed these transitions are retained in the film when they are used to introduce spatial or temporal variations.

Eliminating these fades unavoidably results in an occasional jump cut. For instance, as the television episode fades in from a commercial break, a native emerges from a hut's doorway, whereas in the film the same shot begins once the fade-in is over, with the native already outside of the door. Given that the previous shot took place inside the hut, the newly created transition awkwardly disrupts the viewer's temporal and spatial orientation (which, of course, would have also been the case if the fades were retained in the film). This problem becomes a symptom of the difficulty that can be involved in transporting the content of one medium to another.

In 1964, a new slate of *Ramar* MFTVMs (*Ramar and the Burning Barrier*, *Ramar and the Deadly Females*, *Ramar and the Jungle Secrets*, *Ramar's Mission to India*, *Ramar and the Savage Challenges*, *Ramar and the Hidden Terrors*, *Ramar and the Jungle Voodoo*) saw distribution to television by the Independent Television Corporation, and these were produced using far more editing than those released to theaters in the previous decade. Most of the 1964 films consist of portions of four episodes rather than three (with one film, *Ramar and the Jungle Voodoo*, containing parts of five episodes). Given that each of the 1964 films had a running time of approximately eighty minutes, and the original *Ramar* episodes were typically around twenty-six minutes each in length, five to ten minutes of each episode had to be cut in order to create these new films.

To aid in the (sometimes abrupt) transitions created by this increase in editing, voice-over narration is used to provide audiences with a bridge between episodes. In *Ramar and the Jungle Voodoo*, this overly explicatory narration begins the film in order to quickly establish setting, character, and plot: "In the wilds of Africa, Dr. Tom Reynolds and Professor Ogden, aided by their trusty guide Charlie, have been conducting experiments which may increase the lifespan of man." Transitions between episodes often involve the narrator speaking of Ramar's need to continue his experiments, while foreshadowing a new threat that would soon unfold: "But it appeared that the jungle voodoo had cast a spell on Dr. Reynolds's plans also. For the same boat that ended one adventure brought in a strange visitor."

Narration is even used to help connect much of the new editing that takes place within individual episodes, given that so much of the original pacing has been altered. Audiences are therefore subjected to such often forced narration as "And so Jeff Sharp not only disregarded Dr. Reynolds's warning about the taboos of Naduri territory, but also the time-honored customs of honeymoons, as he left his bride behind." While at times awkward, such narration is largely necessitated by the producer's desire to use portions of more episodes in these later films, perhaps in the belief that a faster pace would make the decade-old content seem more exciting. The narration essentially serves the same role as some intertitles do in silent films, providing expository information to help audiences follow the plot, while at the same time serving to smooth over variances in time and space between scenes.

No such attempt was made to link the episodes used in the 1950s *Ramar* films, however, which are joined only by a simple fade-out and fade-in (transitions that are in fact present in the original episodes themselves). The "Shaitan" episode ends with the imminent resolution of Howard's illness by the intervention of a Guru. The camera pans from right to left as the Guru walks off into the jungle, and then fades to black as the episode ends. The next episode chosen for *Eyes of the Jungle*—"The Flower of Doom"—begins with a tracking shot moving left to right across the jungle landscape, before cutting to a shot of natives carrying a sick man to Ramar's campsite.

Given that the first episode ends and the second one begins at the campsite, the use of an opening tracking shot moving in the opposite direction from the previous camera pan, combined with the punctuating fades, implies that an indeterminate passage of time has occurred. Howard now appears fully recovered as he and Ramar conduct a new scientific experiment. The narrative progression that occurs between the two episodes is easily negotiated due to the congruent settings, as audiences would assume that one or more nights have passed as Howard recuperated.

The second episode ends with Ramar and the Guru once again parting ways, this time with Ramar and his party leaving the Guru behind in the jungle as they depart. The third episode—"Voice from the Past"—opens with Ramar and Howard meeting with the Maharaja, who laments that they must soon leave India. The passage of time between the second and third episodes is once again easily understood (Ramar traveling from jungle to urban center), and an overall narrative progression is enacted. By selecting both the first and last of the India-set episodes, the producers chronicle both Ramar's arrival and his plans for departure, leaving eleven more episodes to choose from in tying together the film's opening and closing acts.

A similar narrative progression occurs in *Phantom of the Jungle*, which uses the first three episodes ("The Lost Safari," "The Golden Tablet," "The Flaming Mountain") of the series' final thirteen-episode arc. New supporting characters are introduced who appear in all three episodes, and a new campsite serves as the recurring setting around which the narratives are organized. At the end of "Safari," Ramar and his group head off into the jungle to return to their camp, while "Tablet" opens with stock footage of jungle brush and roaming animals before cutting to the group as they prepare for a new day at the campsite. A monkey taps on Howard's head as he sleeps, waking him up. With a fade-out/fade-in transition again the only linkage between the two episodes in the film, cinemagoers would naturally assume that they are seeing the characters the next day, while an indeterminate amount of time might have passed for television viewers going a week or more between episodes (if they even saw them syndicated in the correct order).

The mode of production by which the *Ramar* films were created was not the only way in which television episodes were combined to create MFTVMs. In 1954, fifteen episodes from the second season of *Adventures of Superman* were used to create five feature films (*Superman and the Jungle Devil, Superman Flies Again, Superman in Exile, Superman in Scotland Yard, Superman's Peril*), distributed by Twentieth Century–Fox. Each film features three nonserialized episodes that often contain vastly different narratives, settings, and characters. To unite each set of three episodes, producer Whitney Ellsworth gathered the lead actors to shoot new footage for the films upon completion of the second season's production schedule. Linking each episode to the next, the new scenes were approximately one minute each and typically consisted of Clark Kent, Lois Lane, and Jimmy Olson (or two of the three) sitting around the *Daily Planet* office while discussing the events that had just occurred in each episode's narrative and anticipating the events to come.[77]

Whereas the jungle setting of *Ramar* provided the show with a relative consistency in terms of settings and the types of villains and conflicts featured, *Adventures of Superman* was much more varied in its story lines given that both Clark Kent's job as a reporter and Superman's power of flight allowed him to go anywhere in the world, while Superman's other powers allowed him to essentially defeat anyone or anything. Hence Superman might fight gangsters in one episode, prevent a giant meteor from hitting the Earth in the next, and rescue a fighter pilot in another. In the second season alone, Superman travels to Africa, Egypt, and England (and also flies a child around the world after helping to cure her blindness).

With such enormous variations in time and space regularly occurring between episodes, the *Superman* films could not simply use a fade-out/fade-in transition. The newly filmed sequences become a necessity in order to orient cinematic viewers and create some semblance of a larger overall narrative. The *Ramar* and *Superman* films therefore use different production strategies for combining disparate episodes in accordance with the nature of each show's main character. *Ramar*'s jungle-based adventures create a sort of timeless world and a series of conflicts that are often similar in nature, thereby allowing for editing alone to create linkages between episodes in each 1950s film. Alternatively, *Superman*'s globetrotting implies a series of different conflicts that have a more definite resolution, necessitating explicatory dialogue scenes to link each new adventure with the next.

Along with the new footage, each *Superman* film virtually presents the three original episodes in their entirety, barring the credits. A much different approach is found in the films created from Disney's *Zorro* series, which ran from 1957 to 1959. Much like *Rocky Jones*, *Zorro* featured multi-episode narratives, with the first season being comprised of three thirteen-episode story arcs. Portions of the first thirteen episodes were combined to form *The Sign of Zorro* in 1958, a film released internationally in that year and then domestically in 1960 once the series had ended. A second film, *Zorro the Avenger*, was released only in international markets in 1959. Airing its programs on the ABC network rather than in syndication, Disney was evidently more concerned than independent producers such as Flothow and Fromkess that domestic audiences be prevented from seeing their title character in theaters while the show was still on the air. Being a major company with deeper resources allowed Disney the privilege of protecting the brand image of its show, while the tighter financial circumstances of the independents often forced them to capitalize on what little product they had available to market while they still could.

In reducing thirteen serialized episodes to create *The Sign of Zorro*, producer William H. Anderson had to be extremely selective about what scenes to include in the film. Action sequences and key plot details involving main characters were favored, while subplots and lengthy dialogue scenes among supporting characters were largely avoided. Even certain action sequences, however, were not kept in their entirety. Both the first episode and the film begin with an establishing shot of a ship at sea followed by a sword fight, but the film omits the fight's opening moments, resulting in an inadvertent jump-cut edit in the transition between the sailing ship and the thrusting swordsmen. So much of the original episodes having been removed, the pace of the film becomes more hurried as the characters move from one conflict to another with fewer moments of dialogue-driven character development.

In sum, a producer's approach toward turning television episodes into MFTVMs is largely determined by the overall narrative and production strategies of each individual series. The serialized nature of both *Zorro* and *Rocky Jones* dictates that an entire story arc be carried over into a feature film, lest audiences not receive narrative resolution. Given that the story arcs in the latter were much shorter than those in *Zorro*, little to no editing was required to combine *Rocky Jones* episodes into films. While both the *Zorro* and 1964 *Ramar* films often involved the removal of extensive portions of individual episodes, the fact that the former program was serialized while the latter was not afforded more narrative continuity to the *Zorro* films, whereas the later *Ramar* films had to invent a new continuity in the form of voice-over narration to help explain the transitions between various settings and characters.

Advertising Strategies

While production strategies varied, one constant was true of all MFTVMs in regard to theatrical exhibition—they had to be presented as new films in order to compete in the cinematic marketplace. Promotional materials such as posters and lobby cards were required to sell the films, with producers employing various marketing strategies to ensure that their product would not be quickly dismissed as something that audiences could see for free at home on television (even if this was more or less true). Above all, the key to selling these films was to largely avoid reference to the original television programs from which they came.[78] Thus those who were fans of the show from which a film was created might believe that they were seeing their favorite characters in a brand-new adventure. This was often attempted by giving films new titles that were evocative enough to draw fans of the television series while at the same time still remaining generic enough to attract viewers who might be unfamiliar with the program. This was the strategy behind such films as *Superman's Peril* and *Superman Flies Again*—exciting-sounding titles that connote unspecified threats and adventures—as well as the *Ramar* films *Eyes of the Jungle* and *Phantom of the Jungle*, titles that readily convey their genre to prospective audiences.[79]

While the *Superman* films obviously include the main character's name in the title of the film, the producers of the 1950s *Ramar* films deliberately avoided this strategy, even going so far as to omit the name Ramar itself from any of the posters or lobby cards. Viewers who recognized star Jon Hall might believe the films to contain new material; those who didn't know him might assume the film to be a generic jungle picture they hadn't seen before. While such a bait-and-switch approach may seem deceptive, it is actually in keeping with the common promotional practices of the 1950s B-movie marketplace, such as American International Pictures embellishing its posters with promising concepts and images that were largely undelivered upon in the films themselves.

Foremost in this approach was Roger Corman, with the poster for his film *The Beast with 1,000,000 Eyes* (1955) featuring a lurid image of an enormous, multi-eyed monster about to attack a scantily clad woman, despite the fact that no such monster appears in the film. Posters for Corman's films also regularly include painted images of creatures that appear far more elaborate and menacing than they would onscreen, such as with *It Conquered the World* (1956) and *Attack of the Crab Monsters* (1957). Therefore, in not using the titles of the shows from which the films stemmed, MFTVM advertising simply withheld information from audiences, a tactic that some producers might deem somehow more honorable than providing misleading information about a film in its advertising.

Common to most MFTVM advertising (as it is to 1950s B-movie advertising in general) is the use of sensationalistic rhetoric conveying a strong sense of a given film's genre. The poster for *The Beast with 1,000,000 Eyes* features the words "Destroying . . . Terrifying!" while posters for two of Corman's other films use almost identical taglines to describe the horrific thrills seemingly awaiting audiences in 1954's *Monster from the Ocean Floor* ("Up from the forbidden depths comes a tidal wave of terror!") and *Attack of the Crab Monsters* ("Up from the ocean depths . . . a tidal wave of terror!"). Similar to this emphasis on terror in marketing horror films, the *Ramar* films' advertising frequently used such words as "mystery" and "adventure" to sell their jungle-based exploits:

- *Eyes of the Jungle*: "Thrill packed adventure in the savage jungle of India . . . land of mystery!"
- *Eyes of the Jungle*: "Wild adventure . . . Forbidden secrets in India . . . land of mystery!"
- *Phantom of the Jungle*: "Terrifying adventure rages on the dark continent!"
- *Phantom of the Jungle*: "They dared to pierce the weirdest mystery of the dark continent!!"

Also evidenced here is rhetoric that might be described as colonialist—India as "savage," Africa as a "dark continent." In using such language, the producers inevitably appealed to the fears and stereotypes held by many 1950s Americans surrounding other parts of the world. This trend is further seen in posters for the *Ramar* films *Thunder over Sangoland* ("African death ritual . . . with white beauty as a sacrifice!!") and *White Goddess* ("Forbidden Treasure; Forbidden lips . . . in the heart of Darkest Africa they found a thousand wild savages . . . and one woman—mistress of them all!"). Much of the modern criticism of *Ramar of the Jungle* involves a postcolonialist critique of the representations of race and sexuality found in the show, depictions that are amplified in the advertising for the *Ramar* films given the sensationalistic nature of B-movie marketing in the 1950s.[80]

Such representations also figured prominently in another marketing strategy of the *Ramar* films, that being the use of multiple smaller images at the bottom of posters and lobby cards to supplement the single, larger image that dominates the remaining space. These smaller images appear below the film's title, with each photographic or illustrated picture placed in its own individual box to depict some of the film's more lurid or exciting imagery. Many of these images are also accompanied by textual captions in order to further entice audiences with descriptions of a variety of promised thrills. *White Goddess*, for example, invites viewers to "SEE Blood-Thirsty African Armies on the Warpath! SEE Furious wild African elephant stampede! SEE Daring rescue from blazing jungle fire!" *Eyes of the Jungle* largely plays up the film's animal action, while still invoking colonialist rhetoric: "Deathly charge of the ferocious rhinoceros! Blood-thirsty battle of wild tigers! Weird death-dance of savage Puna Khotas tribe! Attack by man-eating crocodile!"

While all of these attractions are indeed featured in their respective films, just how daring, furious, and bloodthirsty they really were is subjective. Although this exploitive rhetoric was a common marketing strategy in creating posters for 1950s B-movies, the lobby card for one particular *Ramar* film employs a more subtle design strategy, one that indirectly references the very fact that the film stems from a television program: the majority of supplementary images found in such advertising are placed in rectangular boxes, but those in the lobby card for *Phantom of the Jungle* have rounded edges rather than straight ones. These images appear roughly analogous to the shape of the screen found in an average 1950s television set.

In using this visual design element, the lobby card conveys the intermedia nature of the film in an almost subconscious way: presenting images from the film via the aspect ratio of the television screen might draw potential cinemagoers who are also regular television viewers to the lobby card on an instinctual level (or, at the very least, this is the hope of the film's producers). While advertising strategies for MFTVMs commonly adhere to the larger marketing principles of 1950s B-movies, there are still significant anomalies that appear to be unique to the process of turning television into films.

Into the 1960s and Beyond

The prime period for MFTVMs was 1953 to 1955, given the twelve *Wild Bill Hickok* films, four *Ramar* films and five *Superman* films released during these years, yet episodes from other television series were occasionally turned into films as the decade progressed. In addition to Disney's *Zorro* films, the late

Phantom of the Jungle (Arrow Productions Inc./Lippert Pictures, 1955)

1950s saw episodes from the 1955 television series *Cheyenne* edited together
into the film *The Travellers* (1957). Three films were also created from episodes
of *Hawkeye and the Mohicans* in 1957 (*Along the Mohawk Trail*, *The Pathfinder and
the Mohican*, *The Redmen and the Renegades*), the same year that the series aired
on television. Another *Hawkeye* film, *The Long Rifle and the Tomahawk*, was
theatrically released in 1964—coincidentally the same year that new *Ramar*
films were shown on television. The 1958 series *Northwest Passage* also led
to the creation of three films: *Frontier Rangers* (1959), *Fury River* (1959), and
Mission of Danger (1961).

The 1960s saw the MFTVM phenomenon continue with a crop of new
television shows edited into films for both domestic and international release.
Western programs were prominent among such cinematic efforts, including
Three Guns for Texas (1968), a film produced from episodes of the 1965–1967
series *Laredo*; *Hondo and the Apaches* (1967), stemming from episodes of the
Hondo television series from the same year; and *The Brazen Bell* (1962), *The
Final Hour* (1962), *The Meanest Men in the West* (1967), and *The Bull of the West*
(1971), all films created from episodes of the 1962–1971 series *The Virginian*.[81]
Most of these westerns, along with those stemming from *Northwest Passage*,
were made primarily for release in European countries that did not typically
see these series on television until a few years after their domestic debut, so
it was often at the level of B-film distribution that American television first
found its way overseas, albeit in a repackaged form.

The most copious example of MFTVMs in the 1960s is those produced
from episodes of the 1964–1968 series *The Man from U.N.C.L.E.*, with eight films
released between 1965 and 1968.[82] As made-*for*-TV movies began to appear
regularly on network television in the mid-1960s, the producers of *U.N.C.L.E.*
appeared confident that the public's appetite for the interplay between television and feature films would sustain the theatrical release of these eight films
(particularly given the rising popularity of the spy genre among audiences
created by the success of the James Bond franchise). Just as the made-fors
of the 1960s represent the desire of television networks for programming
alternatives that would bring in new forms of revenue, this same impulse led
U.N.C.L.E.'s producers to turn their show into films for theatrical release, as
the producers of so many shows in the 1950s had done.

Given the way that they embody both film and television, MFTVMs play a
key, yet historically neglected, role in how the relationship between the two
media developed. Much has been written about the phenomenon of theater
TV in the 1950s, whereby movie theaters would show television broadcasts of
such live events as boxing matches.[83] Modern theaters replicate this trend
by showing live wrestling matches, hockey games, operas—even allowing
gamers the opportunity to rent screens to play Xbox video games.[84] These
events are examples of a blurring of the traditional boundaries between

media, and a shift in the reception contexts through which media content is consumed, something that MFTVMs did regularly throughout the early history of television.

William Lafferty defines feature films as productions that are "intended originally for theatrical distribution and exhibition."[85] It is this question of intent that becomes especially intriguing when applying this definition to MFTVMs, the content of which was certainly not originally intended for the cinema. Are MFTVMs therefore disqualified as feature films despite the fact that they received cinematic distribution and exhibition? Can the MFTVM perhaps be labeled as unintentional cinema, and if so, what are the boundaries of such a concept? Made-from-TV movies are therefore an important phenomenon because they challenge the very question of what exactly a film is—one of the most vital inquiries in film studies since André Bazin asked *What Is Cinema?* Is a film anything released in theaters? If it is exhibition and not production that defines the medium of cinema, do sporting events, operas, and other cultural events shown in theaters become films? If it is instead production that defines cinema, what are the implications for films that were initially produced in a different medium, using a different mode of production?

Made-from-TV movies represent a significant crossroads in the histories of both film and television. Though often posited as rivals in the 1950s, there were many collaborative efforts between the film and television industries, not the least of which was the distribution of MFTVMs—a product made up almost exclusively of content that had already been disseminated in another medium. Their proliferation, along with the ways in which B-films helped establish film-programming patterns on the small screen at the start of the decade, is indicative of just how much of a role the Bs had within the television industry in its early development—even though much has been written by both observers of the period and modern scholars alike about the seemingly bitter rivalry that was thought to prevent collaborative dealings between the two media throughout much of the 1950s.

6

Big *B*, Little *b*

A Case Study of Three Films

In teaching students about B-movies, I typically begin by asking them to define the term, in order to determine their preconceptions. More often than not, there is a general consensus that B-equals-bad, to the point that when I screen such critically celebrated films as *Detour* (1945) and *Cat People* (1942) in the term's early weeks many students are often surprised at how much they genuinely enjoy them—even to the point of questioning whether such films can really be called B-movies given such enjoyment. If B-movies have therefore become a misunderstood cinematic entity, where does such perplexity ultimately come from?

In writing about the Bs, many fans, critics, and scholars use the relatively limited cost of a film, and the ways in which its reduced budget affects that film's style, directing, acting, etc., as a means of determining its categorical status as a B-movie. Others, however, do not take such financial concerns into account. In 2008, David Sterritt and John Anderson's anthology *The B List* offered members of the National Society of Film Critics the chance to celebrate and evaluate some of their favorite B-films. In their introduction, the editors state that they deliberately eschewed defining the B-film or placing any limits on their authors, who could "go in any directions they wanted so long as B productions were at stake." While the book contains entries on such B-noirs as *Detour* (1945), *Gun Crazy* (1950), and *Murder by Contract* (1958), horror and science fiction films such as *I Walked with a Zombie* (1943), *Red Planet Mars* (1952), *Invasion of the Body Snatchers* (1956), and *Night of the Living Dead* (1968), and low-budget cult classics such as *Pink Flamingos* (1972) and *Eraserhead* (1977)—all films that were made on relatively reduced budgets—there are also several choices that are much more unconventional.

Sterritt and Anderson explain that while the B-movie is conventionally defined as "a low-budget quickie," their book examines the B-film "in the broadest sense, referring to any and all movies made with modest means, maverick sensibilities, and a knack for bending familiar genres into fresh and unfamiliar shapes."[1] *The B List* offers up such films as John Huston's *Beat the Devil* (1953), Francis Ford Coppola's *The Conversation* (1974), William Friedkin's *To Live and Die in L.A.* (1985), and Oliver Stone's *Platoon* and *Salvador* (both 1986) as B-films for analysis despite the fact that each was made by a major studio with a budget that was not particularly "modest" for its respective time period.

Economic considerations were key to how the film industry approached the B-film throughout the 1930s, 1940s, and 1950s, but in recent decades the fiscal context of the Bs has proven less central to how B-filmmaking has been understood from both critical and popular perspectives. In 2005, Steven Spielberg's *War of the Worlds* was released to both critical and commercial success, becoming the fourth-highest-grossing film of the year both domestically and internationally. The film also brought renewed attention to the 1953 version produced by George Pal for Paramount, with few reviews of Spielberg's film failing to mention the original. The rhetoric employed by many critics in these reviews was often questionable, however, given that the Paramount film is routinely called a B-movie in reviews of the Spielberg film, yet the former had a budget of $2 million, which clearly made it an A-picture in its time. Most of that money can be seen on-screen, as 70 percent of Pal's budget went to special effects. Still, the 1953 film is frequently referred to as a B-movie by a diverse range of sources, both journalistic and fan based.[2]

One newspaper review credits Spielberg for "taking old, no-budget genres and turning them into big-budget 'quality' films. Just as, in his hands, the old Saturday afternoon adventure serials became *Raiders of the Lost Ark*, the 1950s Grade-B alien invaders movies become *War of the Worlds*."[3] The rhetoric used here is particularly troublesome for two reasons. First, it mistakenly implies that entire genres (such as science fiction, apparently) can be labeled as low budget, an ignorant statement given the high budgets and accomplished production values of such 1950s films as Twentieth Century–Fox's *The Day the Earth Stood Still* (1951) and MGM's *Forbidden Planet* (1956). Second, the phrase "Grade-B" takes B-movie terminology and adds an impertinent tone to it, using an expression traditionally reserved for classifying meat, with Grade-A being the freshest and most desired.

A further question posed by the critical reception of Spielberg's film is whether modern Hollywood blockbusters can themselves be labeled as B-movies. Should the term be reserved for films with budgets that are relatively more modest given when they were made, or should it be defined more broadly? While film historians may argue for the former, modern film criticism frequently opts for the latter, as was indeed the case with reviews in 2005 describing *War of the Worlds* as "a future retro B-movie," "an example of . . . the B-movie genre at its very best," and "a conceptually cheesy B-movie that doesn't take itself too seriously."[4] Yet Spielberg's film was not made on a reduced budget, nor did it feature aesthetically questionable production values, given how many reviews praised its visual style. Still, the film seems to be called a B-movie because it fits the preconception that many people have of what a B-movie is supposed to be—possessing a lurid title, with a plot centered on creatures attacking society.

Hence, a wide range of films become labeled as B-movies, despite the fact that many do not fit any historical or theoretical definition of what a B-movie is—be it in terms of an impoverished mode of production, camp sensibility, or their reception as trash objets d'art. *Platoon* is offered as a B-film in Sterritt and Anderson's book simply because it presents a new take on an old genre—Eleanor Ringel Cater calls it "the first war movie made about the Vietnam War. That is, it was the first nonpolitical film made about a tragedy that had hitherto been treated within a politicized prowar/antiwar context."[5] No consideration of the film's budget is offered, nor is the film contextualized within the film industry beyond brief comparisons of the plot to other films about Vietnam. The film's inclusion in a book about B-movies seems to be based upon a notion that any Hollywood film that appears radical in its politics can be assigned B-status despite how much it cost (or whether it won Academy Awards for Best Picture and Best Director). Sterritt and Anderson see *Platoon* as a "larger production with the fighting B spirit" in the way that it addresses political issues, yet this description is once again focused simply on cinematic content rather than mode of production.[6]

Similarly, content is the primary criterion for retrospectively assigning 1950s B-films that status, as modern reflections on the 1953 version of *War of the Worlds* demonstrate. B-movies of this decade have seemingly become a homogenized product in the minds of many, despite the fact that the films had a wide range of budgets. Popular memory would seem to be the deciding factor: modern critics and audiences remember the films, or at least some of their archetypal images, as something different from what they really were, recalling them as a uniformly trashy-but-thrilling low-budget whole. Films from the 1950s with an extreme range of budgets—from $2 million to $20,000—become envisioned as completely similar "no-budget" entities, despite the fact that they come from wholly different origins. The production values of the $2 million film are infinitely better than those of the $20,000 film, but contemporary audiences often see little difference between them when it comes to B-movies of this decade.

If the time is taken to examine 1950s B-movies as a whole, several different budgetary levels with correlated degrees of professional quality can be found therein. This chapter examines three distinct levels of production within 1950s B-movies, which are designated as films having either high-end, middle-end, or low-end budgets: in other words, in relation to B-movies as a whole from this decade, budgets of particular films are situated either near the top, the middle, or the bottom of the fiscal scale of overall budgets that were typically assigned to B-films, with each category typically linked to a distinct level of production values. Just as the *New York Times* made distinctions between major studio Bs and those of both "large" and "small independents" in 1935, so too can different production categories be seen in 1950s filmmaking.[7] These categories are not meant to necessarily imply, however, that there is an absolute correlated degree of artistic value associated with each. Instead, as with the societal designations of upper, middle, and lower class, these labels are primarily descriptive of economic status rather than of moral worth. Indeed, many middle- and low-end B-movies have achieved greater critical and popular acclaim than certain high-end B-movies have enjoyed. These three levels are meant primarily as a cognitive model in order to recognize the disparity between the various types of 1950s B-movies—films that many tend to envision as a homogeneous group despite what are often highly divergent modes of production.

The first level, the high-end B-movie, was largely produced by Hollywood studios such as Columbia and Universal, with budgets that often ranged from $300,000 to $500,000 or more, and featured relatively high production values and experienced actors; examples are *Revenge of the Creature* (1955) and *The Deadly Mantis* (1957). Many such efforts at times even served a similar function as the programmers of decades past, seeing more favorable distribution if the studio thought that the finished product might be particularly well received. The second level, the middle-end B-movie, was produced by such established independent studios as Robert L. Lippert Productions and American International Pictures, typically involving budgets of around $100,000, which allowed for reasonably credible production values, two examples being *Rocketship X-M* (1950) and *The Amazing Colossal Man* (1957). The third level, the low-end B-movie, was produced by independent companies even smaller and less established than AIP, companies that generally were unsuccessful in the long run. These films typically feature production values that are extremely impoverished or sometimes even amateurish, with budgets around $50,000 or less (often much less). Examples include *Bride of the Monster* (1955) and *Giant from the Unknown* (1958).

Three films form the basis of this case study: Columbia Pictures' *Earth vs. the Flying Saucers* (1956), a high-end B-movie; American International Pictures' *I Was a Teenage Werewolf* (1957), a middle-end B-movie; and Associated Distributors Productions' *Man Beast* (1956), a low-end B-movie. In examining the mode of production for each level of B-movie as well as their specific production values, we see diversity emerge between the various levels of quality that exist among films that are generally categorized together (often derogatorily) under the same B-movie banner.

The High-End B-Movie: *Earth vs. the Flying Saucers*

In 1956, Columbia Pictures released *Earth vs. the Flying Saucers*, a science fiction film about an alien attack on Washington, D.C. The film is a prime example of a high-end B-movie, since it was produced by a Hollywood studio on a budget that was relatively reduced when compared with those of its A-films, was received upon release as a B-film, and is still regarded as such by modern audiences. Critics at the time considered the film a B-movie, with a 1956 *Variety* review describing it as an "exploitation programmer" and "an okay lowercase booking."[8] Modern critics have echoed this B classification, with Leonard Maltin calling the film "a winner that belies its B origins nearly every step of the way."[9]

Columbia is a particularly apt studio for case study in this regard since its films typically had a lower budget than those of most other Hollywood studios between the 1930s and 1950s. A higher proportion of its films could thus be considered as B-movies because of its fiscal prudence. The studio therefore had a higher stake in the battle for the Bs that dominated the 1950s. In the 1930s and 1940s, Columbia had the lowest box office numbers of the seven major Hollywood studios, coming in behind Universal, RKO, Paramount, Warner Bros., Twentieth Century–Fox, MGM, and top-rated United Artists.[10] This was partly due to the fact that unlike most of these studios, Columbia did not own a theater chain through which to distribute its own films, and also perhaps due to Columbia's tendency to focus on making relatively lower-budget films. Cofounder and president Harry Cohn ran the studio from the early 1930s to the mid-1950s and mandated economy of production from the beginning. In 1935, the average production overhead cost per film was $175,000, the lowest among all the major studios. This was achieved in part by forgoing a large stock company of actors and instead hiring performers on a single-picture basis, often renting stars such as Clark Gable, Claudette Colbert, John Barrymore, and Myrna Loy from other studios.[11]

Cohn believed that quality films could still be made without large budgets; the average Columbia film cost around $250,000 in the 1940s, whereas B-films alone at MGM averaged over $400,000 in 1942. Production schedules were meticulously planned at Columbia, with such cost-cutting measures as allowing directors to print and view only a single take of a scene.[12] Even the studio's biggest pictures used relatively short production schedules: "The biggest pictures there were eighteen-day pictures!" recalled cinematographer Lucien Ballard. Columbia regularly employed talent from other studios whose contracts had expired, and avoided long-term contracts. Ballard, for example, worked for several years on a renewable contract.[13]

Ballard has said that while there was no difference in the professional working environment between the various Hollywood studios, working at Columbia did provide some creative challenges due to Cohn's fiscal vision. The studio owned a relatively small number of lighting instruments, for instance, and imposed rationing on each film set; "they assigned just so many to each picture," Ballard recalled, "and then if you needed more you had to go through all sorts of permissions." When some experimental camerawork caused Cohn to extend the production schedule of a particular film, he personally blamed Ballard for going over budget, berating him for the fact that the studio would no longer make as substantial a profit on the film.[14]

Also typical of Columbia's economic vision was the studio's incorporation of independent productions. While the producer-unit system of film production would dominate most Hollywood studios until the 1950s, Columbia began offering directors independent production deals on a limited-term basis in the mid-1930s.[15] It also provided studio space for, or distributed, the films of smaller independent studios and producers, such as Central Films, Coronet Pictures, and Darmour Inc.[16] Columbia's association with independent producers was tightly controlled; Bernard F. Dick describes how producers were often given limited financial and creative control over their films, with Cohn adopting "an 'only passing through' attitude: the studio was permanent; producers were not."[17] In 1948, Columbia began its association with one such independent producer who would become one of its most successful—and permanent—in the 1950s, Sam Katzman. First using the name the Katzman Corporation with the studio, Katzman changed his production company name to Clover Productions in 1953, the banner under which he would make *Earth vs. the Flying Saucers*.

Given the nickname Jungle Sam for his early work in jungle adventure features and serials such as *Jungle Jim* (1948), *The Lost Tribe* (1949), *Mark of the Gorilla* (1950), and *Fury of the Congo* (1951), Katzman has been described as "the dean of 'get it done,'" a "cut-rate impresario," and a "discount mogul."[18] Katzman would have taken little offense at such labels: "I'm in the five and dime business and not in the Tiffany business," he said. "I make pictures for the little theatres around the country."[19]

Katzman served as executive producer on *Earth vs. the Flying Saucers*, which was part of a resurgence in 1956 of what a *Variety* headline that year called "Zombie Pix"—science fiction and horror films with supernatural or otherworldly themes. Mentioning *Earth vs. the Flying Saucers* among other such films, the article noted that the "main asset of the spacers and chillers is their susceptibility to exploitation," a fact not lost on Katzman. Such films were "ideally suited for saturation openings," *Variety* stated, "accompanied by extensive radio-tv campaigns covering a wide market area. In many instances, the coin saved in the production is added to the exploitation campaigns."[20]

Katzman and producer Charles Schneer turned to UFO expert Major Donald E. Keyhoe's 1953 nonfiction book *Flying Saucers from Outer Space* for source material. Schneer and Katzman had teamed up the previous year on *It Came from Beneath the Sea* (1955), in which they first used celebrated special effects creator Ray Harryhausen, who would join them again to work on *Earth vs. the Flying Saucers*. Writer Curt Siodmak was hired to create the story from Keyhoe's book, with the screenplay written by George Worthing Yates and Raymond T. Marcus (Bernard Gordon). Harryhausen created the visual effects for the film in the preproduction stage. As the screenplay was being finalized, Harryhausen had already finished work on the film's flying saucer effects. This affected the way the film was shot, as certain camera angles now became necessary in order to incorporate the special effects footage.[21] Director Fred F. Sears's work therefore had to accommodate Harryhausen's visual effects work, rather than vice versa.

Sears was a house director for Katzman and Columbia throughout the 1950s, hired more for his efficiency than for his artistry. In the summer of 1951, Sears directed a trio of fifty-five-minute westerns that were each completed in seven or eight days. In 1954, his shooting time averaged ten days for films with longer running times.[22] Mark Thomas McGee has written, "If there was a lesson to be learned about the importance of a good story and quality production it was lost on Fred F. Sears and Columbia." McGee implies that Sears's work does not merit critical elevation because it "was simply dull," and his better films such as *Earth vs. the Flying Saucers* were better "because of other people's contributions"[23]—in this case, Ray Harryhausen's visual effects work.

Despite the perceived "dullness" of some of Sears's work in the film, *Earth vs. the Flying Saucers* is in fact very competently made, and fully in keeping with the level of professional quality expected from a major studio release. Hollywood B-movies in the 1950s were relatively low budget in comparison with other productions, but—as the middle-end and low-end B-movies will demonstrate—the budgets of Hollywood's high-end Bs were still several times larger than those of other, smaller companies making similarly themed films. Katzman's films rarely exceeded a $500,000 budget, with most produced for considerably less—often as low as $250,000.[24] Such budgets are comparable to similar kinds of films made by the smaller Hollywood studios from the same period.

A 1957 *Variety* article discussing the economic viability of what it called the "monster-horror-science fiction category"—alternatively, "weirdies"— declared, "Generally, these films are low-budgeters, costing anywhere from $200,000 to $800,000. The returns have been more than satisfactory."[25]

Earth vs. the Flying Saucers (Clover Productions/Columbia Pictures, 1956)

The year prior, *Variety* determined that a "second feature in today's domestic market can yield $450,000 to $500,000 in distribution revenue." The budget for such films needed to be less than $225,000 studio to guarantee the studio a worthwhile return: "Since the pre-production blueprints are drawn to bring a film to at least the breakeven point in the home market, the $450,000 grosser must be brought in at $225,000 (general trade figuring has it that the gross should double the negative cost)."[26]

Critical evaluations of Columbia's B-films often tend toward exaggeration, such as Gene Fernett's statement that the studio's budgets were often "so miniscule as to make a Monogram producer appear a spendthrift."[27] Despite such claims, *Earth vs. the Flying Saucers* is of a distinctly more professional quality than most 1950s B-movies. As a high-end B-movie, it has a relative slickness and visual appeal resulting from its Hollywood production values. It is these qualities that separate it from the products of smaller, independent studios such as the middle-end company AIP and low-end company Associated Distributors Productions, both of which typically worked with much smaller budgets than Columbia.

One of the first differences between these three levels that the viewer encounters in *Earth vs. the Flying Saucers* is the number of different settings established from the outset. In the opening two minutes before the credits sequence begins, voice-over narration establishes the film's story, while the viewer is presented with actions set in various locations. The first shot is of outer space (via a matte painting), followed by—as the narrator describes it—"the skies of California, the fields of Kansas, the rice paddies of the Orient, the air lanes of the world," the latter including the exterior and interior of an airplane. This is followed by a scene at the "Air Intelligence Command Headquarters," which we are told is in Dayton, Ohio, and then by a scene at the "Hemispheric Defense Command Headquarters" in Colorado Springs. In just two minutes the viewer is led through at least seven locations, both indoor and outdoor, establishing from the beginning that the narrative will have a relatively large scope and will not be confined to a small handful of sets, unlike many lower-end B-movies.

While some of the numerous sets used in *Earth vs. the Flying Saucers* were artificially constructed, several others were preexisting. Both exterior and interior scenes depicting the film's NASA-type installation "Project Sky Hook" were filmed at an actual sewage plant in Playa Del Rey, California. With its exposed pipes and metallic echoes, the location serves to create an appropriately industrial look. The site was also beneficial in the design of the film's sound effects, as the sounds of the flying saucers themselves were created from the humming noises of the plant's underground motors.[28] By using an existing location rather than trying to create a reduced version of an enormous military site with an artificial set, the film strives for a certain degree of authenticity despite its depiction of fantastic events.

Even when the film does use settings that are obviously constructed, such as the interior of the aliens' spaceship, the viewer is not overly distracted from the narrative by the noticeably artificial nature of the set. In keeping with the enormity of the ships when viewed from outside, the interior sets are built to be as large (and therefore as realistic) as possible. To emphasize the large scale of these sets, director Sears uses a crane shot looking down far below at a character dwarfed by his surroundings. Moments later, an extreme-low-angle shot looking up at the character further conveys the height of the room. These shots serve to give the viewer not only a sense of the set's immensity, but by extension a sense of the power and intelligence the aliens must possess in order to have designed such architecture.

The authenticity that the film strives for is furthered by the use of lighting to complement each location. In one scene at the "Department of Defense," an interior setting is cross-cut with an exterior setting depicting a telephone conversation. The indoor set is of an underground launch area and uses artificial light with a moderate degree of contrast. There is an attempt to create the impression of source lighting from several overhead fixtures that are part of the set, with the result creating a silvery outline around each character. These indoor shots are juxtaposed with outdoor shots of the military base, where a more naturalistic lighting scheme is achieved. The scene appears to use sunlight as its major source of illumination, and when the characters step into the shade there is far less contrast than that provided by the artificial lighting. The scene presents a visual continuity between the two locations, using the different types of lighting that would be realistic for each respective setting. B-movies do not always provide such continuity, as will be evidenced in *Man Beast*.

In addition to this controlled lighting, *Earth vs. the Flying Saucers* conforms to traditional Hollywood production values in its camerawork and editing. Along with the aforementioned high- and low-angle shots, the film uses a number of tracking shots, beginning with a prime example in the opening two-minute sequence at the "Air Intelligence Command Headquarters." The shot begins with a dissolve into an office full of secretaries and military personnel working at their desks, as the narrator describes how "the Air Intelligence Command gathers data from all quarters of the globe." The camera then begins a diagonal track left, revealing row after row of desks full of employees busily working or conversing with one another. The smooth and carefully controlled tracking shot lasts almost twenty seconds until the entire row of desks is visible. To deliberately draw such attention to the camerawork signals that the filmmakers have a certain confidence in the technical abilities of their craft, as compared with what often appears to be a lack of technical sophistication of lesser B-movie filmmakers.

A further example of such controlled camerawork is found in a long take of the two protagonists, Dr. and Mrs. Marvin. The shot, introducing us to the two characters, is taken from inside their car, beginning as a medium shot, eventually pulling into a close-up of the two as they snuggle closer, and then returning to a medium shot again as they resume their original positions. These camera movements are moderately paced, even, and steady, without any noticeably jarring qualities. As such, the camerawork is meant to be invisible, not drawing attention to itself. This allows the viewer to engage and identify with the characters and the film without being distracted by elements of technical ineffectiveness, as poor camera movement at a moment of character development could potentially limit the viewer's engagement with and enjoyment of the narrative.

At times the film's camerawork even goes beyond being merely satisfactory, becoming relatively complex. One scene of note features deep-focus cinematography during an army personnel meeting, whereby multiple characters are placed at various depths of field and shot diagonally down a table. This setup is deliberately staged for aesthetic effect, so as to build dramatic tension and suspense as the impending alien threat is discussed. The sophistication of this technique becomes particularly apparent when compared with a film like *Man Beast* that regularly uses single shots of multiple characters in succession rather than arranging them all in the same shot.

Deep-focus cinematography is achieved with a wide-angle lens, which the film further employs later in the film to create a special visual effect. When Dr. Marvin puts on one of the alien helmets, there is a point-of-view shot from the perspective of the helmet, giving the audience a sense of how the aliens supposedly view the world. The shot pans from left to right around a room of army officers, who appear extremely distorted and blurred. The effect is created through the use of an extreme-wide-angle lens, which distorts the image with a virtually 180-degree field of vision that makes its subject appear convex. The use of this special lens is an inspired creative choice, employing the lens's distorting properties in a narrative context such as science fiction that supports using such a highly formalist technique to create an otherworldly form of sensory perception.

Earth vs. the Flying Saucers further conforms to the Hollywood production style in its editing, which is representative of classical decoupage: invisible editing techniques are used in order to unify time and space in the viewer's mind, thereby maintaining narrative continuity. The film contains several instances of crosscutting, wipe transitions, and a montage sequence. The latter functions under the model of what is informally known as Hollywood montage, whereby time and space are condensed into a short period through multiple shots in order to rapidly advance the plot. In this case, the development of a new technology to use against the alien invaders over a period of several days is represented by various shots of trucks moving, people working, and machines operating, with voice-over narration explaining the plot advancement to the audience. This use of montage is in keeping with the relatively large scope of the narrative that the film presents, since it is told over a longer period of time than the majority of middle- and low-end B-movies. A larger narrative scope entails more locations, which necessitate more camera and lighting setups. Using shorter and more numerous scenes also requires more time to edit them together, as well as to record narration and other postproduction concerns.

While 1950s B-movies in general are often ridiculed for their reduced production values and ineffectual special effects, *Earth vs. the Flying Saucers* was praised by *Variety* upon release for its visual style: "The technical effects created by Ray Harryhausen come off excellently . . . adding the required out-of-this-world visual touch."[29] Harryhausen is responsible for the film's most famous scenes, depicting a flying saucer attack on Washington in which several national monuments are destroyed. These are achieved through the technique of stop-motion animation, whereby miniature models are shot one frame at a time with slight variations of position between frames.

Raymond Fielding states in the 1968 edition of *The Technique of Special Effects Cinematography* that in the film industry, "miniatures are the most expensive kind of special effect, and there is little room for error in their basic design." That *Earth vs. the Flying Saucers* uses both miniatures and the stop-motion technique is further symptomatic of its status as a high-end B film, due to the higher budgets found at this level. Fielding calls stop-motion animation "the least satisfactory method that can be employed" when working with miniatures, due to the higher amount of time and money that must be spent in order to perfect the process. "The direction, speed and behaviour of the miniature must be planned just as carefully as for an animated cartoon," he says, and "expensive and time-consuming experimentation is almost always necessary and mistakes are easy to make," which explains why the process is rarely used in the middle and lower tiers of B filmmaking.[30]

The larger budgets of high-end Bs allow them a degree of technical sophistication few non-Hollywood B-movies can achieve. *Earth vs. the Flying Saucers* contains the use of force fields and disintegration rays, two examples of visual effects rarely seen in lower-tier Bs. Such effects employ the use of matte shots, in which the bodies of the disappearing soldiers are blocked or "matted" out of the film negative, allowing a disintegration effect to occur. This is achieved through the use of an optical printer, which allows the combination of images in order to create special optical effects—such as flying saucers interacting with the characters. Harryhausen experimented with a new matte technique in *Earth vs. the Flying Saucers*: for a scene in which aliens appear at the base of a flying saucer he "matted in a warped piece of darkened glass using a short dissolve. The result produced an eerie force-field effect underneath the saucer."[31]

Another visual effect, the use of rear projection, was a staple of classical Hollywood filmmaking. Harryhausen uses the process in a unique way in the film with his miniature work, but in addition to this comes a traditional usage of the process as well, whereby actors are photographed in front of a translucent screen, onto which background imagery is projected. *Earth vs. the Flying Saucers* includes one of the most common instances of this technique, whereby actors in a vehicle are placed before rear-projected footage shot from a moving vehicle to simulate the characters' motion on the road. In lower-tier Bs, this process often seems more artificial than in Hollywood films, due to an obvious contrast between the projected footage and that shot with the actors. In order to achieve rear projection that will appear convincing to audiences, the lighting, quality of set design, and so on must be relatively similar in the foreground subject being filmed and the background imagery being projected behind the subject.[32] Hollywood's high-end films are better able to unite the production values of the different footage and construct a more realistic set, creating a stronger sense of naturalism whereby the audience believes that the supposed vehicle is actually in motion.

Rear projection is a considerably complex operation that is relatively expensive and time-consuming, requiring a significant amount of preparation, expertise, and soundstage space to execute properly. As such, shots using rear projection are typically more common and better executed in the high-end Bs than in their middle- and low-end counterparts. The image being projected must be equally sharp and evenly illuminated in all parts of the screen; otherwise the allocation of light will be glaringly unequal. Using three synchronized projectors can overcome such flaws, as in the VistaVision triple-head projector Paramount developed for its rear-projection work. Few low-budget studios could afford such processes, however.

Hollywood films are further able to attain better quality rear projection because they can afford to use more extensive lighting schemes and superior film stocks, two factors that are key to the process. "With increased set illumination," notes Fielding, "slower, fine-grained stocks can be employed for the photography, smaller relative apertures can be used to provide increased depth of field, and greater contrast through lighting can be gained. . . . If the illumination fall-off is sufficiently great, a vignette effect results which destroys the whole illusion of the composite."[33]

Furthermore, Hollywood studios can more readily afford to employ traveling matte shots when attempting composite shots, an option typically used when creating special effects such as Harryhausen's saucers. The film's traveling matte shots use a more advanced version of the basic matte effect from the aforementioned shots of the disintegration ray, which allows for motion by altering the shape of the matte between frames. The composite quality of a traveling matte shot is much higher than that achieved with rear-projection: "There is no 'hot spot' to contend with, and the grain, contrast, and color fidelity of the background image is superior. Most important, the foreground and background in a traveling matte shot are equally sharp," says Fielding. If low-budget film producers are unconcerned with achieving a high level of composite quality, background projection is a less expensive (if merely adequate) format.[34] Hence, the sophistication of special effects is what typically distinguishes high-end Bs from lower ones.

This is not to say that high-end B-movies never use techniques similar to those used in the lower tiers, however. Some of the special effects used in *Earth vs. the Flying Saucers* were extremely inexpensive, such as the lighting effects that are thought to be St. Elmo's fire by the film's protagonist. Special effects assistant George Lofgren created this technique simply by placing a light on the end of a drill and spinning it around in a darkened room.[35] The mark of a successful high-end B-movie is whether it successfully integrates these cheaper effects with its more expensive ones, so that audiences are unable to sense the frugality involved (something that becomes all too evident in lower-end Bs).

It was a regular practice for B-movies of all budgets to use footage from other films (if the studio owned the rights), newsreels, documentaries, and similar sources, which modern practice calls found footage. This material is typically integrated as part of a film's narrative world, meant to look as if the director shot it during the course of production. *Earth vs. the Flying Saucers* uses stock footage of rocket launches, bases, explosions, aerial maneuvers, and anti-aircraft artillery, the majority of which was taken from serials produced by Republic Pictures.

The measure of how well stock footage is used comes in how successfully and seamlessly it is incorporated into the narrative world of the film. High-end Bs are normally able to disguise the use of stock footage more easily than lower-tier Bs, often leading the audience to believe that the stock footage was in fact shot by the filmmakers themselves. Larger budgets allow for the creation of more seamless transitions between the stock shots and regular footage, in the way the latter is shot so as to match the seeming naturalism of the stock footage, as well as during the editing process. The use of stock shots in middle- and low-end Bs is often quite jarring because of their failure to convincingly suture the stock footage into the film. As a result, the production values of the stock footage appear noticeably different from those of the regular footage. This draws attention to the editing process combining the dissimilar shots, which in turns can remove the spectator from the film's narrative.

The difference in this suturing process becomes especially apparent when reusing footage outright from other feature films. High-end B-movies, like their lower-tier counterparts, regularly recycled footage from earlier films, particularly action scenes or special effects shots. Studios used this practice for decades prior to the 1950s, with MGM's *Tarzan* series often reusing footage of Tarzan battling various animals, for example. In turn, Columbia would reuse special effects footage from *Earth vs. the Flying Saucers*, such as the Washington monument collapsing, in the following year's *The Giant Claw* (1957), made by the same director-producer team.

Such recycling predictably reduces expenses, and if the films share similar production values, it will often go unnoticed among audiences. However, when a lower-tier B-movie tries to incorporate material from a higher-level one, the effect is rarely as seamless. The 1966 low-end B film *The Wild World of Batwoman*—directed by *Man Beast*'s Jerry Warren—uses footage from the Universal high-end B-movie *The Mole People* (1956), and the result is a juxtaposition of highly dissimilar styles and production values that complicates the suturing process tremendously.

The Middle-End B-Movie: *I Was a Teenage Werewolf*

Warren, as will be demonstrated, was not overly concerned with making a film of any real quality. His lack of care sets him apart from other B-filmmakers, including many who worked for American International Pictures. In 1957, AIP released *I Was a Teenage Werewolf*, one of the company's most successful films. Advertising for the film boldly declared it to be the "most amazing motion picture of our time!" While certainly hyperbolic, this statement proved to be a telling one. The film would earn $2 million, to become the tenth-highest-grossing film of the year, earnings that were far higher than any of AIP's previous outings. This resounding box office success grabbed the attention of the entire film industry: six weeks into its 1957 run, the *Hollywood Reporter* ran a front-page story about the film's box office strength headlined "'Teen-Age Werewolf' Grosses $1,720,000," listing that amount as the film's take since opening on July 19 and adding that "the 260 prints in circulation domestically all have been booked for Labor Day week."[36]

The film's overwhelming success gained the company newfound recognition in Hollywood. Samuel Arkoff called *Werewolf* "a turning point for AIP," describing how the company was suddenly "no longer the ugly duckling of Hollywood that ached for respectability."[37] In its visual style and production values, *I Was a Teenage Werewolf* is typical of the middle-end Bs that AIP produced during the 1950s, but a combination of factors led to its immediate popularity and enduring legacy as one of the most famous B-movies ever made.

Werewolf is typically the first film that most people think of when envisioning AIP's output. Indeed, in personal discussions with noncinephiles, the film has proven to be the best example to convey a sense of what is meant by the category of 1950s B-movies, with its mention often prompting a flurry of nostalgia and/or delight. This modern reaction has proven contrary to many initial critical responses toward the film at the time. *Motion Picture Herald* declared *Werewolf* to be "shallow entertainment."[38] Other critics called it "'boring,' 'okay' at best, 'pretty lethal,' and 'old fashioned and second rate.'"[39] *Variety* was not as harsh but still largely unenthusiastic, describing it as "another in the cycle of regression themes," in which the "only thing new . . . is a psychiatrist's use of a problem teenager." "There are plenty of story points that are sloughed over . . . ," said the reviewer, "but good performances help overcome deficiencies" such as the final scenes of the film, which he says "are inclined to be played too heavily."[40] These critical responses are largely due to the film industry's relatively late understanding at the time of a teenage marketplace that AIP was savvy enough to tap into first.

The exact budget of *Werewolf* varies according to which source you believe. Producer Herman Cohen estimated that the film cost around $150,000, while Arkoff claimed it was approximately $100,000. Director Gene Fowler Jr. said that the film's budget was $82,000, and this is the figure that is most commonly listed.[41] An April 10, 1957, article from the *Hollywood Reporter* entitled "Nicholson Boosts Budgets and Slate; Adds 3 Producers" states:

> The boosted slate of 24 American International Pictures releases for 1957–1958 also will have higher-budget productions, and three young producers—Herman Cohen, Robert Gurney Jr. and Bert Gordon—will augment Roger Corman in turning out the pictures, president James H. Nicholson told 200 New England exhibitors yesterday. . . ."
> Rock All Night" and "Dragstrip Girl," first AIP combination under the increased budget policy, will be released later this month. Next will be "I Was a Teenage Werewolf" and "Invasion of the Saucer Men."[42]

What becomes problematic is that this announcement comes just weeks after the end of *Werewolf*'s production. Shooting began on March 14 according to *Variety*, less than a month in advance of Nicholson's announcement.[43] This raises the question of whether the initial budget for the film was $82,000 when shooting began but rose to $150,000 by the postproduction stage. If this is the case, it accounts for the discrepancy between Fowler's and Cohen's reported budget amounts—Fowler is referring to the lower amount he was originally given to work with as director, while producer Cohen refers to the larger amount that was eventually determined during postproduction. Fowler has stated that he "didn't know Nicholson or Arkoff that well," having only met them once, so communication was apparently not always optimal within the company.[44]

Similarly, *Dragstrip Girl*—also part of Nicholson's bigger-budget plan—was announced in December 1956 and slated to begin production on January 14, 1957.[45] This is months ahead of Nicholson's announcement, and so if the "boosted budget" mandate had applied to *Dragstrip Girl* during its production stage, it would have surely applied to *Werewolf*, which began filming approximately two months later. It can therefore be hypothesized that the extra money was largely spent on promotion for the film, although the lack of archival materials makes this a highly speculative claim. As a small independent company with limited staff, AIP would inevitably have generated far fewer internal memos and documents than a major Hollywood studio. Hence the thoroughness of its record keeping is naturally to be questioned.

The $82,000 figure falls into the median range of budgets for AIP films between 1955 and 1956. *The Phantom from 10,000 Leagues* (1955) had a budget of $75,000, *Day the World Ended* (1956) cost $96,000, *Runaway Daughters* (1956) was budgeted at $90,000, and *Hot Rod Girl* (1956) was made for $80,000.[46] Preproduction on *Werewolf* was announced in January of 1957, putting it squarely in line with the economic pattern demonstrated by the company the previous year. There is no reason to believe that the company would suddenly approve a budget that was roughly 60 percent higher than those of films being made just months prior.

However, the circumstances surrounding the film's preproduction were far from typical, and perhaps explain in part the later decision to increase the film's budget. A short *Variety* piece on January 14, 1957—"Teenage Werewolf' to Roll"—announced the film as a one-sentence blurb at the bottom of page three, among other short blurbs about casting for the Elvis Presley film *Something for the Girls* and Alfred Hitchcock's getting a physical checkup.[47] Seemingly unremarkable, this minor blurb caught the attention of the media in a way that no other AIP film had done before. As Arkoff described it, "Once the preproduction schedule was announced in the trades, still weeks before the movie was shot and eventually released, AIP's phone began to ring off the hook. Newspapers and magazines across the country were calling us for stories and interviews with the people behind the movie. Comedians on TV shows were making jokes based on the Teenage Werewolf title. Overnight, the picture was getting millions of dollars worth of free publicity, long before it had ever reached theaters."[48]

It is highly possible, then, that the April announcement to boost AIP's budgets came on the heels of *Werewolf*'s widespread (and not wholly positive) publicity in order to improve the company's image within the industry. Prior to the start of *Werewolf*'s production schedule, Nicholson and Arkoff completed a 30,000-mile sales tour to promote their films to exhibitors across North America, including Hawaii and parts of Canada. Their sales pitch included a plan to produce and release eighteen films in 1957, as compared with only ten films the previous year.[49] This emphasis on an increased output, combined with the stress on higher budgets, signals a desire to transform AIP from an "ugly duckling," as Arkoff said, into a respected industry competitor. By the end of the summer, *Werewolf*'s impressive box office performance would guarantee the studio the respectability it was seeking.

As evidenced by trade articles, the film's title went through a slight evolution during preproduction, being simply *Teenage Werewolf* in its early months. No two accounts agree on exactly who came up with the film's title and when exactly it was created, however. Arkoff claimed that it was Nicholson who came up with the title: "Jim Nicholson was tossing around titles one morning in 1957 during our morning meeting. 'Sam, I came up with this title last night: *I Was a Teenage Werewolf.* What do you think?' I was stunned. 'My God, it's terrific,' I told him," said Arkoff, adding that "Jim had created the title to put on a story idea brought to AIP by a producer named Herman Cohen."[50]

For his part, Cohen claimed that he created the title *Teenage Werewolf* that was initially reported by the trades. Describing how he came up with the story idea, Cohen recalls: "Jim was asking me, 'Herm, can you do a picture for us?' That's when I thought of doing a teenage werewolf picture; I felt that for a fledgling company which was trying to get the teenage market, it could be ideal. I came up with the title *Teenage Werewolf*, and Jim Nicholson added *I Was a.*"[51]

Trade papers listed a film entitled "Blood of the Werewolf" as being readied by Cohen's production company at the time.[52] Cohen has adamantly denied such a title, stating that it was "never" called that: "In reference

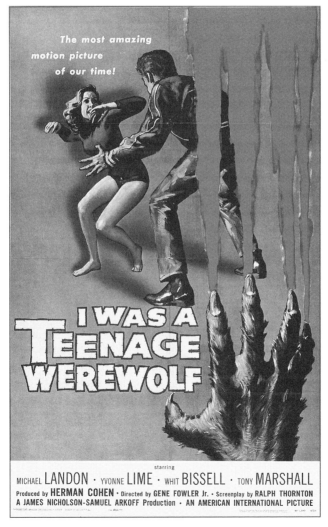

I Was a Teenage Werewolf (Sunset Productions/American International Pictures, 1957)

books, I've seen that and a couple other names for it too. It was titled *Teenage Werewolf* from the beginning—I still have the original script. Jim Nicholson worked on the advertising campaign himself, came up and showed me a great ad on *I Was a Teenage Werewolf* and I said, 'Jim, that's genius.'"[53] This runs contrary to Arkoff's version of events, which states that Nicholson's work on the advertising campaign began as the script was being written: "While Jim and I began working on the film's promotion and advertising . . . Herman cowrote the script (with Aben Kandel, both sharing the single pen name, Ralph Thornton)," said Arkoff.[54]

Given all of the evidence, it is fairly reasonable to accept Cohen's word. Considering how the title was simply *Teenage Werewolf* for weeks in the trades before a name change occurred, Cohen's statement that Nicholson added the *I Was a* to Cohen's *Teenage Werewolf* would seem to hold up. The controversy over the title's creation is another symptom of a lack of archival material and of the less-regimented business practices of lower-tier B-studios.

AIP's mode of production was quite atypical in comparison with that of the major studios, although the fact that Harryhausen created the special effects for *Earth vs. the Flying Saucers* before the screenplay was completed signifies that high-end Hollywood B-movies occasionally strayed from the norm as well. As a middle-end B-movie studio, however, AIP often employed preproduction methods that were far less disciplined than those of even the smallest Hollywood studio. When asked who was in charge of casting *I Was a Teenage Werewolf*, Fowler replied, "Oh, we all did that," stating that cast selection was a collaborative effort with the producer. Rather than follow a strict division of labor, Fowler also worked closely in preproduction with various crew members to ensure that each department was sufficiently prepared for the shoot: "We worked together. I worked with the art director, the cameraman and the head of pre-production, and tried to lay out everything in the most economical way we could," said Fowler, whose actions here are more in the capacity of a producer than a director. Such a blurring of roles often becomes necessary with low-budget filmmaking: "The theory being," said Fowler, "if you know what you're doing, you can do it faster! . . . I had no choice, it had to be done quickly, and that's how we did it, by planning."

Fowler even rewrote much of the film's dialogue without telling anyone. The initial screenplay, Fowler said, "was the usual kind of mad scientist picture, which I disagreed with." When interviewer Tom Weaver told Fowler, "I'm surprised that Cohen let you rewrite. [I've been told that] Cohen was touchy about things like that," Fowler replied that Cohen "didn't know it, while I was doing it! Otherwise he'd have fought me every step of the way."[55]

This lack of supervision goes against Cohen's claim that he was on the set "all the time" while shooting *Werewolf*. "I'm on the sets of *all* my pictures *all* the time," he said, adding, "If I'm not on the set, then my associate or my assistant or somebody is there, so if anything happens where they need me, they can call me and get me there right away."[56] Fowler contradicts this notion, however, stating that during the shoot Cohen "generally came on the set in the morning and was there for about an hour and left. He was busy promoting other stuff, and he left me alone pretty much."[57] Cohen's assistants were apparently also unaware of the script changes, suggesting that some involved with the film did not read the script very closely.

Herbert L. Strock, who directed the *Werewolf* follow-up *I Was a Teenage Frankenstein* (1957), described Cohen as having "an ego that knew no end. He wanted things his way and that's the way he wanted them, and he wanted a director who would do things his way." Fowler countered this by taking advantage of what was apparently a lack of close communication with the producer. Strock, on the other hand, challenged Cohen directly about the *Frankenstein* script's continuity, having what he called "violent arguments" with the producer "over story points, over illogical things in the script, over time warps that were absolutely ridiculous—you didn't know where you were or when this was supposed to happen or how it happened. And he just didn't want to listen." Despite Cohen's objections, Strock changed the script anyway, rewriting it with script supervisor Mary Whitlock Gibsone. Together, Strock said, "we did things that had to be done"; in the end, he added, "after much arguing, [Cohen] finally accepted."[58]

Similarly, Fowler has described how he too ignored Cohen's wishes while shooting *Werewolf*: "There's a scene in *Teenage Werewolf* where Michael Landon argues with his father, Michael gets mad and the old man leaves. And Michael is left standing there, boiling. I said 'The scene needs a capper, to show that the kid is a little unstable.' So I figured that, since Michael had in his hand a big bottle of milk, I'd have him throw it at the wall. I told Herman and he was against it, but finally I figured I was going to do it anyway—I was all set up, and I might as well do it. And Herman liked it after he saw it."[59]

These examples of directors ignoring the producer's dictates further demonstrate how informal the working environment often was at AIP, given the low-budget nature of production where the goal was to finish as quickly as possible. Actress Susan Cabot recalled the sometimes chaotic nature of making a film for the studio as compared with her work at Universal, which regularly produced high-end B-movies. She described working for AIP as "totally *mad*. It was like a European movie. I mean, we'd have some sort of a script, but there was a lot of, 'Who's going to say what?' and 'How 'bout I do this?'"—plenty of ad-libbing and improvising."[60] Compared with the "professional" attitude that Ballard describes at the Hollywood studios, where producers typically exercise a much stricter control over their set and crew, AIP's filmmaking process was more of the "flying by the seat of your pants" variety, in keeping with the title of Arkoff's autobiography.

The surreptitious independence that Fowler achieved under such working conditions allowed him to give more depth to the film's characterization while rewriting the script. "In the dialogue I wrote, I tried to give the characters dimension, to show where they came from," he said, "instead of just moving them around and having them say obligatory lines. I tried to give them a reason for things."[61] Strock supported this notion, adding that when he received scripts from Cohen they were often quite weak—or as Strock once told the producer, "These stink." "You find that a writer, especially of this caliber on these pictures," said Strock, "really doesn't read the dialogue out loud, and you have to do that because actors speak the lines and they have to mean something."[62]

Despite losing half of one of the film's few shooting days because of rain, Fowler was able to finish filming *Werewolf* on time, though not without being rushed. The film's wrap party was scheduled immediately following the final day's shooting. As Fowler recalled it, the last shot he filmed "was the destruction of the lab, and everybody came down to look at it. I think I went about a half hour over schedule, and everybody was trying to hurry me up so they could open the bar!"[63]

As a result of this pressure to finish as quickly as possible, the shooting schedule was subject to change at a moment's notice, particularly in regard to the availability of daylight. This was the case with the filming of a key scene in the gymnasium in which the werewolf attacks Theresa (Dawn Richard), who hangs upside down on the parallel bars. While working on the scene, however, "suddenly somebody realized that they were losing the light outside and they still needed to shoot a scene outside," actor Ken Miller recalled. "They said, 'Come on, we gotta go outside and do this shot right away!' Everybody ran out, the cameraman, Gene Fowler and everybody, and they left Dawn *hanging* there! She was so high up off the floor, she couldn't get down!"[64]

Despite the rushed nature of the production, *Werewolf*'s cinematography is generally quite proficient. Much of the film's look can be credited to experienced cinematographer Joseph LaShelle, a Hollywood veteran who had previously shot *Laura* (1944), *Road House* (1948), *River of No Return* (1954), and *Marty* (1955), and who would go on to shoot *The Long Hot Summer* (1958), *The Naked and the Dead* (1958), and *The Apartment* (1960). LaShelle and Fowler had both worked at Twentieth Century–Fox, and Fowler was able to get his old friend to do him a favor in coming to AIP. When told of the film's infamous title, LaShelle replied, "You're kidding! I don't want to do something like that!" Fowler explained that neither did he, "but this is my first feature and I could sure use some help." So LaShelle agreed, "strictly as a friend."[65]

Given the limited time and budget, and working conditions very different from those he was used to in Hollywood, LaShelle's efforts are admirable. The film's lighting effects appear thought-out and controlled, unlike those in many low-end B-movies. LaShelle demonstrates a deliberate attempt to create the impression of natural light sources in the film—in other words, to create lighting effects that would correspond to the given sources of light in each scene, as they would realistically occur.

In a scene set in a basement club, for example, a kerosene lamp appears in the background. LaShelle lights the scene as if this were the only source of illumination, making the room slightly darker than other locations—almost low-key, perhaps inspired by his previous work creating film noir. Similarly, during scenes set in a doctor's office and a police station, he creates the effect of sunlight coming in through the window, making the sets noticeably brighter than the basement club. LaShelle even creates faint shadows on the walls from the venetian blinds, further suggesting the presence of the sunlight in each room.

One area where LaShelle apparently could not overcome the film's low-budget nature is in his use of day-for-night cinematography, whereby a scene shot in daylight is manipulated to create the effect that it is night. Successful day-for-night becomes more difficult to achieve on a lower budget, because it involves the use of special color filters. The setup time required for such an effect is inevitably much longer than for conventional daylight shots, and time was usually a decisive factor in determining a film's aesthetics at AIP. Many of the studio's films relying on day-for-night photography "invariably suffered from inadequate filtering techniques," says Randy Palmer: "Lowering the camera's f-stop had the effect of darkening a shot, but day-for-night invariably appeared murky on-screen, with telltale giveaways every time the camera tilted upward to reveal a sky that was too bright to look like anything except mid-afternoon. Night-for-night photography was too expensive."[66]

Economics was also the deciding factor in determining the use of sets in the film. Unlike *Earth vs. the Flying Saucers*, which introduces multiple settings in the film's opening minutes alone, *Werewolf* uses only a small number of locations throughout. In high-end B-movies, as in Hollywood filmmaking generally, the settings are largely driven by the demands of the story; hence the mode of production begins with the script being written. At AIP, any given film's marketing took precedence and was decided upon before the script was finalized; hence the studio had a very different conceptual approach to the process of filmmaking and in turn used a different mode of production. In lower-tiered Bs, financial concerns limit the use of locations, as the budget determines the number of sets, props, costumes, and special effects that can be used, and therefore determines the scope of the narrative that can be presented.

Werewolf's primary locations are the doctor's office, the basement club, the father's home, the girlfriend's home, the school, and the woods. Some of these are preexisting locations, such as the school, but even the scope of this setting is reduced in comparison with *Earth vs. the Flying Saucers*'s entire sewage plant. The rest of *Werewolf*'s sets were hastily constructed—Fowler has admitted that he and art director Les Thomas "really cheated on sets" for the film, "building them out of spit and polish"[67]—although LaShelle's cinematography likely makes them look better than they otherwise would have.

Location shooting didn't stray far, with scenes at the school being shot in a park behind the studio, perhaps in an effort to save on transportation costs. The location that works most effectively in the film is the one that cost the least—the woods, shot in Griffith Park in Hollywood. Here, the werewolf, who has not yet been fully revealed in the film, stalks a victim who has just left a party and is taking a shortcut home through the woods, unaware that he is being followed. Bill Warren writes that the scene "creates a sense of unease at once, and makes the film unique among the teenage monster movies," because it "is suddenly and impressively *scary*." He adds, "This is not only the best scene in the film, it's one of the best (if most conventional) fright scenes in any American film of the 1950s."[68]

Actor Michael Rougas, who portrayed the werewolf's victim in the woods, says that the scene was shot twice in two very different ways. The first time it was shot, Michael Landon appeared in the scene as the werewolf, chasing his prey. This was eventually changed, however, as Rougas describes:

> When the producer, Herman Cohen, came on the set that final day of shooting I asked how the death scene went. He didn't answer and he walked away. . . . Later he called me into his office and told me they had to shoot the scene over. . . . He reminded me that when he hired me he told me that the death scene would be a solo bit. The scene would be all mine. . . . The camera was to be the werewolf, following me through the woods, causing me to react to the camera as if it was the beast and then the camera closing in for the kill as I backed away screaming and pleading into a slow fade out. That is not the way it was originally shot and I'm glad I had a second chance because I think the scene plays better.[69]

The scene works precisely because, like Val Lewton's horror films of the 1940s, it takes full advantage of the power of off-screen space. Instead of putting the werewolf in the scene, it merely suggests the creature's presence through the use of point-of-view shots, a technique that has gone on to become one of the most frequently used visual tropes of horror filmmaking in recent decades.

The power of this scene in *Werewolf* is its visual strength, emphasizing formal elements in order to compensate for its impoverished content. Low-budget filmmaking, particularly with genre films such as horror, is typically at its best when it attempts to do more with less, so as not to expose the cheapness of the film's production values. That Cohen ordered a reshoot of the scene, a rare occurrence at AIP, suggests that he understood this fact well enough to sacrifice more time and money.

Further use of the subjective camera comes when the werewolf attacks the gymnast, seen from her perspective upside down, and also in an attack on the doctor. The latter features alternating point-of-view shots from the perspective of each character, with each framed as a medium shot and edited together by use of match cuts, demonstrating an adherence to the principles of continuity editing in the classical Hollywood style. AIP's films may have been made quickly and cheaply, but they still generally display a conscious effort to conform to the standards and principles of the Hollywood style through the adherence to spatial and temporal contiguity. While not always successful in this regard, the attempt at seamlessness is one of the major factors separating the middle-end B-movie from its low-end counterpart.

Werewolf further demonstrates this adherence to classical Hollywood style in its use of camerawork throughout the film. Many scenes regularly feature extended takes of a minute or longer, which at first glance would seem to be in the effort to reduce the number of camera setups in order to speed up production. However, these prolonged shots rarely employ a mere static camera, and instead feature multiple camera movements. Early in the film, for example, when a schoolyard fight between Landon's character, Tony, and another student named Jimmy is broken up by Detective Donovan, the three of them engage in extended dialogue. The conversation begins in a long shot on all three characters and soon moves into a medium shot of Jimmy and Tony as they become angry. Jimmy moves to his right toward Donovan as the camera pans right to follow him, maintaining a medium shot as the detective enters the frame. The camera soon pans left to follow Jimmy as he moves back toward Tony and reestablishes the original medium shot of the two teens. The shot is approximately one minute long and contains smooth, steady camerawork as it negotiates between the three characters. It is reminiscent of the camerawork in *Earth vs. the Flying Saucers* in the scene where Dr. and Mrs. Marvin are driving, as the camera follows their body movements within the vehicle.

This shot in *Werewolf* is then followed by a shot lasting fifty seconds and consisting of pans and tracking movements between the following: 1) close-up; 2) medium-long shot; 3) medium shot; 4) medium-long shot; 5) medium shot. This is followed by a seventy-second shot in which the camera begins with a long shot and then intermittently tracks backward into a medium shot of Tony and Donovan as they occasionally walk while talking to each other. Throughout each of these scenes, the camerawork is controlled and skillful; in a word, it is invisible, adhering to the classical Hollywood style. While the camerawork in *Werewolf* does not always match the Hollywood style, the fact that—as with the editing—the film's production values are often quite technically proficient is further example of how the middle-end B-movie becomes separated from the low-end B film.

The production values of the middle-end B-movie were not always flawless, of course. While the camerawork is regularly proficient, the use of sound in *Werewolf* is awkward at times. The film contains a musical number—the song "Eeny, Meeny, Miney, Mo"—that is billed in the opening credits but is poorly executed. The bongo player Vic performs the song for his friends, but the synchronization between the music and his vocals is slightly off. The reason for this again stems from AIP's atypical mode of production. Actor Ken Miller, describing the unusual method by which his song was created, noted:

> Normally . . . [when a film is shot] you sing to a playback, you lip synch. Because this production was so cheap, we didn't have a chance to do that. What *we* did was, when they were actually doing the movie, I sang the song—and there was no music. Then when they scored the film, they scored the song. The problem was, when they were putting the score on the film, whoever did it was like three measures off. It was not coordinated with me, it was out of sync, which is a very simple thing to fix. But when it was released it was still out of sync. . . . Herman Cohen said, "Oh, we're gonna fix it, Kenny, I promise," but they never did—it would have cost like $150 to go in and put the music in correctly.[70]

This synchronization error is likely due in part to the fact that *Werewolf*'s editor, George Gittens, was, as Fowler put it, "deaf as a post." Fowler, in another subversive move, managed to hide Gittens's hearing loss from Cohen throughout the film's postproduction. "When we'd run *Teenage Werewolf* with Herman Cohen," said Fowler, "Herman would say something to George and I had to write it down. George couldn't hear and I didn't want Herman to know he was deaf!" This led to an unusual method of editing the film: after their meetings with Cohen, Fowler said, "[I] would have to transcribe all my notes, go up to [Gittens's] cutting room and show him what had to be done."[71] Despite the editor's deafness, the film does possess a capable musical score that is primarily used to accompany some action scenes. During the town's hunt for the werewolf, however, the score only comes in halfway through the action, making its placement somewhat arbitrary.

Comparatively, the musical scores of *Werewolf* and *Earth vs. the Flying Saucers* are not overly dissimilar. The use of special effects, however, is where the limited nature of the middle-end B-movie's production values becomes most overtly noticeable in comparison with high-end Bs. When Roger Corman went looking for a special effects technician to design the title creature for some last-minute reshoots on his first AIP science fiction film, *The Beast with 1,000,000 Eyes* (1956), he turned to *Famous Monsters of Filmland* editor Forrest Ackerman for suggestions:

> Perhaps forgetting for a moment who he was dealing with, Ackerman first suggested "Dynamation" animator Ray Harryhausen. The notion of paying the man who brought to life *Mighty Joe Young* and *The Beast from 20,000 Fathoms* was, of course, ludicrous to budget-strapped Corman. Ackerman's second suggestion was Jacques Fresco, who had created effects for the 1953 film *Project Moon Base*. Alas, his asking price of $1,000 was beyond Corman's reach. Finally, Ackerman cut to the quick and asked just how much Corman was willing to spend to salvage his movie. "I'm willing to go as high as $200," he answered.[72]

While *Saucers* features Harryhausen's miniature work in the film's opening minutes, *Werewolf* does not use any special effects until nearly two-thirds into the film, at the forty-seven-minute mark. Here the audience finally witnesses Landon's transformation into the creature, via the use of several ripple dissolves. This technique features shots of Landon in transition between progressive stages of makeup, linked together with dissolve edits that create an undulating or "rippling" effect between shots. This ripple effect served two purposes for the transformation sequences: "First it made the transition look more supernatural, and second, it hid the lack of detail at every interval."[73] Similar transformation effects were common in horror films of previous decades, such as Universal's *The Wolf Man* and its sequels. The technique was more effective in those films, however, because they typically created the effect without the use of ripples (along with applying more detailed makeup), allowing the transformation to appear more seamless.

The ripple effect somewhat obscures the werewolf's features as he changes, serving to partly hide the fact that the makeup effects are not of the same standard as in most Hollywood werewolf films. In comparison, the makeup effects in *Saucers* further signify its high-end B status due to their relative complexity. When the aliens are finally shown without their protective suits, they are very similar to the gray-skinned humanoid aliens perpetuated by modern popular culture via *The X-Files* and alien autopsy footage. The makeup is very precise and intricate, reminiscent of Jack Pierce's work for Universal on Boris Karloff in *The Mummy* (1932). The result is a far more realistic alien than those presented by AIP in such films as *Invasion of the Saucer Men* (1957), which had giant heads and huge bug-eyes, or *It Conquered the World* (1956), which features an alien whom many have described as resembling a giant pickle.

While many of the initial reviews were unkind, *Werewolf*'s reputation has gained in recent years. Many critics and scholars have praised the film's sincerity, with Thomas Doherty stating that it shows "genuine insight into the inner life" of the target teenage audience. Bill Warren describes Landon's acting as "sincere," noting, "He does not play down to the part."[74] Such admiration is largely due to Fowler's effort to not take the material lightly—"we treated the picture as though it were *Gone With the Wind* and we didn't make fun of it," said the director about the crew's attitude during production. Fowler sought to make something that went beyond merely exploiting a lurid title in order to make a quick buck: "I did not try to make just an exploitation picture. I was trying to make something with a little substance to it," he explained.[75] It is this commitment to making a quality product despite limited resources, and to maintaining a relatively respectable standard of technical proficiency, that distinguishes the middle-end B-movie from low-end B-films.

The Low-End B-Movie: *Man Beast*

If Fowler was committed to substance, then producer-director Jerry Warren's approach to his films was nothing short of apathetic. In *The New Poverty Row: Independent Filmmakers as Distributors*, Fred Olen Ray begins the chapter on Warren and his company—the generically named Associated Distributors Productions Inc.—with the following assessment: "Jerry Warren's strange and aloof approach to filmmaking (and the movie-going public in general) was astounding. He could not make up his mind as to what exactly he wanted to be: film director, patchup artist, or straight huckster. The bulk of his 'work' was in the 1950s and the 1960s and was sporadically distributed by his own company as if it were more of a hobby than a business."[76]

Warren has been described as a "quick-buck producer," the "cheapjack hack of the genre film world," and "Hollywood's most notoriously underskilled auteur." His films have been described as "some of the poorest ever offered in a cinema."[77] Weaver states, "It is hard to think of any horror filmmaker who made movies that were as cheap or as ridiculed as Jerry Warren's." "His credo seems to be to promise that no matter how terrible his previous film was, his next will be worse," writes Bill Warren, who states emphatically that he is not related.[78]

While director Edward Wood Jr.'s films are routinely dismissed as being utterly terrible and perhaps among the worst in cinematic history, there is a distinct difference between the work of Wood and that of Warren. Wood is admired by many for the overly earnest nature with which he made his films and for the failed ambition of his projects, with Roger Ebert stating that the director "always and sincerely made the very best film he possibly could," even if the results were deemed aesthetically questionable.[79] Wood's films fall squarely into the low-end category of B-movies, with his films made for states' rights distributors such as Howco. As was the case with film noir, his films have been subject to critical (although not necessarily celebratory) reevaluation in recent decades. Kristin Thompson and David Bordwell state that Wood's films were "ignored or mocked on their release," but this was not always the case.[80] Reviews of his films typically did not single them out as worse than other low-end B-movies of the 1950s, but rather as merely part of a larger trend toward mediocre low-budget genre films. A 1959 *Motion Picture Herald* review of *Plan 9 from Outer Space*, for example, describes it as "but another in the apparently endless stream of minor-effort sci-fi, played out with an obvious eye on the type of audience that is not particularly concerned with logic and clamors only for weirdness, the further out in unknown areas the better."[81]

A 1956 review of *Bride of the Monster* is even mildly enthusiastic toward the film: "The atom has finally caught up with the unending stream of horror melodrama. That element, plus the sizeable marquee draw of the late Bela Lugosi, are visible selling prospects for this attraction produced and directed by Edward D. Wood Jr. It follows a familiar vein, true, but Lugosi and a sizeable supporting cast go through the assigned action and dialogue of the Wood–Alex Gordon screenplay with something approaching briskness and the film benefits accordingly."[82]

While the rhetoric in these reviews might well apply to most middle-end B-movies as well, Thompson and Bordwell describe AIP's films as "more upscale" than those of Wood.[83] Alex Gordon, who served as both a producer at AIP and a screenwriter for Wood's films *Jail Bait* (1954) and *Bride of the Monster* (1955), described the key discrepancy between the mode of production used in Wood's films and that of AIP: "[Wood] had absolutely no sense of business. . . . He was just completely unable to conduct himself in a businesslike manner. He was just a sort of wild-eyed innocent, and I think that he was just not able to cope with the serious realities of the business."[84]

"If anyone ate, drank and dreamt motion pictures, it was Ed Wood. This was his whole life. Movies—24 hours a day," said actor Carl Anthony, who worked with the director on *Plan 9 from Outer Space* and *The Sinister Urge* (1960). Although Wood may not have been as savvy a businessman as Roger Corman, he was still able to find ways to reduce his budget during preproduction. "He was always looking at available stock footage from film libraries, to see what he could tie together," Anthony recalled. "He would see enough stuff and then he would start writing a script where he could incorporate a lot of stuff and then he wouldn't have to spend the money shooting. His mind could probably take all sorts of loose ends and make some sort of continuity out of it."[85] In order to compete with the likes of AIP, Wood needed to apply such resourcefulness to other areas of the filmmaking process as well. His failure to do so was what caused his career to wane after *Plan 9 from Outer Space*.

If Wood's love of filmmaking superseded his business acumen, then it might be said that Jerry Warren's emphasis on the monetary result of filmmaking bred a certain kind of apathy toward his work. His actors have described him as being cynical and indifferent about his films. Bruno Ve Sota has called Warren "the only person in Hollywood that ever set out to make a bad picture," while Katherine Victor has accused him of not caring about his work. "Many times," said Victor, "I'd say to him, 'For God's sake, Jerry, let's do something *good* for a change,' and he'd say 'Why? People aren't interested in anything good, they don't know and they don't care. Just give them garbage!' That was his philosophy."[86]

Warren has not denied these accusations, having stated, "I only direct because it costs too much to hire a director. . . . [If you want to] just make a vehicle designed to be merchandized and make a little bit of money, the easiest way is to control it yourself." He has also said: "My directing is what is adequate for the type of films I wanted to put together. I have never seriously wanted to be a director, or to do great things."[87] This belief was quite different from the mindset at AIP: "One thing that Jim Nicholson tried to do at AIP was keep in mind Shakespeare's axiom of 'a simple story, simply told,'" recalled AIP's lead special effects technician, Paul Blaisdell. "That was a general kind of motto, if you will, for all of the AIP films, and Jim really tried to make sure that his producers and directors and, really, just about everybody involved with motion pictures at AIP in those days kept that motto in mind day by day. If you think back on it and look at some of the pictures that were made at American International, you've got to admit that they tried."[88]

Warren, on the other hand, believed that it was unnecessary to put a lot of thought or energy into making B-movies, because "you didn't have to go all-out and make a really good picture" in the 1950s, "you'd just make the kind of thing that was *weird*." To a certain extent, Warren was correct in his belief that low-end Bs did not need to be "really good" to find an audience. With high-, middle-, and low-end Bs each typically being made for different audiences based upon the expectations of acquiring distribution for a particular scope of exhibition sites (be it smaller rural and neighborhood theaters, drive-ins, larger urban theaters, or particular ratios thereof), each level of filmmaking therefore entailed different aesthetic approaches. Films made for largely rural audiences or teenage drive-in patrons were not necessarily deemed to require the technical polish of films that sought large returns from major urban centers, given that audiences from the latter were seen as being more discriminating. While some low-end films were able to become mainstream hits and earn hundreds of thousands (if not millions) of dollars, most were made to address the product shortages suffered by smaller theaters where the emphasis was often on quantity rather than quality. The style of the low-end B-film is therefore often the result of more factors than just simple lack of technical skill—although few producers were as blatant about describing their films' lack of quality as Warren, which is what makes *Man Beast* a particularly compelling case study.[89]

His films are indeed suitably "weird" at times, though largely due to the lack of effort and care Warren put into them. His first film was 1956's *Man Beast*, intended to capitalize on the public interest in Abominable Snowmen that was related to various Mount Everest expeditions at the time.

Man Beast (Jerry Warren Productions/Associated Producers Inc., 1956)

As a low-end B-movie, the film had a significantly lower budget than those produced by AIP. When asked exactly how much the film cost, Warren replied, "Let's just say it was about one-half of what the normal low-budget picture cost in those days. This was very, very low-budget."[90] Given that *Werewolf*'s proposed $82,000 cost was an average budget in the company's early years of production, this might place *Man Beast* in the low $40,000 range. Other independent companies, however, were making low-budget films for even less than AIP in the mid- to late 1950s. Screencraft Enterprises, for example, made *Giant from the Unknown* (1958) for $54,000 and *She-Demons* (1958) for $56,000. Therefore, *Man Beast*'s budget could have been well under $30,000, a plausible estimate given its diminutive production values.

Warren relied heavily on the use of stock footage in his films as a cost-cutting measure. Whereas *Earth vs. the Flying Saucers* uses select pieces of stock footage in order to add context to Harryhausen's miniature work during the film's action scenes, some scenes in *Man Beast* use stock footage as the primary source of action. Warren obtained footage of mountain-climbing scenes from Allied Artists Studios, taken from an unknown 1940s Monogram film. It was not the only element reused from a previous film, however, as the Yeti costume featured in *Man Beast* had previously been used in the 1945 Producers Releasing Corporation film *White Pongo*, in which it served as a white gorilla. Warren said that he "got it from a Western Costume–type outfit on Highland Avenue" and merely "changed the face" to transform it from gorilla to Yeti.[91] Whereas AIP employed Paul Blaisdell to create the costumes for many of its films, Warren's costume shop rental allowed him to avoid this costly labor, just one of the differences in preproduction between low-end and middle-end B-movies.

The Yeti suit was worn by rotating actors in the cast during production. One of them, however, is particularly important in analyzing Warren's mode of production, given that the actor does not in fact exist. Warren gave the film's lead acting credit to someone named Rock Madison, and when asked by Weaver what role the mysterious actor played, Warren replied, "He was in the Yeti suit!" In response to whether Madison played any other role in the film, Warren artfully said, "Yeah, but we had to make some changes that cut what he did way down. Other than playing the Yeti, he may not even be in the picture anymore."[92] The name, in fact, was originally created as a pseudonym for actor Tom Maruzzi, meant to sound like a combination of Hollywood actors Rock Hudson and Guy Madison. The pseudonym was surely in the efforts of marketing the film, attempting to play off of the success of these famous actors and using an overtly masculine-sounding name as the film's star. Yet when he felt the need to further expand his cast list, Warren then gave Maruzzi third billing in the credits, leaving the nonexistent Rock Madison as the film's enigmatic star.

If AIP's films lived and died by their marketing, then low-end B-movies, with their doubly reduced production values, occasionally felt the need to flagrantly deceive their audiences in order to succeed. The hoax fooled many, apparently including some researchers: Ray's book includes a picture of the Yeti with the caption "Top-billed star Rock Madison as the formidable *Man Beast*," while Bill Warren writes, "Most of the actors are unknowns, with only top-billed star Rock Madison, here in a very small role, having appeared elsewhere, to my uncertain knowledge" (it is entirely possible, however, that Ray and Warren are in on the joke themselves and have helped to perpetuate the myth of Rock Madison).[93]

The rest of the cast were not professional film actors, with Warren turning to local California theater groups for fresh (therefore inexpensive) talent: "I had to use actors who really had no film experience at all; as a matter of fact, I cast practically the whole thing out of the Pasadena Playhouse because I couldn't afford professional actors. I used 90 percent from there and 10 percent from other little theater groups," he said. While high-end and even many middle-end B-movies used experienced and often recognizable actors such as Hugh Marlowe, John Agar, Hugh Beaumont, Richard Denning, Peter Graves, Paul Birch, and Whit Bissell—not to mention such future stars as *Werewolf*'s Michael Landon, Clint Eastwood (1955's *Revenge of the Creature*), Steve McQueen (1958's *The Blob*), and Charles Bronson (1958's *Machine Gun Kelly*)—many low-end B-movies feature actors with little to no professional experience.

Warren's extreme cost-cutting efforts extended beyond the film's casting, determining its production methods as well. As did AIP, Warren used nearby California locations such as Bishop County and Bronson Canyon for his mountainous sets. Unlike AIP, however, Warren was willing to take unscrupulous and unlawful measures to acquire certain locations:

> I remember I needed a Mongolian village, because I had to establish where the characters were. We filmed around Bishop, California, which is a snowy ski area; we had ice and glaciers, that was no problem, but nothing to establish that it was Tibet. We couldn't possibly build a village, and naturally we couldn't go to Tibet. So I took my actors and we climbed over the fence into a major studio and shot our scene on *their* Mongolian set! We got our scene, and then climbed over the fence and out again. I was a good fence-climber in my younger days, and it didn't really seem that weird to me, at that age, to do such things.

In 1958, Warren made *Teenage Zombies*, a film that was written in five days and shot in another five. He has admitted to putting the least possible amount of effort into the production, stating, "I just put together a picture that was long enough to play the lower half of my double bill. . . . The budget was so low that it was preposterous. . . . It was one tenth of the lowest possible budget you could think of! I made it so cheap that it was really ridiculous."[94] The cast was given no rehearsal time, and Warren rushed his actors through their lines. Katherine Victor recalled, "There was a lot of dialogue, and Jerry just wanted it done." Unlike Fowler's attempt to create something worthwhile in his middle-end film, with Warren there "was no finesse, no chance to develop any characterization. . . . We didn't do scenes with an eye towards perfecting them, we just did 'em to get through 'em and to get it done fast," said Victor.

In addition to the indifferent treatment of his actors, Warren's technical prowess was also meager. Most of the scenes in *Teenage Zombies* are filmed in a single take, creating a static, visually monotonous look. "Jerry shot master shots," said Victor; "he would shoot a scene continuously for ten minutes and he didn't shoot close-ups. In *Teenage Zombies* I think I had one close-up and the rest was master shots. That saved him money and saved time in editing."[95] Victor's claim that Warren did not intercut into his master-shot scenes is no exaggeration. Warren actually seemed to take great pride in this cost-effective technique: "In one sequence, I ran the whole magazine of film shooting the scene. There were no cuts—it was all a master shot, the whole thing going for ten minutes. I just did it like a stageplay. I mean, you can't do it any cheaper than that—that's one to one shooting!" he boasted.

With fewer camera setups to worry about, Warren was able to use a reduced crew in making his films. Actor Robert Clarke noted that when shooting *The Incredible Petrified World* in 1959, "the crew consisted of *a* cameraman, who did his own lighting, and *a* sound man. When one of us [actors] wasn't in the scene, *we* would hold the boom!"[96] While middle-end B-movies typically use a reduced crew in comparison with their high-end counterparts, low-end B-movie crews—which are frequently nonunion—tend to be desperately understaffed in the effort to keep costs to an absolute minimum, even at the expense of the film's production values.

In light of Warren's impoverished mode of production, it is little wonder that *Variety* described *Man Beast* as being "somewhat amateurishly done" in a 1956 review.[97] To begin with, many of the film's sets appear even more artificial than those used by AIP. This is largely due to the fact that Warren stages many of his dialogue scenes in a tent, which requires only a sheet hung behind the actors in order to suggest this location. Furthermore, Warren often uses no visible sets at all in the film, with only lighting effects creating a visual backdrop to the scene. Characters are often framed against an all-black background to suggest night, or an all-white background in daytime. Many of the night scenes are staged around a campfire—suggested but not actually seen. To generate this look, the actors are filmed with a key light directly in front of them, creating a high-contrast effect. To create the campfire's flames, Warren simply waves something in front of the light for a rippling effect, as the actor stretches his fingers out before him to further suggest the fire.

This lighting effect may sound cleverly appealing, and could well be in the hands of a talented director, but Warren's use of the technique throughout the film displays some confusing irregularities. In one scene, Warren has his actor wear a black shirt, with the inevitable result of this poor costume choice being that the character resembles a floating severed head as he moves when shot in close-up against the black backdrop. When the characters sit around the campfire in daylight, there is suddenly a cut to a medium shot of actor George Skaff, who plays the sinister role of Varga (later revealed to be the title character). The shot is framed with the same black background that had previously been established as nocturnal in the earlier scene. Here the effect is presumably meant to foreshadow the sinister nature of the film's eventual villain, but it creates a glaring continuity error, made even more noticeable when Varga is soon seen in close-up amid full daylight. To add further confusion, the next scene is again nocturnal, and the same lighting technique is now meant to suggest night rather than forthcoming menace. The result is less the product of low-budget filmmaking than of bad decision making. If *Werewolf's* unsuccessful day-for-night shots were the result of not being able to afford to use the technique properly, then *Man Beast*'s "day or night?" conundrum is due to Warren's artistic incompetence, or perhaps just his indifference.

Continuity errors in cinematography are found throughout the film, such as the use of natural lighting in an early rock-climbing sequence. Here the tone of the light varies greatly from shot to shot—from being washed out to possessing a fuller range of shades. Much of the problem would seem to lie in the fact that such footage is primarily from the older Monogram film that Warren acquired, as matching the lighting tone of these shots with his existing locations is seemingly beyond the scope of his ability. Yet these incompatible lighting tones persist later in the film, with footage that was entirely shot by the director. Warren cross-cuts between two characters inhabiting the same general space, a woman who waits as a man approaches her from a short distance. In the first shot, the woman is bathed in bright sunlight, while in the next shot of the man—who is meant to be less than one hundred yards away—the light is conspicuously duller, suggesting an overcast sky. When the man soon enters the shot with the woman, it is again bright and sunny. To make matters worse, Warren then cuts to a close-up of the two actors against the backdrop of an all-white sky with neutral lighting tones, again suggesting overcast weather, before cutting back to a wider shot of them in bright sunlight once more.

The inconsistent lighting is not the only problematic element of this scene, however, as it is very poorly edited at times as well. The footage of the man approaching begins as a long shot, but there is a sudden cut to a medium shot of the same actor walking in the same space. The viewer may be inclined to believe that this is merely the fault of some missing frames from a bad print, yet this is not the case upon closer inspection. In the long shot the actor moves in the left side of the frame, but in the subsequent shot he inhabits the center of the frame. Furthermore, his hat is in a different position on his head than in the previous shot, making this jump cut a continuity offense on multiple counts. Warren's lack of technical finesse is here further demonstrated by the fact that the camera is not stationary in these shots but is shaking slightly, evidence of an improperly mounted camera. This erratic camera movement is made even more obvious by the ensuing cross-cuts of these shots with those of the awaiting woman, who is actually filmed with a stationary camera.

Such technical oversights are symptomatic of how most low-end B-movies do not adhere to the principles of classical Hollywood decoupage. Be it due to a lack of money, resources, time, or care, low-end Bs typically do not achieve a predominantly seamless visual style. Instead, it is as if their financial and aesthetic limitations somehow prevent a unification of time and space in these films. For example, when one group of characters in *Man Beast* fires a gun into the air to alert a second group, there is a delayed reaction before the sound is heard. Once the gun is fired, there is a cut to an extreme long shot of the second group walking for three seconds. This is followed by a cut to a long shot of the group, who continue walking for two more seconds before one of the characters suddenly stops and says, "I hear a gunshot. Listen." The scene could have easily been tightened during editing, but low-end B-movies routinely pad out their films with unnecessary footage so as to more easily generate a longer running time for the film.

The most glaring example of the film's lack of a seamless aesthetic is found in the Yeti attack sequence. Continuity in time and space is repeatedly violated here, in what is meant to be the film's most exciting moments. As the Yeti approaches its victim, Warren cross-cuts this action with the reactions of other characters. In between these cuts, the space between Yeti and victim seemingly keeps getting larger; in the first shot the creature is relatively close, but in subsequent shots it is further back. Hence, the Yeti approaches its victim several times, thereby stretching out the action to create what Warren must have believed was suspenseful pacing. Instead, Warren creates a feeling of disequilibrium as he cuts to various reaction shots of characters alternately looking left or right, framed in close-up against the ever-present black backdrop. The result is a complete violation of the principles of decoupage, since the viewer has no sense of the spatiotemporal relations between any of the characters. When someone pulls out a gun and prepares to shoot the Yeti, the villainous Varga throws a club at him to prevent the shooting; the club is thrown off-screen from right to left, but in the subsequent shot the club moves in violation of the 180-degree rule from left to right before striking.

The entire attack sequence consists of a series of jump cuts between various individual shots that do not construct a unified whole when connected together. AIP's films usually solve this problem by adhering to the principles of continuity editing, but Warren—like many other low-end B-movie directors—creates a fractured sense of filmic space by not using this invisible approach. Perhaps the strangest example of this in *Man Beast* is when Warren tries to create the impression that there are several Yetis attacking the group, despite there being only one Yeti suit. In attempting to achieve the effect of a group attack, Warren employs three successive medium close-ups of a Yeti crossing the screen from left to right. The result is that it appears as if the same Yeti merely runs around the camera in a circle three times, but closer inspection proves that there are indeed edits between the shots. Rather than being awed by the apparent invasion of an army of Yetis, viewers are left puzzled as to why they have just witnessed what seems like the exact same shot repeated three times. The clumsiness of the attempted effect draws explicit attention to the awkward nature of its construction, removing the viewer from the narrative to ponder the film's technical inelegance.

If seamlessness is the ultimate goal of Hollywood cinema, then those independent studios that aspire to make films that can compete in the same marketplace must create films that ascribe to the tenets of continuity editing. AIP's success in this endeavor is indicative of the fact that middle-end B-movies often did compete effectively with Hollywood product at the box office, since these films were of a reasonable aesthetic standard. Low-end B-studios rarely hoped to compete with Hollywood product and were usually lucky if they could attain anything near the same level of financial success of a middle-end company like AIP. Warren sought nothing more than to make a modest profit from his films, and their aesthetics reflect the fact that he was not seeking to compete with Hollywood. His indifference toward his own filmmaking is symptomatic of how low-end B-movies were typically not supposed to be well made, but simply had to be good enough to find distribution in smaller markets. "I never, ever tried in any way to compete," said Warren, "or to make something worthwhile. I did only enough to get by, so they would buy it, so it would play, and so I'd get the few dollars. It's not very fair to the public, I guess, but that was my attitude toward this."[98] Warren's cynicism becomes all the more apparent in comparing his efforts to those of AIP, whose films seem even more accomplished by contrast.

Ed Wood's low-end B-films contain far more interesting visual imagery than Warren's, despite the fact that both men faced similar budget constraints. While his sets are by no means elaborate, Wood went to the effort to surround actor Bela Lugosi with such macabre props as a skeleton, skulls, and voodoo iconography in *Glen or Glenda?*, along with creating a reasonably passable laboratory environment in *Bride of the Monster* and a misty graveyard for *Plan 9 from Outer Space*. When one compares Wood's work with Warren's monotonous tent scenes in *Man Beast*, one begins to appreciate the fact that Wood often put far more effort into his mise-en-scène than Warren. Wood also chose for his films such colorful actors as Lugosi, Tor Johnson, Criswell, and Vampira, who collectively add further visual appeal due to their various eccentricities. The parade of reanimated bodies, transvestites, devilish figures, and space aliens that fill Wood's films is also more compelling than the modified secondhand ape costume that Warren uses for the main creature in *Man Beast*.

While Wood may be saddled with the reputation of being the worst director of all time, his films "are only intermittently as bad as has been claimed," says Geoffrey O'Brien. He adds: "Far from being the worst movie ever made, *Plan 9* is a work of startling if inadvertent originality. Its flagrantly cheap and artificial look is indistinguishable in the end from a deliberately chosen style, and who is to say it is not? It isn't exactly Jean Cocteau, but those images of Vampira and the Swedish wrestler Tor Johnson wandering endlessly with glazed expressions through a landscape of fake fog and fake tombstones do linger in the mind; they even return in dreams."[99]

Wood is simply another in a long list of directors in the 1950s making low-budget films that were hampered by the economic limits of their production methods—but under these terms his films can actually be seen as being more inventive than many other low-end B-movies. Therefore, in light of this comparison between the high-end, middle-end, and low-end B-movies of the 1950s, the key to understanding these films lies in analyzing their respective modes of production. In so doing, both the role of the 1950s B-movie in film history and the larger theoretical concerns surrounding the B-movie become more apparent. It would appear that, for the most part, economics determined the aesthetics of the 1950s B-movie. Therefore, these films cannot be compared with one another in a wholesale manner, as many critics and audiences do, because the process of creation involved in each varies greatly. Each of the three films in this case study is a different entity, stemming from specific economic conditions. Consequently, each of the three types of films presented in this chapter is a unique product with its own distinctive aesthetics that derive from different economic contexts, and should be evaluated accordingly. While a wide of range of films might be labeled as B-movies by a variety of different sources, recognizing the way in which a film's budget affects its aesthetics is central to fully understanding any given B-film and its place within the industry.

7

Notes from the Underground

The Legacy of the 1950s B-Movie

One of the fundamental principles of filmmaking is that of risk, with gambling metaphors proving common when film producers and analysts describe the industry. Perhaps more than any other category of films, the 1950s B-movie exemplifies this risk, given that it was an extremely marginalized entity during a highly transitional period. With films of the 1930s and 1940s ensconced in the block-booking policies of the classical Hollywood studio system, B-movies in these decades were not subject to the same level of uncertainty as were the Bs of the 1950s. Whereas most studio-system-era B-movies were essentially guaranteed distribution and a minimum profit level, no such guarantees existed once the effects of the 1948 antitrust ruling were felt. The modern era of low-budget filmmaking—with all of its risks and rewards—can be seen as being born in the 1950s by way of the independent producers and directors who gambled on making films outside of the major Hollywood studios.

The late 1950s saw major developments in what has been called the "underground" cinema movement in America, particularly regarding a number of films made in New York City.[1] Independent director Shirley Clarke described in 1961 how "in New York now a very exciting movement is starting, a movement of filmmaking that will benefit the entire NY area."[2] *Variety* had reported on this movement a year earlier, with Vincent Canby's February 17, 1960, article "Film's Poverty Row Now in N.Y.—Fast-Buck Lurids sans Union Cards." Referring to these films as "exploitation pictures," it detailed the growing cinematic movement of a particular kind of low-budget filmmaking that would flourish into the category of underground films—the article in fact described such directors as "new wavers." While underground and exploitation films are typically seen as being very different products, the similarities between the two became quite evident as the 1950s came to a close.

Quick Bucks and Underground Films

"Want to make a movie?" asked Canby.

> It's easy, if you have a lot of drive, ambition, nerve, and say about
> $23,000. Of course you can spend more, but that isn't always neces-
> sary, and you can always spend less, but that usually means putting
> your mother-in-law behind the camera, and if she doesn't have a
> natural aptitude for photography, you might waste more money than
> you save.
>
> The point is that N.Y. City and environs currently seem to be in
> the midst of a do-it-yourself boom in very-low-budget feature film
> production. Last year approximately 20 such v.l.b.s [sic] were turned
> out in and around N.Y.; several are in production right now and perhaps
> a dozen more or so are scheduled to go before begged, borrowed or
> rented cameras during the year. These pictures are all in the $20,000
> to $90,000 category, with most being around the lower figure. Their
> producers eschew local studios (they can't afford them obviously),
> shooting instead around the city in apartments, hotels, streets, parks,
> lofts, and anywhere else that might be imagined.

Canby divided such low-budget production into two groups. The first
he designated as the "'elder' generation," being those established producers
who had already been making B-films for a number of months or years.
They are further referred to as "the 'quick buck boys'" who "build comparatively innocuous screenplays around sensational-type titles." Canby also
described a second category of filmmakers, however, consisting of "the
'youngsters,' guys in their twenties and early thirties who are out to
learn about films in the only way possible—by making films themselves."
As compared with the "quick buck boys," these "youngsters" represent
the underground filmmakers that emerged out of New York during this period.
That both categories of low-budget filmmaking are described as constituting
a new Poverty Row as per the article's title signifies how wide-ranging
the industry's conception was regarding what constituted a B-movie
at the end of the 1950s. Canby indirectly addressed the seeming discrepancy between underground films and B-movies when he noted, "College
backgrounds and copies of *Sight and Sound* in their hip pockets, however,
do not mean that they, too, aren't out to make as quick a buck as their
elders."

Canby went on to chronicle the mode of production of these underground
films:

Last week in New York, this *Variety* reporter paid a visit to the "set" of a pic now being shot by one of these domestic "new wavers." "Set" was a loft on Manhattan's lower west side and on hand were the producer, who also wrote the script and was tripling as cameraman and director; two associate producers, one of whom held the sound boom during takes while the other operated the sound pickup; a script girl and three actors. There wasn't a union card in the group. By the kind of fortuitous circumstances which such producers rely upon, this reporter wandered in just in time to stand by the camera and alert the director-producer-cameraman when the camera ran out of film during the take.

The overlapping responsibilities described here are highly similar to the shooting practices employed by many low-end B-movie filmmakers, including Jerry Warren. They can even be compared to an extent to the production methods of a middle-end B-movie director such as Roger Corman, whose actors regularly fulfilled duties behind the camera as well as in front of it. This comparison between underground films and B-movies extends beyond their economics, however, with Canby discovering a surprising parallel between their content: "Film being shot had social overtones (about trials of a Puerto Rican family in New York), but was not being approached with an artsy-craftsy point of view. Producer explained enthusiastically that all the violence and sex in the picture would grow naturally out of the story. These things (rape, murder, and mayhem), he said, would really happen to the characters. With showmanship, and not shame, he was designing the film for the exploitation market."

Hence, there is significant overlap between the Bs of the late 1950s and the underground cinema that emerged at the same time, regarding the types of films that were made and which markets they targeted. Canby noted that the decade's product shortages had made "the selling of these pix a good deal easier than at any time in the past."[3] Just as B-movies benefited from this shortage as the decade progressed, so too did underground films enjoy a similar benefit at the end of the 1950s, with the former paving the way for the latter.

Film Quarterly was particularly active in covering this developing American underground movement, with several articles of note in the late 1950s and early 1960s. In "The Hollywood War of Independence," Colin Young drew a direct parallel between underground and B-movie filmmaking, describing "the 'growing edge' of Hollywood" as consisting of "dozens of young men working somewhat on the fringes of things, some as associate producers, some as writer-director-producers of the very low budget (sometimes nonunion) horror and teenage films." While many of them may have started off making B-films, Young states that their true intent is "to register some personal declaration on film" and to cut "through the gloss and timidity and conventions of Hollywood."[4]

Young and Gideon Bachmann profiled several emerging American directors in an article entitled "New Wave—or Gesture?" One of them is Curtis Harrington, who wrote and directed the 1961 film *Night Tide* depicting a man's tragic relationship with a mermaid. He began making experimental short films in the late 1940s, such as *Fragment of Seeking* (1946) and *Picnic* (1948), and was also Kenneth Anger's cinematographer for the 1949 short *Puce Moment*. Harrington would go on to appear as an actor in Anger's *Inauguration of the Pleasure Dome* (1954) before working as an assistant to producer Jerry Wald at Twentieth Century–Fox throughout the late 1950s.

Returning to film production as the 1960s began, Harrington released *Night Tide* through both Roger Corman's Filmgroup and American International Pictures. Despite the fact that the film was deliberately created for the B-movie market, Young and Bachman saw him as a peer of John Cassavetes, Shirley Clarke, and similar independent directors of the period, stressing Harrington's "freedom" as a director, as well as the "esoteric" nature of the film.[5] His appeal has proven enduring, as there is even a chapter devoted to Harrington in Xavier Mendik and Steven Jay Schneider's 2002 anthology *Underground U.S.A.: Filmmaking Beyond the Hollywood Canon*. Drawing an explicit connection between underground cinema and the B-film in his article "Curtis Harrington and the Underground Roots of the Modern Horror Film," Stephen R. Bissette calls Harrington "one of the few true underground filmmakers to actively engage with mainstream media venues, savoring the occasionally rich opportunities to further explore his own particular visionary and thematic obsessions and interests for a much broader audience."[6] As in *Night Tide,* featuring production design by Paul Mathison and an appearance by actor Marjorie Cameron—both having acted with Harrington in *Inauguration of the Pleasure Dome*—the realms of underground cinema and B-filmmaking often intersected in this period.

Cassavetes, *Shadows*, and B-Filmmaking

The predominant example of American underground filmmaking is John Cassavetes's *Shadows* (1959), regarded as highly influential to both then-current and future generations of directors. The magazine *Film Culture* established the Independent Film Award in 1959, in order "to mark 'the entrance of a new generation of filmmakers in America,'" with *Shadows* being the first recipient.[7] While Cassavetes's film is by no means a B-movie by almost all accounts, it does have many similarities with the mode of production of many middle-end and low-end B films. In his assessment of the film for the British Film Institute, Ray Carney gives the title "Your Style Is Your Budget" to a subsection on the film's production techniques—a deterministic statement similar to my own conclusion that economics largely determined the aesthetics of 1950s B-films.[8] At first glance, *Shadows* might even be mistaken momentarily for a B-movie as its opening credits roll. The film opens at a house party where a band performs rock music before a cheering and dancing crowd. Such subject matter is typical of the many rock 'n' roll films aimed at teenage audiences in the late 1950s, which regularly use rock songs over the films' titles.

Cassavetes's production methods are certainly reminiscent of Warren's or Corman's in that his crew rarely consisted of more than five or six people, with his actors also working behind the camera as well.[9] Some of Cassavetes's actors even began as crew members, such as Seymour Cassel, who started off as a mere observer of the film's production stemming from one of Cassavetes's acting workshops, but within a few hours found himself aiding in such tasks as loading the camera and performing a range of grip duties. Cassel was eventually given a small acting role in the film, and would go on to starring roles in several of Cassavetes's later films—even earning an Academy Award nomination for Best Supporting Actor in *Faces* (1968). As Canby observed, the lines between cast and crew frequently became blurred in low-budget productions of the 1950s, both in underground and B-movie filmmaking.

Further similarity between Corman and Cassavetes is found in the efforts of each to avoid various authorities while filming. Just as Corman would often shoot at different locations each day to avoid union interference, Cassavetes's lack of permits to shoot in the streets of New York saw him regularly trying to avoid being stopped by the police. This led him to "post lookouts so the production could pack up and make a getaway to a less conspicuous location when necessary."[10] With limited budgets, both directors felt hindered by the cost of obtaining the proper permits and required union presence, resorting to more iconoclastic measures of shooting their films.

Cassavetes struggled with the same continuity problems that typically affect low-end B-movies as well. The music heard over the opening credits is not synchronized, with shots of the band consequently kept to minimum (we see a shot of a trumpet player, for instance, yet the instrument is not heard in the rock music used). This strategy also conceals the way in which the music and crowd noise have been looped, as the same laughs and cheers often seem to be repeated multiple times. The same music and cheers are then later heard briefly as background noise in a nightclub, although the source of these sounds is never shown.

The film's first dialogue scenes are also nonsynchronous; filmed on the streets of Manhattan, the actors have been shot at angles that mostly avoid

Shadows (Lion International, 1959)

a clear view of their mouths (which strategically have cigarettes hanging from them to obscure lip movements) as they say their lines. Cassavetes uses an approach to audio recording common to films made on extremely low budgets, whereby the actors' dialogue is dubbed in postproduction. Another underground filmmaker who used this approach was Morris Engel, in *Little Fugitive* (1953) and *Lovers and Lollipops* (1956), films that Cassavetes acknowledges as influencing his work on *Shadows*.[11]

The limitations inherent in this approach to audio have not stopped audiences from celebrating Cassavetes's film, however. Viewers are frequently engaged by the bold subject matter of the film and its improvisational acting rather than being put off by the technical restrictions imposed by a limited budget. Such technical limitations are usually deemed far more problematic in B-movies because their subject matter is typically so routine that it does not engage the audience nearly as much; hence the technical flaws appear more obvious and distracting to the viewer. If a low-budget genre film is primarily structured around its special effects or a costumed monster, and if those effects are done relatively poorly due to fiscal constraints, then audiences will likely not be satisfied with the film and its production values. Offer the audience something more than just substandard thrills and chills, and the same limited production values often become far less problematic for the viewer, even allowing for the possibility of artistic meaning if one is able to look past the film's low-budget nature.

Further example of the commonalities between *Shadows* and various low-end Bs regarding continuity errors comes in a fight scene near the end of the film containing several jump cuts. While Cassavetes co-edited the film, and may have wanted the jumpy edits to reflect the fight's violence, at least one such instance seems problematic. As the last punches are thrown, a visually jarring moment occurs in a shot of one man pulling back his fist before delivering a final blow, which suddenly cuts to the beginning of a motion to throw his fist forward again. The viewer is left to wonder if several frames of the film are missing. While not as confusing as some of the sloppy edits in Warren's *Man Beast*, the fight scene in *Shadows* nevertheless could have been edited more tightly to avoid these occasional temporal lapses.

Shadows faced its share of problems during postproduction, not the least of which was the fact that many shots simply did not match: "Actors showed up on different days wearing different clothing. Ben wore three different sweaters underneath his black leather jacket, forgetting that the jacket would be unzipped in some shots and show the difference. Some days he wore white gloves, other days black gloves, and other days no gloves in shots that ended up being edited together. The editing challenge was compounded by the fact that almost no thought had been given to shooting basic cut-away coverage or transitional footage," says Carney.[12]

After several unsuccessful screenings of the finished film, Cassavetes began extensive reshooting to create a new version. Approximately thirty minutes of footage from the first version was incorporated into the second cut, which resulted in further continuity problems as the director tried to match the previous (and now unavailable) sets to his new ones. Not surprisingly, many American reviews focused primarily on the "low-budget origins and technical deficiencies" of the film, a condition common to the majority of reviews of low-end Bs.[13]

The aesthetics of *Shadows* therefore become largely inseparable from its low-budget mode of production, just as economic considerations are essential to understanding the B-movie in the 1950s. With a multitude of low-budget producers working outside of the major studios throughout the decade, struggling to acquire distribution for their alternative product during a period of marketplace uncertainty, a distinct parallel emerges between B-movies and the underground films of Cassavetes and others at the end of the 1950s. Just as there was often a blurring of the boundaries between art films and B-movies at the level of exhibition (at such theater chains as American Broadcasting–Paramount Theatres), both B-movies and underground films existed in opposition to the cinematic mainstream—a legacy that was passed on to independent filmmakers of subsequent decades.

The 1960s, "New Hollywood," and Modern Cinema

Experimentation in cinema is not strictly limited to avant-garde filmmakers but can also occur at the level of the B film. In a 1951 *Sight & Sound* article entitled "A Line of Experiment," Gavin Lambert analyzed how artistic experimentation can occur in low-budget films:

> Experiment in the cinema is usually thought of as a non-commercial activity, the isolation of an artist who will not compromise with the industry, and is either engaged in constant struggles with it to keep his work intact, or somehow manages to make films outside it. . . . [Yet the] shrewdest film producers, whatever impatience they may profess with the claims of the artist, realise the necessity of imaginative expansion within the cinema. The greater the range (and, incidentally, the freedom), the less the danger of staleness, of over-indulging in proved formulas. . . .
>
> Those producers, then, who are not content to make easy money with a regular program of crude and shoddy second features, but impose a standard of liveliness and craftsmanship, are achieving several things beside making better entertainment films. They are renovating the whole tradition of mass-produced films, by its very nature always in danger of stagnation; they are appealing to something other than the grossest instincts of their audience; and they are training technicians—and perhaps one or two artists—in a way more valuable than merely giving them working experience on mechanical potboilers.[14]

American International Pictures, along with Corman's own production company New World Pictures, aided in the development of several such artists, many of whom were among the forefront of Hollywood in the 1970s. Such notable names as Woody Allen, Peter Bogdanovich, Francis Ford Coppola, Joe Dante, Jonathan Demme, John Sayles, and Martin Scorsese all received their first big breaks through either New World or AIP: Allen's first film, *What's Up, Tiger Lily?* (1966), was distributed through AIP; Bogdanovich's directorial debut was *Targets* (1968) for AIP; Coppola apprenticed with AIP before directing his first film for the company, *Dementia 13* (1963); New World distributed Dante's first film, *Hollywood Boulevard* (1976), and produced his second, *Piranha* (1978)—a film that also marks Sayles's first screenplay credit and acting role; Demme began his career as a producer at New World on *Angels Hard as They Come* (1971), for which he also wrote the screenplay.

Accordingly, Beverly Gray describes Corman as "the only man in Hollywood who was entrusting directing gigs to recent graduates of film schools," allowing many young filmmakers a swift path to a directorial career at the major studios that eluded most B-movie directors in previous decades.[15] Even those directors working at the major studios in the classical Hollywood period who moved on to make A-films, such as Edward Dmytryk and Stuart Heisler, typically worked in B-production for many years before being given an A-film assignment. Furthermore, such directors often worked as editors for several years before even being promoted to B-unit director; this process of climbing the studio ranks was very different from the way in which Scorsese quickly moved on from working with Corman to making films for Warner Bros. (which distributed *Mean Streets* in 1973 and produced 1974's *Alice Doesn't Live Here Anymore*). By the early 1970s, Hollywood was routinely recruiting talent from the realm of low-budget independent filmmaking, solidifying a trend that emerged over a decade prior.

Scorsese, who made his first film at a studio of any size for producer Corman at AIP (1972's *Boxcar Bertha*), tells of how the aesthetics of *Mean Streets* were heavily influenced by the fact that he had recently made a B-film: "I used a Corman crew and shot it in the Corman style, doing nearly everything on location to get the totally realistic seaminess I wanted."[16] With *Boxcar Bertha*, "I learned how to make a real movie, in a sense, with a real budget and a real schedule. . . . Up to that point I had never really made a film on a schedule."[17]

Scorsese considers Cassavetes to be a mentor as well, with *Shadows* serving as an inspiration to such early films as *Who's That Knocking at My Door?* (1967). In fact, he had worked with Cassavetes on the postproduction of *Minnie and Moskowitz* (1971) at the same time he was offered the job to direct *Boxcar Bertha*. Credited as an assistant sound editor, Scorsese had largely trivial duties: he briefly participated in some Foley sound effects work, "guarded" the set overnight since he had nowhere else to sleep, and sat in on some of Cassavetes's editing sessions (largely as an observer). This lasted only a few weeks, ending once his contract to direct *Boxcar Bertha* for Corman arrived.[18]

The fact that Scorsese quickly shifted from Cassavetes's production methods (which, although *Minnie and Moskowitz* was made for Universal, were still largely true to the spirit of underground cinema that *Shadows* made famous) to those of Corman's films demonstrates how the low-budget nature of the two were often comparable. It also shows how Corman and AIP were keenly aware of newcomers making independent or underground films and often sought to develop this talent by giving them the opportunity to make B-films, even if the results only hinted at the potential of these directors. While often thought of as being born of the various restructuring efforts of the major studios, the New Hollywood of the 1970s can perhaps instead be seen as owing more to the practices that emerged out of 1950s B-filmmaking.

Scorsese would return to the Corman style with *The Last Temptation of Christ* (1988): "I shot a biblical epic in sixty days, cutting all day and night and using time the way I learned from Roger," he says.[19] Another thing he had learned was AIP's storyboarding method:

> I remember at that time literally preparing for the picture by drawing out every shot, because we had a very short shooting schedule, and about four hundred, five hundred drawings—primitive drawings—and I pretty much knew what I was going to do when we got to the set. . . . The same techniques and the same preparation I did for *Boxcar Bertha* came in handy for *Mean Streets*, for *Taxi Driver*, for *Raging Bull*, and for *After Hours*, for *The Color of Money*, and particularly for The *Last Temptation of Christ*. Every shot was drawn, and if not drawn, notated on a separate piece of paper. In any event, without that experience on *Boxcar Bertha*, there's no way I could have made this picture [*The Last Temptation of Christ*], or any of the pictures I've made, really.[20]

The legacy of 1950s B-movies also extends to the blockbuster Hollywood films made by many of Scorsese's contemporaries. Steven Spielberg's *Jaws* (1975), often credited with launching the modern blockbuster era of filmmaking, can be seen as an updating of such "creature features" as *Tarantula* (1955), *The Deadly Mantis* (1957), and *Earth vs. the Spider* (1958). The narrative of another 1970s genre film—Ridley Scott's *Alien* (1979)—is remarkably similar to that of 1958's *It! The Terror from Beyond Space* in its depiction of a spaceship crew being stalked and killed by an alien creature hidden on board. Sam Arkoff once pointed out that the premises of many modern films "are really not ideas that were advanced by Spielberg or Lucas—although I won't take anything away from 'em. But the fact is that most of those ideas came out of the fifties." On another occasion he noted, "Now genre pictures don't have to be cheap pictures. *Jaws* was a genre picture."[21] Corman adds that modern blockbusters such as Spielberg's are essentially "exploitation" films: "'Exploitation' films were so named because you made a film about something wild with a great deal of action, a little sex, and possibly some sort of strange gimmick. . . . It's interesting how, decades later, when the majors saw they could have enormous commercial success with big-budget exploitation films, they gave them loftier terms—'genre' films or 'high concept' films."[22]

The Bs can also be seen as forerunners in the way the Motion Picture Production Code came to an end in the late 1960s, with one B-movie studio openly challenging the Motion Picture Association of America (MPAA), the film industry's internal censorship board, earlier in the decade. *The Pawn broker*—Sidney Lumet's 1964 examination of a Holocaust survivor's bleak life in Manhattan—was rejected by the MPAA because of scenes in which two actresses bared their breasts. The independent film was then picked up for distribution by Allied Artists, which made arrangements to release it without the endorsement of the MPAA. Upon appeal, the film was deemed to be "a special and unique case" by the MPAA and granted approval, but by this point it had already been released in theaters by Allied Artists (who risked boycotts as a result from such groups as the Catholic Legion of Decency).[23] Allied Artists was rewarded for its risk, as *The Pawnbroker* earned more than $2 million at the box office.

In further challenge to the Production Code, many B-films of the 1960s tested the limits of violent imagery well before such films as *Bonnie and Clyde* (1967) and *The Wild Bunch* (1969) brought what some scholars see as a new degree of violence to American cinema.[24] The boundaries of gore and bloodshed were explored ad nauseam earlier in the decade by director Herschell Gordon Lewis in such low-budget horror films as *Blood Feast* (1963), *Two Thousand Maniacs!* (1964), and *Color Me Blood Red* (1965). *Blood Feast* was made for less than $25,000 and earned over $4 million through states' rights distribution, due largely to the notoriety gained from such images as one woman having her tongue cut out, and another having her leg cut off in a bathtub.[25] Such imagery was certainly in violation of Production Code standards, although many independent producers who distributed their films through states' rights theaters would often forego MPAA approval.[26] Serious repercussions did occasionally emerge from such a strategy—one exhibitor in Philadelphia was fined $1,000 by a grand jury for showing *Blood Feast* on the grounds that it was "obscene, sadistic and perverted" and "contribut[ed] to the delinquency of minors."[27]

The severed limbs and bloody entrails of Lewis's films would resurface in George Romero's *Night of the Living Dead* (1968), with body parts being cannibalistically consumed by zombies. Romero's film cost $114,000 to make and earned over $1.5 million, once again demonstrating that there was a potent market for such gruesome imagery.[28] On October 7, 1968, the MPAA announced that the Production Code would be replaced by a new age-based rating system, one that was voluntary and not legally binding for exhibitors (allowing them to determine on an individual basis which films were indeed "obscene"). In turn, Hollywood began to embrace films that featured a larger degree of violent imagery, sexuality, and coarse language as the 1970s began.

This period has been described as the "Hollywood Renaissance" by some scholars, and as "New Hollywood" by others.[29] Indeed, a shift in both tone and content can be seen in many 1970s Hollywood films compared to those of the early to mid-1960s, not only in the new freedoms permitted by the Production Code's elimination, but also in the move away from the epic films that emerged with the introduction of such widescreen processes as CinemaScope. Twentieth Century–Fox's 1963 production of *Cleopatra* cost the studio $44 million to make and earned $26 million, making it a colossal financial failure even though it was the year's highest-grossing film. Though it nearly bankrupted the studio, Fox survived through the middle of the decade by securing distribution deals with several independent companies for their low-budget product, including Associated Producers, Iselin-Tenney Productions, Panoramic Productions, and Steve Productions for such genre films as *Horror of Party Beach* (1964), *The Curse of the Living Corpse* (1964), *Convict Stage* (1965), and *Up from the Beach* (1965), among others. By relying upon these films to fill its release schedules and provide steady (if often unremarkable) returns, Fox was able to survive long enough to see *The Sound of Music* (1965) reestablish the studio by becoming one of the highest-grossing films of all time.

While many Hollywood studios reduced their production output in the mid-1960s, American International Pictures had been steadily increasing its throughout the decade and by 1964 was producing twenty-five films a year—far more than were being directly produced by many of the majors.[30] Alongside its steady slate of Edgar Allan Poe adaptations between 1960 and 1964, AIP established a popular cycle of beach films with 1963's *Beach Party* as a way of branching out beyond the horror and science fiction fare for which it was best known. In so doing, it was able to capture additional segments of the youth market that was still being underserved by the larger studios. In 1966, AIP innovated another new film cycle with Roger Corman's *The Wild Angels*—that of the biker film. Earning over $5 million, *The Wild Angels*'s success led to numerous biker films at AIP and elsewhere, culminating in the release of *Easy Rider* (1969) as the defining film that represented the counterculture movement of the late 1960s.

With stars Dennis Hopper directing and Peter Fonda producing (and both co-writing the script with Terry Southern), *Easy Rider* was financed independently for less than $400,000 and grossed approximately $60 million worldwide with distribution from Columbia. The film's cinematographer, Laslo Kovacs, brought his early experiences working on such AIP films as *Hells Angels on Wheels* (1967) and *Psych-Out* (1968) to *Easy Rider*—"we had to shoot fast and cheap," he recalled, particularly regarding the film's extensive use of location shooting.[31] *Easy Rider*'s success convincingly proved the possibilities that existed for low-budget films receiving major studio distribution, as well as the foresight of companies like AIP in establishing new genre cycles and appealing to audience demographics that were traditionally deemed unconventional (if not undesirable) by the major studios.

Like *The Wild Angels*, Melvin Van Peebles's *Sweet Sweetback's Baadasssss Song* (1971) also served as the beginning of a new genre cycle, that of the blaxploitation film. While films such as Van Peebles's *Watermelon Man* and Ossie Davis's *Cotton Comes to Harlem* proved relatively successful in 1970, the fact that *Sweet Sweetback* earned over $10 million from a $500,000 budget signaled the beginning of a new cinematic trend in films starring and marketed to African Americans.[32] Just as *Blood Feast* and *Night of the Living Dead* had done before them, numerous low-budget horror films also found success with independent distribution throughout the 1970s, such as Wes Craven's *Last House on the Left* (1972) and Tobe Hooper's *The Texas Chainsaw Massacre* (1974)—the latter earning over $30 million.

Even more popular was John Carpenter's *Halloween* (1978), which earned $47 million in domestic returns alone from a budget of $325,000. *Halloween*'s success quickly led to the rise of the slasher film as a popular subgenre of the horror film, with Paramount purchasing Sean S. Cunningham's *Friday the 13th* (1980) after seeing the finished product. Cunningham had previously produced *Last House on the Left*, and with *Friday the 13th* earning close to $40 million domestically from a budget of approximately $500,000, the trend of Hollywood studios purchasing low-budget horror films for distribution became cemented (and has persisted in recent decades with the success of such films as *The Blair Witch Project* in 1999 and *Paranormal Activity* in 2009).

Horror films were not the only profitable low-budget product in the 1980s, however, as Spike Lee's *She's Gotta Have It* (1986) earned over $7 million despite a budget of just $20,000. By the 1990s, the acquisition of independently produced low-budget films by the major studios became a regular occurrence, launching the careers of such directors as Quentin Tarantino (*Reservoir Dogs*, 1992), Robert Rodriguez (*El Mariachi*, 1992), and Edward Burns (*The Brothers McMullen*, 1995), among others. The fact that the latter two films were made for approximately $7,000 and $24,000, respectively—costs that were deemed to be extraordinarily low even for the poorest of Poverty Row producers in the 1930s—is indicative of how radically different the treatment of low-budget cinema is in modern Hollywood than it was under the classical studio system. The ability for a director to find success at a major studio by making a small film independently began to flourish in the 1950s, when B-movies changed the way in which the industry approached films that were produced with modest means outside the majors.

B-films of the 1950s have left an important legacy for modern popular culture: from summer blockbusters being hailed by critics as big-budget Bs to the success of television shows like *Mystery Science Theater 3000* that lovingly mock the original B-movies themselves, 1950s B-movies possess an enduring cultural currency that has allowed them to proliferate in the public's imagination. The success of specialty cable television channels such as Drive-In Classics demonstrates that there is still an active market for these films. American Movie Classics and Turner Classic Movies regularly devote programming blocks to 1950s B-films, such as the latter channel's weekly late-night TCM Underground series.

Numerous cinematic parodies of 1950s B-movies have been created in recent decades, including *Amazon Women on the Moon* (1987), *Attack of the Killer Tomatoes* (1977) and its numerous sequels, *Big Meat Eater* (1985), *Killer Klowns from Outer Space* (1988), *The Lost Skeleton of Cadavra* (2003), *Strange Invaders* (1983), and *Top of the Food Chain* (1999). William Castle's career served as the inspiration for the film *Matinee* (1993), while Tim Burton's *Ed Wood* (1994) won multiple Academy Awards for its sympathetic depiction of the eponymous director. Furthermore, independent company Troma Films has found success in making low-budget genre films largely for the home video market, many of which are clearly inspired by the Bs of the 1950s, such as *Chopper Chicks in Zombietown* (1989), *A Nymphoid Barbarian in Dinosaur Hell* (1991), *Pterodactyl Woman from Beverly Hills* (1994), *Student Confidential* (1987), and *Teenage Catgirls in Heat* (1997).

Modern independent production is in many ways indebted to the low-budget producers of the 1950s, who helped to establish new patterns of production, distribution, and exhibition during an extremely uncertain period in film history. Speaking in 2002 shortly before his death, Arkoff noted, "There are still movies that are made on budgets that aren't that far different than what we had at the end."[33] Companies such as AIP proved that independent producers making modestly budgeted films could compete in the mainstream marketplace—often finding huge success at the box office and setting new trends along the way. In 1934, reporter Lewis Jacobs warned readers of the *New York Times* about the "Shoestring Products" emerging from Poverty Row, describing how "the quickie flourishes, but its producer seldom grows rich." The "quickie producers wistfully maintain and surround themselves with all of the grandeur of the majors," wrote a cynical Jacobs. "There isn't a quickie producer who doesn't think that, given half an opportunity, he could startle the motion picture industry with his picture sense and ideas," he added.[34] Yet quickie producers certainly could grow rich in the 1950s, as low-budget films did indeed "startle" the film industry and command strong box office returns.

B-movies were an integral part of the overall success of the major studios in the 1930s and 1940s, but independent producers demonstrated that low-budget films were also essential to the industry even after the end of block booking and the classical Hollywood studio system. "There is a difference between a one million dollar production and a $100,000 film," director

Shirley Clarke stated in 1961. "And it will be the $100,000 film that will make the industry stay alive," she predicted. "It will feed into it certain things that will make $1,000,000 productions possible."[35] Low-budget filmmaking could have easily died out in the early 1950s: the major studios largely abandoned the Bs, Poverty Row's collapse was imminent, and most Hollywood observers seemed all but certain that the B-movie was at an end. Instead, independent production flourished among a new group of filmmakers, and low-budget cinema was reborn.

NOTES

THE Bs TAKE FLIGHT

1. Many scholars see B-films as a distinct product of the 1930s/1940s, such as Brian Taves, who suggests that using the term to widely encompass "bad" films of all decades is inaccurate, given that "there is little comparison in either content or style between the 1930s B and the low-budget pictures of the 1950s and beyond; applying the B label to such widely different forms as exploitation, 1950s horror and sci-fi, and 1980s slasher films is a misnomer. Properly speaking, the historical context of the B belongs to the studio era of double bills, when such movies operated in relation to, and as a variation on, the principles of classical filmmaking" ("The B Film: Hollywood's Other Half," in *Grand Design: Hollywood as a Modern Business Enterprise, 1930–1939*, ed. Tino Balio, History of the American Cinema series [New York: Charles Scribner's Sons, 1993], 350). This book proceeds from the idea that while the 1950s B-film often retained many aspects of the production process of prior decades, it evolved into a product that frequently challenged A-films at the box office. With my own definition of the B-film, including films of later decades that similarly functioned within relatively limited economic contexts, I hope to bring renewed attention to the very low-budget nature of such films themselves, and how exactly such limitations determined their content and style—thereby challenging the "B = bad" mentality that persists among many film audiences and has limited the scholarly attention that B-films receive.

2. Michael Conant explains that under block-booking policies, distributors "charged less than the highest possible price for superior films and more for inferior films than if sold singly. Many mediocre films," namely B-movies, "would never have earned their costs of production had the distributor tried to market them singly, each on its own merits. In this way block booking enabled distributors to shift a part of the market uncertainties to the exhibitors by guaranteeing that poorly accepted pictures would be bought. By insuring a market for the season's output, block booking helped the producer-distributors to secure financing for production. As to the policy of deliberately making class B pictures and block booking them with class A films, the . . . motives were to assure full utilization of production and distribution plant by making a supplementary group of low-cost films, and to secure and maintain long-run control of the marketplace. The effect of block booking as a long-run market policy, when followed by seven distributors in combination, was to preempt independent exhibitors' playing time and thus foreclose entry into the market to independent distributors" (*Antitrust in the Motion Picture Industry: Economic and Legal Analysis* [New York: Arno Press, 1978], 79).

3. Thomas Emerson Hall and J. David Ferguson, *The Great Depression: An International Disaster of Perverse Economic Policies* (Ann Arbor: University of Michigan Press, 1998), 4.

4. Thomas Doherty, "This Is Where We Came In: The Audible Screen and the Voluble Audiences of Early Sound Cinema," in *American Movie Audiences: From the Turn of the Century to the Early Sound Era*, ed. Melvyn Stokes and Richard Maltby (London: British Film Institute, 1999), 146–148; Frank S. Nugent, "What's Wrong with the Movies?" *New York Times Magazine*, 20 November 1938, 24–26. The movie quiz contest was prompted in 1938 by Fox West Coast Theatres head (and later Twentieth Century–Fox chairman) Spyros Skouras, who got other theater chains involved in the event as well.

5. Douglas Gomery, "The Economics of U.S. Film Exhibition Policy and Practice," *Cine-Tracts* 12 (Winter 1981): 37.

6. Ibid., 37–38; Tino Balio, "Surviving the Great Depression," in Balio, *Grand Design*, 28–29. "The first-run houses of the major chains tendered double bills" in the early 1930s, says Gomery, "but not in the numbers of their independent competitors. The mix varied. Some exhibitors presented two or more A films, others an A and B, still others three B's. Theatre owners constantly varied combinations in order to gain an edge on nearby competitors."

7. Douglas Gomery, *The Hollywood Studio System* (London: Macmillan, 1986), 19; Gomery, "Economics," 39.

8. Paul Kerr, "Out of What Past? Notes on the B Film Noir," in *The Hollywood Film Industry*, ed. Paul Kerr (London: Routledge, 1986), 227.

9. Balio, "Surviving the Great Depression," 29.

10. Andre Senwald, "As the Old Year Draws to a Close," *New York Times*, 29 December 1935, X5.

11. "Double Features," *New York Times*, 16 April 1933, X3; John T. McManus, "Thumbs Down on Doubles," *New York Times*, 31 May 1936, X4; Frank S. Nugent, "There Should Be a Law Against It," *New York Times*, 3 May 1936, X3.

12. Don Miller, *"B" Movies: An Informal Survey of the American Low-Budget Film, 1933–1945* (New York: Curtis Books, 1973), 36; Nugent, "There Should Be a Law Against It."

13. Balio, "Surviving the Great Depression," 29.

14. Taves, "The B Film," 314.

15. Tino Balio, "Columbia Pictures: The Making of a Motion Picture Major, 1930–1943," in *Post-Theory: Reconstructing Film Studies*, ed. David Bordwell and Noel Carroll (Madison: University of Wisconsin Press, 1996), 423; Douglas W. Churchill, "Facts and Frills from Hollywood," *New York Times*, 3 May 1936, X3; Theodore Strauss, "Little Dogies Get Along," *New York Times*, 4 August 1940, 105. See chapter 6 for a more detailed account of the mode of production of Columbia's B-movies.

16. Douglas W. Churchill, "Hollywood on the Wire," *New York Times*, 30 June 1935, X3.

17. Taves, "The B Film," 317–319. A very thorough account of the programmers is provided herein, as well as a four-tiered structural model of the differentiations between various kinds of B-movies in the 1930s that is comparable at times to the one offered by the *New York Times* in 1935. See also Miller, *"B" Movies*, 41–42.

18. Bosley Crowther, "How Doth the Busy Little 'B,'" *New York Times*, 2 January 1938, 126.

19. Douglas W. Churchill, "Hollywood from A to Z," *New York Times*, 14 March 1937, X3.

20. Crowther, "How Doth the Busy Little 'B,'" 126.

21. Charles Flynn and Todd McCarthy, "The Economic Imperative: Why Was the B Movie Necessary?" in *Kings of the B's: Working Within the Hollywood System*, ed. Todd McCarthy and Charles Flynn (New York: E. P. Dutton, 1975), 17. Regarding the specific allocation of ticket sales to individual films paired together for a double bill, John W. Cones describes how distributors "must allocate (based on a predetermined formula, at the distributor's discretion or otherwise) the film rentals generated by the joint exhibition of the films between the two films for the purposes of calculating payments for the two profit participants, if any" (*The Feature Film Distribution Deal: A Critical Analysis of the Single Most Important Film Industry Agreement* [Carbondale: Southern Illinois University Press, 1997], 52). Most often B-films were sold for flat fees and did not qualify for such profit participation, but at studio-owned theaters showing a double bill of two programmers, such allocations often became more significant. If a B-film quickly proved to be a hit, it could be moved to the top half of a double bill in other theaters and sold strictly on a percentage basis.

22. Tom Weaver, *Science Fiction and Fantasy Film Flashbacks: Conversations with 24 Actors, Writers, Producers, and Directors from the Golden Age* (Jefferson, NC: McFarland, 1998), 99.

23. McCarthy and Flynn, "The Economic Imperative," 24; Wheeler Dixon, ed., *Producers Releasing Corporation: A Comprehensive Filmography and History* (Jefferson, NC: McFarland, 1986), iv.

24. Kerr, "Out of What Past?" 229.

25. Dixon, *Producers Releasing Corporation*, ix.

26. Peter Bogdanovich, "An Interview with Edgar G. Ulmer," in Dixon, *Producers*, 63–65.

27. Kerr, "Out of What Past?" 228–229.

28. Statistics compiled from Ted Okuda, *The Monogram Checklist: The Films of Monogram Pictures Corporation, 1931–1952* (Jefferson, NC: McFarland), 1987.

29. Richard B. Jewell, "RKO Film Grosses, 1929–1951: The C. J. Tevlin Ledger," *Historical Journal of Film, Radio and Television* 14, no. 1 (1994): 43–44; H. Mark Glancy, "MGM Film Grosses, 1924–1948: The Eddie Mannix Ledger," *Historical Journal of Film, Radio and Television* 12, no. 2 (1992): 136–137. Jewell and Glancy describe how numerous other A-films lost money for both RKO and MGM, including *The Conquerors* (1933), *The Merry Widow* (1934), *Sylvia Scarlett* (1935), *Mary of Scotland* (1936), *A Woman Rebels* (1936), *Conquest* (1937), *The Toast of New York* (1937), *Bringing Up Baby* (1938), *Carefree* (1938), *Room Service* (1938), *Gunga Din* (1939), and *Abe Lincoln in Illinois* (1940). Warner Bros. saw fewer titles lose money than most of the other major studios but occasionally saw one of its A-films become a huge flop, such as *The Horn Blows at Midnight* (1945), which lost $861,000. See also H. Mark Glancy, "Warner Bros. Film Grosses, 1921–1951: The William Schaefer Ledger," *Historical Journal of Film, Radio and Television* 15, no. 1 (1995): 64–65.

30. Sources vary wildly as to the box office performance of *Cat People*. In his book *Val Lewton: The Reality of Terror* (London: Secker and Warburg, 1972), Joel E. Siegel describes how the film "earned enough money to save RKO" from a state of "deeper financial trouble than ever before." Yet Siegel also notes that the studio's financial records were unavailable at the time of publication, "making it impossible to quote an exact figure on how much *Cat People* grossed." The film's screenwriter, DeWitt Bodeen, "says $4,000,000; almost every published estimate exceeds $2,000,000," Siegel states (38–39). Similarly, an article from the *New York Times* in 1943 reported *Cat People* was "headed for a domestic gross of $4,000,000, it is stated" (Fred Stanley,

"Hollywood Views the New Season," *New York Times*, 23 May 1943, X3). Whether it was Bodeen stating this $4 million figure in 1943 is uncertain, but the fact that the article points to the anecdotal nature of the reported sum is key. Richard B. Jewell contradicts such accounts, however, as the result of discovering certain files in RKO's Accounting Department several years after the publication of Siegel's book. Upon consulting the financial records of RKO's film grosses from 1929 to 1951, Jewell concludes that the common conception of Val Lewton's horror films being " 'sleeper' hits that earned huge profits for the company" is incorrect. "In reality," says Jewell, "the Lewton films were indifferent performers that never approached the company's top ten money making releases in their respective years. The first of the group, *Cat People*, was the most profitable, earning $183,000, but thereafter a slow decline set in and the final entry in the series, *Bedlam*, actually lost $40,000" ("RKO Film Grosses," 46).

31. This definition might prompt some readers to ask whether within its parameters modern major studio releases produced for a fraction of the average budget of a summer blockbuster could also be called B-movies. Indeed, it is this book's contention that the success of independent B-filmmakers in the 1950s within a new industrial era of risk and reward in turn allowed for the massive success of such films as *The Blair Witch Project* (1999), *My Big Fat Greek Wedding* (2002), and *Paranormal Activity* (2009), among others, which were produced independently and distributed by major studios.

32. John Fiske, *Understanding Popular Culture* (Boston: Unwin Hyman Ltd., 1989), 26.

33. "Movie Review: Red Eye," *Chicago Tribune*, http://metromix.chicagotribune.com/movies/mmx-050818-movies-review-redeye,0,4616520.story?coll=mmx-movies_top_heds; Emmanuel Levy, "Review: Red Eye," http://emanuellevy.com/article.php?articleID=344; Rob Blackwelder, "Overnight Sensation," http://splicedwire.com/05reviews/redeye.html; Phillip Martin, "Neatly Broken," *Arkansas Gazette*, http://www2.arkansasonline.com/news/2007/apr/20/neatly-broken-20070420/?entertainment/movies.

34. David Edelstein, "Oh Jesus," *New York Magazine*, http://nymag.com/movies/reviews/17071/; "Review: The Incredible Hulk," *Entertainment Weekly*, http://www.ew.com/ew/article/0,,20205934,00.html.

35. Marke Andrews, "Return of the B-Movies," *Vancouver Sun*, 13 March 2004, D1.

36. Kristin Thompson and David Bordwell, *Film History: An Introduction* (New York: McGraw-Hill, 1994), 381.

37. Greg Merritt, *Celluloid Mavericks: A History of American Independent Film* (New York: Thunder's Mouth Press, 2000), 126–127. Responding indirectly to this kind of flippant rhetoric, Randy Palmer describes how a certain critical prejudice against 1950s B-movies ultimately formed over past decades, even among some fans: "It became fashionable to disdain the black-and-white 'cheapies' made during the 1950s. . . . Trashing easy targets like *The Beast with 1,000,000 Eyes* seemed to prove that they were no longer indiscriminating monster lovers, but serious devotees of horror film art. The problem, as many fans later recognized, was that in their eagerness to prove to the world that horror films should be taken seriously, they damned anything that failed to match a set of preconceived standards that purported to define what was good and what was bad. Could these elitists admit to actually liking pictures with titles like *How to Make a Monster* or *I Was a Teenage Werewolf*? Of course not. Not if they

wanted to be taken seriously" (*Paul Blaisdell, Monster Maker: A Biography of the B Movie Makeup and Special Effects Artist* [Jefferson, NC: McFarland, 1997], 252–253).

38. Harry Medved and Michael Medved, *The Golden Turkey Awards: The Worst Achievements in Hollywood History* (New York: Berkley Books, 1980), xi; Harry Medved and Randy Dreyfuss, *The 50 Worst Films of All Time* (New York: Warner Books, 1978), 9. Wheeler Winston Dixon writes that such books "may be entertaining to read, and even factually accurate, [but these books] encourage the reader simply to belittle all 'B' movies, as if any film produced on a low budget in a short period of time must be inherently worthless" (*The "B" Directors: A Biographical Dictionary* [Metuchen, NJ: Scarecrow Press, 1985], 1).

39. Jeffrey Sconce, "'Trashing' the Academy: Taste, Excess, and an Emerging Politics of Cinematic Style," *Screen* 36, no. 4 (Winter 1995): 375; Paul Roen, *High Camp: A Gay Guide to Camp and Cult Films* (San Francisco: Leyland, 1993). Paul Coates notes that camp culture "thrives on the failure of art," and on "the failure of low culture to become high culture," and in so doing "paradoxically transforms failure and dissonance into a sign of success" (*Film at the Intersection of High and Mass Culture* [New York: Cambridge University Press, 2004], 3).

40. Greg Taylor, *Artists in the Audience: Cults, Camp, and American Film Criticism* (Princeton, NJ: Princeton University Press, 1999), 154.

41. Alan Warde, "Production, Consumption, and Cultural Economy," in *Cultural Economy: Cultural Analysis and Commercial Life*, ed. Paul Du Gay and Michael Pryke (London: Sage, 2002), 186.

42. Kerr uses this term, stating that he seeks to "refocus the debate on the specifically film-industrial determinants of the [film noir] genre" ("Out of What Past?" 222).

43. David Gordon, "Why the Movie Majors Are Major," *Sight & Sound* 42 (1973): 194.

CHAPTER 1   HOLLYWOOD IN TRANSITION

1. See Garth Jowett's *Film: The Democratic Art* (Boston: Little, Brown, 1976) for a detailed account of the 1940 consent decree.

2. John Izod, *Hollywood and the Box Office, 1895–1986* (New York: Columbia University Press, 1988), 121.

3. Society of Independent Motion Picture Producers, Letter to Thurmond Arnold, 1 June 1942, http://www.cobbles.com/simpp_archive/simpp_1942openletter.htm.

4. Quoted in *The American Movie Industry: The Business of Motion Pictures*, ed. Gorham Kindem (Carbondale: Southern Illinois University Press, 1982), 172.

5. Tino Balio, "Surviving the Great Depression," in *Grand Design: Hollywood as a Modern Business Enterprise, 1930–1939*, ed. Tino Balio, History of the American Cinema series (New York: Charles Scribner's Sons, 1993), 20, 29.

6. Douglas Gomery, *The Hollywood Studio System: A History* (London: BFI Publishing, 2005), 71; 74.

7. Compiled from Izod, *Hollywood and the Box Office*, 122, and Michael Conant, *Antitrust in the Motion Picture Industry: Economic and Legal Analysis* (New York: Arno Press, 1978), 98–99.

8. Quoted in Select Committee on Small Business, United States Senate, *Motion-Picture Distribution Trade Practices—1956: Problems of Independent Motion-Picture Exhibitors* (Washington, DC: Government Printing Office, July 27, 1956), 24.

9. Ibid., 1.

10. David Bordwell, Janet Staiger, and Kristin Thompson, *The Classical Hollywood Cinema: Film Style and Mode of Production to 1960* (New York: Columbia University Press, 1985), 93. "What occurred in the Hollywood mode of production was the result of its conditions of existence: the economic and ideological/signifying practices which individual firms and institutions took as their initial models. Furthermore, the industry changed these models to suit its particular medium and situations," says Staiger. "Each [successive] management system in one or a few areas differed from the prior one, changed out of it," she notes (335).

11. Select Committee, *Motion-Picture Distribution Trade Practices*, 35.

12. Bordwell, Staiger, and Thompson, *Classical Hollywood Cinema*, 330.

13. Janet Wasko, *How Hollywood Works* (London: Sage, 2003), 2–3.

14. Select Committee, *Motion-Picture Distribution Trade Practices*, 20.

15. Ibid., 28.

16. "Herald Reports Box Office Off 17% in Four Months," *Motion Picture Daily*, 24 March 1950, 2.

17. Select Committee, *Motion-Picture Distribution Trade Practices*, 50; 52.

18. Jack Gould, "Television's Role," *New York Times*, 20 February 1949, XII.

19. Samuel Goldwyn, "Hollywood in the Television Age" (1949), http://www.cobbles.com/simpp_archive/goldwyn_television.htm.

20. Select Committee, *Motion-Picture Distribution Trade Practices*, 30; "TV Thaw," *Time*, 21 April 1952, http://www.time.com/time/magazine/article/0,9171,889476,00.html.

21. Izod, *Hollywood and the Box Office*, 134.

22. Select Committee, *Motion-Picture Distribution Trade Practices*, 19; 36.

23. *Variety*, 14 April 1953, quoted in John Belton, *Widescreen Cinema* (Cambridge, MA: 1992), 116.

24. "Rather than attending a local theater regularly," note Thompson and Bordwell, such viewers "would choose an 'important' film'" on a less regular basis. "Catering to this audience, the big producers cut back on the number of films they released, concentrating on ways to provide big attractions" (*Film History: An Introduction* [New York: McGraw-Hill, 1994], 375–376).

25. "Sees Bigger, Fewer Films with 3-D," *Motion Picture Daily*, 26 February 1953, 2.

26. "Gotta Be Smash Hits or Else—No In-Betweens on Pic Product," *Variety*, 20 May 1951, 5.

27. "1952—Big Grosses, Low Profits—Show Biz Turns to New Patterns," *Variety*, 31 December 1952, 1.

28. "Only 20% of All Films Show Profit, Making It Tougher for Indies with Their Fewer Pix, ELC's MacMillan Stresses," *Variety*, 28 March 1951, 7.

29. Leonard Spinrad, "End of an Era," *Films in Review* 7, no. 4 (April 1956): 145.

30. Barbara Boyle, "The Independent Spirit," in *The Movie Business Book*, ed. Jason Squire, 3rd ed. (New York: Simon & Schuster, 2004), 175, 179–180.

31. Terry B. Sanders, "The Financing of Independent Feature Films," *Quarterly of Film, Radio and Television* 4, no. 4 (Summer 1955): 381–382.

32. "When You Say 'Indie' Use Quotes—Majors Backing Lone Filmmakers," *Variety*, 7 April 1954, 3.

33. Fredric Marlowe, "The Rise of the Independents in Hollywood," *Penguin Film Review* 3 (August 1947): 72–73.

34. Hal Bartlett, "The Fighting Independent," *Films in Review* 6, no. 2 (February 1955): 49.

35. Stanley Kramer, "The Independent Producer," *Films in Review* 2, no. 3 (March 1951): 1.

36. Bartlett, "The Fighting Independent," 49, 52–54.

37. "Indie Production So Low That Producers Not Even Seeking Loans, Sez Banker," *Variety*, 15 November 1950, 5.

38. "Independent Producers Need 'Stronger' UA: Kaufman," *Motion Picture Daily*, 25 October 1950, 3.

39. "War Industries Cut Indie Coin—Newcomers Get Nix from Banks," *Variety*, 17 January 1951, 5.

40. "Aid to Independents Unless Films Improve: Sullivan," *Motion Picture Daily*, 4 April 1951, 1.

41. "Eased Coin for Indies Ups Production," *Variety*, 18 January 1950, 3.

42. "New High on Indie-Major Deals—Firms Lure More Outside Projects," *Variety*, 14 February 1951, 3.

43. "See 1951 as Banner Indie Year," *Variety*, 28 February 1951, 7.

44. "Films' 'Heftiest' Distrib Sked—Numerous Indies Back in Action," *Variety*, 21 March 1951, 3.

45. "25% Rise in Independent Films Seen," *Motion Picture Daily*, 19 July 1951, 1.

46. "Independents Must Be 'Different': Kramer," *Motion Picture Daily*, 12 April 1949, 1.

47. "Says Independents Need New Approach," *Motion Picture Daily*, 28 April 1952, 5.

48. Gilbert Vivian Seldes, *The Great Audience* (New York: Viking Press, 1950), 9–10, 13.

49. Leo A. Handel, *Hollywood Looks at Its Audience: A Report of Film Audience Research* (Urbana: University of Illinois Press, 1950), 98.

50. Seldes, *Great Audience*, 15, 43.

51. Select Committee, *Motion-Picture Distribution Trade Practices*, 32.

52. Fred Hift, "Hard to Come in Offbeat: Public Taste is Crazy Guesswork," *Variety*, 20 February 1957, 3.

53. Select Committee, *Motion-Picture Distribution Trade Practices*, 27.

54. "What Makes a Movie Fan," *Newsweek*, 3 February 1958, 87.

55. Martin Quigley Jr., "Who Goes to the Movies . . . and Who Doesn't," *Motion Picture Daily*, 10 August 1957, 21–22.

56. Ned Armstrong, "Suburbia—Key to Legit Future?—Trend Is Away from Midcity," *Variety*, 23 January 1952, 1.

57. Hy Hollinger, " 'Lost Audience': Grass vs. Class," *Variety*, 5 December 1956, 1.

58. Walter Brooks, "Double-Bills—They're In and Out," *Motion Picture Herald*, 17 August 1957, 31.

59. Kerry Segrave, *Drive-in Theatres: A History from Their Inception in 1933* (Jefferson, NC: McFarland, 1992), 65.

60. "1 in 8 Pic-Goers Went to Drive-Ins in July," *Variety*, 6 September 1950, 4.

61. "Ozoners No More Stepchildren—Providing 10% of Film Rentals," *Variety*, 7 May 1952, 5.

62. "Drive-ins Accounted for 20% of Grosses in 1953," *Motion Picture Daily*, 2 July 1954, 1.

63. Leonard Spinrad, "Burgeoning Drive-Ins: Building Boom in Open Air Houses Expected," *New York Times*, 1 March 1953, X5.

64. "Drive-In Movie Fan Is Solid Consumer, TsAB Report Says," *Advertising Age*, 14 March 1960, 31.

65. Wilfred P. Smith, "Getting into the Drive-In Business," *Motion Picture Herald*, 9 February 1952, 11.

66. Rita Reif, "Drive-In Theatre Extends Horizon," *New York Times*, 9 June 1957, 251.

67. "Stage Shows for Drive-In," *Motion Picture Daily*, 26 January 1953, 2; "Free Admission, Free Gas Is Latest Drive-In Lure," *Hollywood Reporter*, 12 September 1956, 1.

68. "19 Million Weekly at Drive-Ins," *Hollywood Reporter*, 1 August 1956, 1.

69. "31,000,000 in Week at Drive-Ins," *Hollywood Reporter*, 30 August 1956, 1.

70. "Drive-In Season 40 Percent Off," *Hollywood Reporter*, 30 September 1957, 1.

71. "Drive-In Patrons Now Choosy Like Hardtops," *Variety*, 31 December 1958, 4.

72. Handel, *Hollywood Looks at Its Audience*, 98.

73. Quigley, "Who Goes to the Movies . . . and Who Doesn't," 22.

74. "Teen-agers Best Film Audience," *Variety*, 23 April 1952, 3.

75. "Pix 'Gotta Have Youth Appeal,'" *Variety*, 7 December 1955, 9.

76. Hy Hollinger, "Hollywood's 'Age of the Teens': Need Stars with Coke-Set Draw," *Variety*, 22 August 1956, 3.

77. "Stress Sales to Youth, Says Rydge," *Motion Picture Herald*, 24 August 1957, 21.

78. "More Youth Lure in Product, Biz Up: Goldenson," *Variety*, 14 November 1956, 3.

79. "How Big Is the Teenage Audience? [$9,000,000 in Pocket Change]," *Variety*, 24 October 1956, 22.

80. "Bel-Air-UA Aim for Young Fans," *Hollywood Reporter*, 11 October 1956, 7.

81. "15-to-24 Is Top Audience: Weingarten," *Motion Picture Daily*, 3 June 1957, 1.

82. "Bel-Air-UA Aim for Young Fans," 1, 7.

83. "Teenage Promotion for RKO's 'Young Stranger,'" *Hollywood Reporter*, 9 October 1956, 3.

84. "What Kind of Film Teenagers Want Is Goal of Experiment in Cleveland," *Motion Picture Daily*, 17 March 1959, 1.

85. "Interstate's Teenage Idea Advertised," *Motion Picture Herald*, 2 July 1955, 41.

86. "Teenagers vs. A-2 Legion Rating," *Variety*, 28 December 1955, 12.

87. "Berserk Teenagers Close Theatre," *Variety*, 12 December 1956, 3.

88. Hy Hollinger, "Teenage Biz vs. Repair Bill—Paradox in New 'Best Audience,'" *Variety*, 19 December 1956, 1

CHAPTER 2   THE BATTLE BEGINS

1. Thomas M. Pryor, "By Way of Report," *New York Times*, 8 September 1946, X3.

2. "Universal to Drop Four 'B' Film Units," *New York Times*, 26 July 1946, 16; Brian Smith, "Burning Down the House: House of Dracula and the Death of Universal Pictures," *Monsters from the Vault* 6, no. 12 (2001): 29–30.

3. Michael Brunas, John Brunas, and Tom Weaver, *Universal Horrors: The Studio's Classic Films, 1931–1946* (Jefferson, NC: McFarland, 1990), 541.

4. Thomas F. Brady, "Low Budget Films Expanding at Fox," *New York Times*, 23 September 1947, 31; "Hollywood Buzzes," *New York Times*, 28 September 1947, X5.

5. Thomas F. Brady, "Low-Budget Unit Added by Metro," *New York Times*, 29 January 1948, 27; "Old Order Changes," *New York Times*, 8 February 1948, X5.

6. Thomas F. Brady, "Hollywood Memos," *New York Times*, 18 January 1948, X5.

7. "B's Buzzing out of Business?—Tougher to Book by Distributors," *Variety*, 26 March 1952, 3.

8. "'B' Pictures Join Top Product in Upturn at B.O.," *Variety*, 12 September 1951, 1, 54.

9. Mike Kaplan, "Hollywood's to 'B' or Not to 'B': Majors Cutting Program Films," *Variety*, 21 November 1951, 7.

10. "Freeman, Roach See Upped Quality, No 'B' Pix in Industry Future; TV Forecast as New Cradle of Talent," *Variety*, 12 December 1951, 5; "Freeman Predicts Passing of 'B's,'" *Motion Picture Daily*, 7 December 1951, 1, 4.

11. "Medium Budgeters B.O. Dimout—Hit-or-Miss Biz Stymies Indies," *Variety*, 20 March 1950, 7.

12. Robert Coughlan, "Now It Is Trouble That Is Supercolossal in Hollywood," *Life*, 13 August 1951, 106.

13. "'Bad' Movies Linked to Failure of 'Good,'" *New York Times*, 6 January 1951, 19.

14. "No B's in Major Studios' Bonnet, Veering More to Major Product," *Variety*, 19 August 1953, 7. The notion of B-movies as a site where "fledgling talent was developed for better things" is later discussed in the article "If No 'B's,' Where Are New Stars to Get Showcasing?" *Variety*, 17 November 1954, 1. It posits that "Hollywood's concentration on 'A' pictures might jeopardize the development of new screen stars who broke in via the type of 'B' product that is now being abandoned." Television actors and those who work as supporting cast in films were now thought to be primary sources for developing new movie stars—a situation that has come to be standard practice in modern Hollywood.

15. Kaplan, "Hollywood's to 'B' or Not to 'B,'" 7; 20.

16. "No B's in Major Studios' Bonnet."

17. "Medium Budgeters B.O. Dimout."

18. "If No 'B's.'"

19. Lewis Jacobs, "A History of the Obscure Quickie," *New York Times*, 30 December 1934, X4.

20. George Turner and Michael H. Price, *Forgotten Horrors: Early Talkie Chillers from Poverty Row* (New York: A. S. Barnes, 1979), 10; Charles Flynn and Todd McCarthy, "The Economic Imperative: Why Was the B Movie Necessary?" in *Kings of the B's: Working Within the Hollywood System*, ed. Todd McCarthy and Charles Flynn (New York: E. P. Dutton, 1975), 18–19. See also Michael R. Pitts, *Poverty Row Studios, 1929–1940* (Jefferson, NC: McFarland, 1997).

21. Gene Fernett, *Poverty Row* (Satellite Beach, FL: Coral Reef Publications, 1973), 9.

22. Flynn and McCarthy, "The Economic Imperative," 24, 36; Brian Taves, "The B Film: Hollywood's Other Half," in *Grand Design: Hollywood as a Modern Business Enterprise, 1930–1939*, ed. Tino Balio, History of the American Cinema series (New York: Charles Scribner's Sons, 1993), 323. A single states' rights distributor typically handled

multiple studios, selling their films "on a state-by-state or regional basis, with flat fees paid for the limited exclusive rights to distribute for exhibition in a particular area, allowing small but predictable profits. The distributors to such second- and third-rate houses absorbed the cost of release prints and publicity materials, paying a use fee to the producer that might range as high as $50,000. Such a system virtually guaranteed production, but had no incentive for quality, since the pictures were bought without regard to the care or expense that went into making them."

23. Gene Fernett, *American Film Studios: An Historical Encyclopedia* (Jefferson, NC: McFarland, 1988), 175–176; Wheeler W. Dixon, *The "B" Directors: A Biographical Directory* (Metuchen, NJ: Scarecrow Press, 1985), 482; "Eagle-Lion Offers Financing of Films," *New York Times*, 26 August 1949, 14.

24. Todd McCarthy and Charles Flynn, "Phil Karlson," in McCarthy and Flynn, *Kings of the B's*, 331, 333.

25. "Hollywood Shoots for the Moon," *New York Times*, 19 February 1950, SM24; Thomas F. Brady, "Dark Days for Independents," *New York Times*, 21 January 1951, 85.

26. "E-L Plans Embrace Distribution Only," *Variety*, 14 September 1950, 1.

27. Thomas F. Brady, "Eagle Lion Films Gets Five Movies," *New York Times*, 19 September 1949, 18; "5 More for Eagle-Lion," *Motion Picture Daily*, 19 September 1949, 1; 3.

28. "Eased Coin for Indies Ups Production," *Variety*, 18 January 1950, 3.

29. "Eagle-Lion and Film Classics Consolidated," *Motion Picture Daily*, 22 May 1950, 1.

30. "Eagle-Lion Classics Set to Market an 'A' Film Monthly," *Variety*, 1 June 1950, 1; "More Indies Get Pitch from ELC," *Variety*, 4 October 1950, 4.

31. "ELC Files Big Suit Against Loew's, RKO," *Motion Picture Daily*, 4 October 1950, 1, 6.

32. "Films' 'Heftiest' Distrib Sked—Numerous Indies Back in Action," *Variety*, 21 March 1951, 3.

33. "1950–51 Will Be ELC's 1st 'Profit' Year," *Motion Picture Daily*, 26 March 1951, 1; 3.

34. Tino Balio, *United Artists: The Company Built by the Stars* (Madison: University of Wisconsin Press, 1976), 233–235.

35. "1950–51," 3.

36. "Scramble for ELC's Market," *Variety*, 18 April 1951, 3.

37. "Only 20% of All Films Show Profit, Making It Tougher for Indies with Their Fewer Pix, ELC's MacMillan Stresses," *Variety*, 28 March 1951, 7.

38. Len D. Martin, *The Republic Pictures Checklist* (Jefferson, NC: McFarland, 1998), 1.

39. "Republic Lists 53 Features for New Year," *Motion Picture Daily*, 21 September 1949, 1.

40. "Minors' Profits on the Rise," *Variety*, 22 February 1950, 7.

41. Murray Horowitz, "Republic to Make Fewer but Bigger Pictures: Yates," *Motion Picture Daily*, 31 June 1952, 1, 4; "Republic Doubles Production Budget for 1952–1953: Yates," *Motion Picture Daily*, 23 July 1952, 1.

42. "Republic Six Month Net Up 100G over Last Year," *Variety*, 15 July 1953, 7.

43. "Rep. Will Bankroll 'Outstanding' Indies," *Variety*, 9 September 1953, 74.

44. Quoted in Richard Maurice Hurst, *Republic Studios: Between Poverty Row and the Majors* (Metuchen, NJ: Scarecrow Press, 1979), 113.

45. R. M. Hayes, *The Republic Chapterplays* (Jefferson, NC: McFarland, 1991), 7.

46. Hurst, *Republic Studios*, 25.

47. "Republic Re-edits and Re-titles," *Variety*, 10 February 1954, 16.

48. Thomas M. Pryor, "Hollywood Blues," *New York Times*, 10 April 1955, X5; "Offer Made to Buy Republic Pictures," *New York Times*, 24 May 1956, 50; Thomas M. Pryor, "Republic Studios to Resume Work," *New York Times*, 8 January 1957, 26; "Republic President 'Optimistic' about '58 Net," *Wall Street Journal*, 2 April 1958, 14; Hurst, *Republic Studios*, 25–26.

49. Gene Arnell, "RKO-Allied-Republic as One—Talks Project 3-Way Merger," *Variety*, 18 December 1958, 3, 19.

50. Hurst, *Republic Studios*, 27–29; Fernett, *Poverty Row*, 95.

51. Fernett, *American Film Studios*, 145.

52. "Monogram Lists 40 Films for Year," *New York Times*, 6 September 1950, 48.

53. "Monogram Sharply Reduces Its Losses," *Motion Picture Daily*, 12 July 1949, 1, 4; "16 This Fall: Monogram," *Motion Picture Daily*, 21 September 1949, 1; "46 from Mono. and Allied in the New Year," *Motion Picture Daily*, 6 September 1950, 1; "Mono. Reports $175,866 Loss for 13-Week Period," *Motion Picture Daily*, 10 November 1950, 1.

54. "ELC Bow Out Ups Monogram in 'B' Market," *Motion Picture Daily*, 17 April 1951, 1; "'Best Season' for M.-Allied Reported Broidy," *Motion Picture Daily*, 12 September 1951, 1; "Monogram Reports $1,061,648 Net," *Motion Picture Daily*, 16 October 1951, 1; "1-a-Month Color Pic Slated from Mono for '51–'52," *Variety*, 12 September 1951, 5.

55. "600,000 Profit Reported by Mono," *Motion Picture Daily*, 25 September 1952, 5.

56. Len D. Martin, *The Allied Artists Checklist* (Jefferson, NC: McFarland, 1993), ix; Richard Kaehling, "Interview: Steve Broidy," in McCarthy and Flynn, *Kings of the B's*, 273.

57. "If No B's," 15.

58. Kevin Heffernan, *Ghouls, Gimmicks, and Gold: Horror Films and the American Movie Business, 1953–1968* (Durham, NC: Duke University Press, 2004), 76–77.

59. Lester Dinoff, "Allied Artists' 39-Wk. Billings Show 42% Rise," *Motion Picture Daily*, 9 April 1956, 1; "Allied Artists Slates 36 in Year," *Hollywood Reporter*, 17 September 1957, 1.

60. "AFI's 10 Top 10—Top 10 Sci-Fi," *The American Film Institute*, 2008, http://www.afi.com/10top10/category.aspx?cat=7.

61. Stuart M. Kaminsky, "Don Siegel on the Pod Society," in *Invasion of the Body Snatchers*, ed. Al LaValley (New Brunswick, NJ: Rutgers University Press, 1989), 154. Similar metaphorical statements about cold-war American values might be found in such films as *Invasion of the Body Snatchers*, *Invaders from Mars* (1953), and *I Married a Monster from Outer Space* (1958). Current social issues were also explored more overtly in 1950s B-films such as *The Phenix City Story* (1955) from Allied Artists. In its portrayal of corruption in a small Alabama town, *Phenix*'s handling of issues of racial intolerance and violence against African Americans (even showing the murder of a young African American child) stands as a plea for civil rights and a commentary on the sociopolitical climate that existed in some parts of the South. In this way, many 1950s B-films were a continuation of the legacy of social problem films that flourished in Hollywood in the late 1940s (and were also seen throughout much of the 1930s). Films such as *Crossfire* (1947) and *Gentleman's Agreement* (1947) explored issues of anti-Semitism, while films like *Home of the Brave* (1949), *Lost Boundaries* (1949), and *Pinky* (1949) confronted prejudices against African Americans.

62. " 'Haunted Hill' Good Spook Fun—Plus Ballyhoo Gimmick," *Hollywood Reporter*, 1 December 1958, 3–4; "Review: House on Haunted Hill," *Newsweek*, 29 January 1959, 100; Heffernan, *Ghouls, Gimmicks, and Gold*, 78–79.

63. "Allied Artists May Rely 100% on Indie Units," *Variety*, 18 November 1957, 3.

64. Kaehling, "Interview: Steve Broidy," 280.

65. William R. Weaver, "Castle Ideas Good Match with Ability," *Motion Picture Herald*, 13 July 1957, 23.

66. "O'Donnell Asks for Support for Allied Artists," *Motion Picture Herald*, 20 April 1957, 19.

67. "Allied Artists' 'Want to Live,'" *Variety*, 3 December 1958, 5.

68. "Allied Artists Sets 36, 6 Big Budget," *Variety*, 14 January 1959, 4.

69. "Broidy: AA Looms in Black for '59," *Variety*, 25 March 1959, 3.

70. "AA's Future Looking Up; 'Capone' and 'Macabre' Hit into the Tall Mazuma," *Variety*, 15 April 1959, 5.

71. "Allied Artists Up 134% on Quarter," *Variety*, 18 November 1959, 15.

72. "If RKO, Republic Gone, There's AA and Disney Now," *Variety*, 3 June 1959, 13.

73. Martin, *Allied Artists*, ix, x.

CHAPTER 3   THE REBIRTH OF THE B-MOVIE IN THE 1950s

1. "'Sick' Screen Given Senatorial Advice," *New York Times*, 5 August 1953, 19.

2. Thomas Schatz, ed., *Boom and Bust: American Cinema in the 1940s*, History of the American Cinema series (Berkeley: University of California Press, 1999), 78.

3. Douglas Gomery, *Shared Pleasures: A History of Movie Presentation in the United States* (Madison: University of Wisconsin Press, 1992), 66.

4. Stanley W. Penn, "Movie-Makers to Cut '59 Output 15% to Post-War Low, Stress Big-Budget Films to Counter Slump," *Wall Street Journal*, 4 February 1959, 24.

5. "It's Light Musicals 2 to 1, Panels Find," *Motion Picture Herald*, 26 January 1952, 18.

6. "Lippert Sees Television a Real Threat," *Motion Picture Herald*, 11 February 1950, 42.

7. Janet Staiger, "Duals, B's, and the Industry Discourse About Its Audience," in Schatz, *Boom and Bust*, 72.

8. Walter Brooks, "There's Opportunity in Small Towns for Showmen," *Motion Picture Herald*, 27 January 1951, 49; Brooks, "In Praise of Paramount's Small Town Premieres," *Motion Picture Herald*, 11 August 1951, 37; Charlie Jones, "What About Movies on Main Street?" *Motion Picture Herald*, 9 January 1954, 16–17; Brooks, "The Small Town Manager Has Friends," *Motion Picture Herald*, 17 April 1954, 33; Martin Quigley Jr., "Plight of the Small Exhibitor," *Motion Picture Herald*, 8 May 1954, 2; "One Theatre Towns Are the Soul of Show Business," *Motion Picture Herald*, 13 August 1955, 33.

9. David Kenyon Webster, "Film Fare: Hollywood Producers Concentrate on Fewer, More Lavish Pictures," *Wall Street Journal*, 13 July 1954, 8.

10. Quigley, "Plight," 2; "Relief for Small Situations," *Motion Picture Herald*, 30 October 1954, 7.

11. Simon N. Whitney, "Antitrust Policies and the Motion Picture Industry," in *The American Movie Industry: The Business of Motion Pictures*, ed. Gorham Kindem (Carbondale: Southern Illinois University Press, 1982), 176–177.

12. "Reade Decries Film Shortage," *Motion Picture Herald*, 12 June 1954, 28.

13. Select Committee on Small Business, United States Senate, *Motion-Picture Distribution Trade Practices—1956. Problems of Independent Motion-Picture Exhibitors* (Washington, DC: Government Printing Office, July 27, 1956), 10–11.

14. "Need 26 More A's: O'Donnell," *Motion Picture Herald*, 5 June 1954, 20.

15. "Feldman Points to Small Market Today for Low Budget Films," *Motion Picture Daily*, 29 December 1954, 5; 39.

16. "Crop of New Distributors—Product Decline Serves as Hypo," *Variety*, 22 September 1954, 5.

17. Quoted in Kevin Heffernan, *Ghouls, Gimmicks, and Gold: Horror Films and the American Movie Business, 1953–1968* (Durham, NC: Duke University Press, 2004), 66.

18. "More Product Crying Need but Exhibition Differs on Solution," *Motion Picture Herald*, 26 March 1955, 15.

19. "Mode Theater," *Cinema Treasures*, http://cinematreasures.org/theater/4467/.

20. Stephen Davis, Personal Interview, 2 January 2006.

21. Abel Green, "Sarnoff on Hollywood vs. TV: Sees All Cinemas Adding TV to Pix," *Variety*, 29 August 1951, 22.

22. Murray Horowitz, "Find Art Films Can Aid Some 'B' Theatres," *Motion Picture Daily*, 28 February 1955, 1.

23. Barbara Wilinsky, *Sure Seaters: The Emergence of Art House Cinema* (Minneapolis: University of Minnesota Press, 2001), 1.

24. Ibid., 12–13.

25. Horowitz, "Find Art Films Can Aid Some 'B' Theatres," 5.

26. Wilinsky, *Sure Seaters*, 3–4.

27. John E. Twomey, "Some Considerations on the Rise of the Art-Film Theater (1956)," in *Moviegoing in America: A Sourcebook in the History of Film Exhibition*, ed. Gregory A. Waller (Oxford: Blackwell, 2002), 259–262.

28. Stanley Frank, "Sure-Seaters Discover an Audience (1952)," in ibid., 258.

29. Wilinsky, *Sure Seaters*, 35.

30. Horowitz, "Find Art Films Can Aid Some 'B' Theatres," 5.

31. The label of "exploitation film" is one that was used regularly in the 1950s for a wide range of B films—*Variety* magazine refers to films from both Columbia Pictures and AIP as exploitation films, for instance. Even big-budget A-films were occasionally labeled as exploitation films, as a trade advertisement for Vincente Minnelli's 1953 musical *The Band Wagon* starring Fred Astaire invites exhibitors to "Get Aboard the Exploitation Picture of the Year!" (*Variety*, 8 July 1953, 19). The use of the term "exploitation" in these contexts, however, contradicts the work of Eric Schaefer in *"Bold! Daring! Shocking! True!" A History of Exploitation Films, 1919–1959* (Durham, NC: Duke University Press, 1999). Schaefer notes that classical exploitation films tended to be controversial, because, "to one degree or another, [they] centered on some form of forbidden spectacle" such as drug abuse, venereal disease, and/or nudism "that served as their organizing sensibility" (2, 5). Given that 1950s B-movies are largely not concerned with such taboo subjects (preferring instead to focus on genre-based narratives and current youth trends in popular culture), a clear distinction exists between such Bs and the classical exploitation film.

32. Wilinsky, *Sure Seaters*, 37, 122.

33. Twomey, "Some Considerations," 261.

34. Arthur Mayer, *Merely Colossal* (New York: Simon and Schuster, 1953), 233.

35. Wilinsky, *Sure Seaters*, 38–39, 107.

36. "Drive-Ins Saviour for 'B' Features," *Variety*, 1 August 1956, 5.

37. "Drive-Ins Demand More Films," *Hollywood Reporter*, 4 January 1955, 1, 4.

38. Garth Jowett and James M. Linton, *Movies as Mass Communication*, 2nd ed. (Newbury Park, CA: Sage, 1989), 54.

39. "The Colossal Drive-In," *Newsweek*, 22 July 1957, 85–86.

40. "Drive-Ins Demand More Films," 4.

41. Sam Arkoff, *Flying Through Hollywood by the Seat of My Pants* (New York: Birch Lane Press, 1992), 58–59.

42. Kerry Segrave, *Drive-in Theatres: A History from Their Inception in 1933* (Jefferson, NC: McFarland, 1992), 59.

43. Frank J. Taylor, "Big Boom in Outdoor Movies," in Waller, *Moviegoing in America*, 251.

44. Gillian Doyle, *Understanding Media Economics* (London: Sage, 2002), 18.

45. Mark Thomas McGee, *Beyond Ballyhoo: Motion Picture Promotion and Gimmicks* (Jefferson, NC: McFarland, 1989), 73–74.

46. "'Haunted Hill' Good Spook Fun—Plus Ballyhoo Gimmick," *Hollywood Reporter*, 1 December 1958, 3; Christopher Schaefer, "Macabre: William Castle's First Horror Film," *Cult Movies* 37 (2002): 47.

47. McGee, *Beyond Ballyhoo*, outlines these various gimmicks on the following pages, respectively: 100, 101, 103–104, 108–109, 111–112, 118.

48. "Mad, Mad Doctors 'n' Stunts—Blood Runs High but Ideas Low," *Variety*, 23 July 1958, 7.

49. William R. Weaver, "Castle Ideas Good Match with Ability," *Motion Picture Herald*, 13 July 1957, 23.

50. "'Haunted Hill' Good Spook Fun."

51. One Poverty Row holdout that managed to survive through the 1950s was Astor Pictures, a small distributing company formed in the early 1930s. Throughout the 1930s and 1940s, Astor offered re-releases of other Poverty Row studios' films, such as Monogram's Bowery Boys series. By the mid-1940s, the company began distributing first-run product, mostly westerns such as those starring Sunset Carson. Between 1945 and 1947, Astor moved into producing a few of its own films for American theaters, in addition to its ongoing distribution business. Its production schedule was mainly comprised of films for the African American theater circuits, with films like *Tall, Tan, and Terrific* (1946), *Beware* (1946), *Look-Out Sister* (1947) and *Reet, Petite, and Gone* (1947). In the 1950s, Astor was able to recognize—unlike studios such as Republic—the marketplace's need for B-movies that were different from those in decades past, particularly in the horror and science fiction genres. As such, they distributed films like *Robot Monster* (1953) *Cat Women of the Moon* (1953), *She-Demons* (1958), *Giant from the Unknown* (1958), *Frankenstein's Daughter* (1959), and *Missile to the Moon* (1958). Astor remained in business until 1962.

52. J. D. Spiro, "Hollywood Acts," *New York Times*, 23 October 1949, X5.

53. Ida Lupino, "Interview with Ida Lupino, Los Angeles, September 1974," in *Film Crazy: Interviews with Hollywood Legends*, ed. Patrick McGilligan (New York: St. Martin's, 2000), 224. See also Annette Kuhn's *Queen of the B's: Ida Lupino Behind the Camera* (Santa Barbara, CA: Greenwood, 1995) for analysis of Lupino's films for Filmakers.

54. Howard Thompson, "The Local Movie Scene," *New York Times*, 22 August 1954, X5.

55. "Crop of New Distributors," 5.

56. Thomas M. Pryor, "Film Aid Planned for Independents," *New York Times*, 25 August 1954, 24.

57. "Roach Studios Buys Distributors Corp.," *New York Times*, 14 January 1959, 30.

58. Heffernan, *Ghouls, Gimmicks, and Gold*, 72.

59. Ted Okuda, *The Monogram Checklist: The Films of Monogram Pictures Corporation, 1931–1952* (Jefferson, NC: McFarland, 1987), 124.

60. "Medium Budgeters B.O. Dimout—Hit-or-Miss Biz Stymies Indies," *Variety*, 20 March 1950, 7.

61. A. H. Weiler, "By Way of Report," *New York Times*, 30 January 1949, X5.

62. See, for example, Mark Jancovich's *Rational Fears: American Horror in the 1950s* (Manchester: Manchester University Press, 1996).

63. "Predict More Science Fiction Pix; Sparked by Increasingly Big Grosses," *Variety*, 3 October 1951, 22.

64. Quoted in Peter Lev, *Transforming the Screen: 1950–1959*, History of American Cinema series (New York: Charles Scribner's Sons, 2003), 174.

65. "Predict More Science Fiction Pix."

66. "Mono., Lippert Talk a Deal," *Motion Picture Daily*, 27 July 1950, 1; "Monogram, Lippert Co. May Merge; Negotiations Now in Progress," *Variety*, 26 July 1950, 7.

67. "Lippert Sets 12; Budget is $2-Million," *Motion Picture Daily*, 8 August 1950, 2.

68. Robert Coughlan, "Now It Is Trouble That Is Supercolossal in Hollywood," *Life*, 13 August 1951, 106.

69. "Lippert Fiscal Aid for Independents," *Motion Picture Daily*, 7 August 1951, 1.

70. Thomas M. Pryor, "Lippert in a Deal with Film Agency," *New York Times*, 4 December 1951, 55.

71. "8 Productions from Lippert in 8 Weeks," *Motion Picture Daily*, 15 August 1951, 1.

72. "4,000,000 Program for Lippert in '52," *Variety*, 2 January 1952, 3.

73. "B's Buzzing out of Business?—Tougher to Book by Distributors," *Variety*, 26 March 1952, 3.

74. "4,000,000 Program."

75. Thomas M. Pryor, "Busy Hollywood," *New York Times*, 15 September 1957, X7. Regal produced thirty-four films for Fox between 1956 and 1959, mostly westerns.

76. Tom Weaver, *Science Fiction Stars and Horror Heroes: Interviews with Actors, Directors, Producers, and Writers of the 1940s Through 1960s* (Jefferson, NC: McFarland, 1991), 75.

77. Fred Olen Ray, *The New Poverty Row: Independent Filmmakers as Distributors* (Jefferson, NC: McFarland, 1991), xi.

78. Barbara Berch Jamison, "And Now Super-Colossal Headaches," *New York Times*, 10 January 1954, SM20.

79. "Feldman Points to Small Market Today for Low Budget Films," 1, 5.

80. "3 Majors Thrive on 'B' Pix—Many Exceptions in All-Big Era," *Variety*, 12 January 1955, 5.

81. Select Committee, *Motion-Picture Distribution Trade Practices*, 32.

82. "Universal's 'Weirdies' Ain't Crazy; $8,500,000 Since '54 a Lot of Clams," *Variety*, 3 April 1957, 3.

83. "Universal's Money-Making Habit vs. Industry Blockbuster Theory," *Variety*, 24 October 1956, 28.

84. "Today's 'B' Returns $450,000: Economy a Must on L'il Films," *Variety*, 8 August 1956, 5.

85. "Para. Interested in Taking On Some Low-Budget Films," *Hollywood Reporter*, 27 December 1956, 1.

86. " 'B's' Ride Again, Studios Busier," *Variety*, 16 January 1957, 17.

87. "Paramount Resumes Small-Budget Pix," *Variety*, 23 January 1957, 3.

88. " 'B's' Ride Again."

89. "Blockbusters vs. Mainstreet: 'B' (for Budget) Films Return," *Variety*, 5 February 1957, 5, 22.

90. "Medium Budgeters B.O. Dimout," 7.

91. "Hidden Production Increases—More than 75 Unannounced Exploitation Pictures Placed on Market During Past Year," *Hollywood Reporter*, 8 February 1957, 1, 17.

92. These "hidden" films reflect the commercial implications of Jeffery Sconce's description of the B-movie as embodying a "subcultural sensibility" in his essay " 'Trashing' the Academy: Taste, Excess, and an Emerging Politics of Cinematic Style," *Screen* 36, no. 4 (Winter 1995): 372.

93. John "J. J." Johnson, *Cheap Tricks and Class Acts: Special Effects, Makeup, and Stunts from the Films of the Fantastic Fifties* (Jefferson, NC: McFarland, 1996), 92.

94. Steve Ryfle, *Japan's Favorite Mon-star: The Unauthorized Biography of "The Big G"* (Toronto: ECW Press, 1998), 52–53; 58; David A. Cook, *Lost Illusions: American Cinema in the Shadow of Watergate and Vietnam, 1970–1979* (Berkeley: University of California Press, 2002), 324.

95. Floyd Stone, " 'Blob' Maker Brings Fresh Approach," *Motion Picture Daily*, 19 September 1958, 1.

96. "Gimmicks Did Well in 1957—Sputnik Latest 'of Monsters,'" *Variety*, 6 November 1957, 3, 16.

97. Denis Meikle, *A History of Horrors: The Rise and Fall of the House of Hammer* (Lanham, MD: Scarecrow Press, 1996), 46.

98. "Horror Cycle in Global Boom—Bloodiest Pix Gross Best; Columbia, Paramount, U-I in Carreras Production Deals," *Hollywood Reporter*, 4 November 1957, 1; " 'Curse of Frankenstein' a Payoff Blessing at Times Square Paramount," *Variety*, 14 August 1957, 4.

99. "Horror Cycle," 1, 7.

100. "Hidden Production Increases."

101. Heffernan, *Ghouls, Gimmicks, and Gold*, 70.

102. "Gimmicked and Exploitable Aim—Levin Describes AB-PT Releases," *Variety*, 15 May 1957, 13.

103. "Itself out of Production, Republic Handling Films of New Am-Par Setup," *Variety*, 12 June 1957, 7.

104. "Review: The Beginning of the End," in *Variety's Film Reviews*, vol. 9, *1954–1958* (R. R. Bowker, Daily Variety Ltd., 1983).

105. "AB-PT Beefing Up; 5 of Next 15 Features 'Major,'" *Variety*, 25 September 1957, 4.

106. "Review: She-Demons," *Hollywood Reporter*, 13 March 1958, 3.

107. "Review: Giant from the Unknown," *Hollywood Reporter*, 13 March 1958, 3.

108. "Associated Producers to Roll 5 in 3 Months," *Hollywood Reporter*, 30 December 1958, 3; " 'Return of Fly,' 'Alligator People' Better than Average Horror Dualers," *Hollywood Reporter*, 13 July 1959, 3.

109. Frederick Woods, "Take That You Swine," *Films & Filming* 11, no. 6 (August 1959): 6.

110. "B's Out for Now—Sam Katzman," *Variety*, 2 April 1958, 15.

111. "Quiet Buzz of Persisting B's: In Buster Epoch Many Stay Small," *Variety*, 9 December 1959, 7.

112. "20th to Make 30 'A' Pics in 1959," *Hollywood Reporter*, 3 November 1958, 1.

CHAPTER 4   ATTACK OF THE INDEPENDENT

1. Sam Arkoff, *Flying Through Hollywood by the Seat of My Pants* (New York: Birch Lane Press, 1992), 8.

2. Mark Thomas McGee, *Fast and Furious: The Story of American International Pictures* (Jefferson, NC: McFarland, 1984), 26.

3. Beverly Gray, *Roger Corman: An Unauthorized Biography of the Godfather of Indie Filmmaking* (Los Angeles: Renaissance Books, 2000), xiii.

4. Arkoff, *Flying Through Hollywood*, 29–31.

5. Robert Ottoson, *American International Pictures: A Filmography* (New York: Garland, 1985), xi; Tom Weaver, *Attack of the Monster Movie Makers: Interviews with 20 Genre Giants* (Jefferson, NC: McFarland, 1994), 53.

6. Arkoff, *Flying Through Hollywood*, 30–31.

7. Randy Palmer, *Paul Blaisdell, Monster Maker: A Biography of the B Movie Makeup and Special Effects Artist* (Jefferson, NC: McFarland, 1997), 19.

8. Gray, *Roger Corman*, 47; McGee, *Fast and Furious*, 14.

9. Arkoff, *Flying Through Hollywood*, 33–34.

10. McGee, *Fast and Furious*, 16.

11. Tom Weaver, *Interviews with B Science Fiction and Horror Movie Makers: Writers, Producers, Directors, Actors, Moguls, and Makeup* (Jefferson, NC: McFarland, 1988), 25.

12. "Nicholson Forms New Distrib Unit," *Hollywood Reporter*, 25 March 1956, 3.

13. Cyndy Hendershot, *I Was a Cold War Monster: Horror Films, Eroticism, and the Cold War Imagination* (Bowling Green, OH: Bowling Green State University Popular Press, 2001), 107.

14. Arkoff, *Flying Through Hollywood*, 41.

15. Frank S. Nugent, "Eight to Eighty," *New York Times*, 22 May 1938, 153. A skeptical Nugent pondered, "Where will the entertainment tastes of an 8-year-old, a 38-year-old and an 80-year-old coincide? What, cinematically speaking, will an Egyptian, a Fiji-islander, a Broadwayite and a Peruvian have in common?"

16. Richard Staehling, "Interview: Samuel Z. Arkoff," in *Kings of the B's: Working Within the Hollywood System*, ed. Todd McCarthy and Charles Flynn (New York: E. P. Dutton, 1975), 261.

17. Arkoff, *Flying Through Hollywood*, 30. Teenagers also felt the need to get out of the house due to the fact that families typically owned only one television set, with teens being forced to watch whatever programs their family chose. Furthermore, programs depicting teenage characters, such as Wally Cleaver and Eddie Haskell on *Leave It to Beaver*, were not as exciting as films such as *I Was a Teenage Werewolf*. Hence, AIP offered teenagers something unique that they could only see in theaters.

18. Richard Maltby, "The Classical Hollywood Cinema," in *The Film Studies Reader*, ed. Joanne Hollows, Peter Hutchings, and Mark Jancovich (London: Arnold, 2000), 169.

19. Ray Greene, "Sam Arkoff: The Last Interview," *Cult Movies* 36 (2002): 11.

20. "Action-and-Horror Staple Stuff; 20,000,000 Thrill-Seekers (12 to 25) Backbone of Exploitation Pix," *Variety*, 6 March 1957, 20.

21. Gray, *Roger Corman*, 58.

22. Quoted in Kevin Heffernan, *Ghouls, Gimmicks, and Gold: Horror Films and the American Movie Business, 1953–1968* (Durham, NC: Duke University Press, 2004), 68.

23. Advertisement, *Blue Denim*, *Motion Picture Daily*, 8 July 1959, 6.

24. Grace Palladino, *Teenagers: An American History* (New York: Basic Books, 1996), 106.

25. Weaver, *Attack*, 60.

26. Weaver, *Interviews*, 19–21.

27. "Nicholson Forms New Distrib Unit."

28. Gary Morris, *Roger Corman*, Twayne Filmmakers series (Boston: Twayne, 1985), 3.

29. "Nicholson Forms New Distrib Unit."

30. "American Int'l, Ziv Sharing AN Studios," *Hollywood Reporter*, 8 November 1956, 1; 7.

31. McGee, *Fast and Furious*, 61–62.

32. "Roger Corman Signed," *Hollywood Reporter*, 21 March 1956, 2.

33. "AIP Shopping for Production Space," *Hollywood Reporter*, 19 November 1956, 1.

34. "Am. Int'l Pictures Takes 5-Year Lease on Kling Lot," *Hollywood Reporter*, 26 November 1958, 1, 4. AIP soon sold the studio to Red Skelton, however, as (according to Arkoff) the facility was decrepit and termite-ridden (Arkoff, *Flying Through Hollywood*, 73–74).

35. Weaver, *Interviews*, 25–26.

36. Paul Kerr, "Out of What Past? Notes on the B Film Noir," in *The Hollywood Film Industry*, ed. Paul Kerr (London: Routledge, 1986), 230; McGee, *Fast and Furious*, 18.

37. Arkoff, *Flying Through Hollywood*, 138.

38. Weaver, *Interviews*, 23.

39. Arkoff, *Flying Through Hollywood*, 38.

40. Palmer, *Paul Blaisdell, Monster Maker*, 56. *Famous Monsters of Filmland* has been the world's most well-known monster movie magazine since its debut in 1958.

41. Greene, "Sam Arkoff: The Last Interview," 11. Arkoff added in further reference to Nicholson's knack for titles: "If he didn't come up with the titles himself, he used to be able to select the titles we would get from our staff."

42. Arkoff, *Flying Through Hollywood*, 38–39. Whereas Producers Releasing Corporation would often invent titles for films before writing the scripts, AIP took this rationale much further by designing advertising and conducting focus groups to ensure the marketability of a given film concept before commissioning a script to be written. See Wheeler Dixon, ed., *Producers Releasing Corporation: A Comprehensive Filmography and History* (Jefferson, NC: McFarland, 1986), 65.

43. Greene, "Sam Arkoff: The Last Interview," 11.

44. Irving Rubine, "Boys Meet Ghouls, Make Money," *New York Times*, 16 March 1958, X7.

45. Palmer, *Paul Blaisdell, Monster Maker*, 37.

46. Michael Brunas, John Brunas, and Tom Weaver, *Universal Horrors: The Studio's Classic Films, 1931–1946* (Jefferson, NC: McFarland, 1990), 250.

47. Arkoff, *Flying Through Hollywood*, 52; 76.

48. Ibid., 39.

49. Palmer, *Paul Blaisdell, Monster Maker*, 146.

50. Arkoff, *Flying Through Hollywood*, 83. Corman, however, was apparently exempt from this storyboarding requirement, with AIP affording him more autonomy with his films presumably because of Corman's unfailing record of financial success.

51. Ibid., 1–2, 43.

52. "Hot Rod Girl Will Roll for Nacirema March 10," *Hollywood Reporter*, 2 March 1956, 2.

53. Joe Medjuck, "An Interview with Roger Corman," *Take One* 2, no. 12 (July–August 1970): 7.

54. "Roger Corman Signed," 2; "Corman Produces, Directs 'Hypnosis,'" *Hollywood Reporter*, 4 May 1956, 3.

55. "Corman Double Schedule for '56," *Hollywood Reporter*, 18 January 1956, 2.

56. Weaver, *Attack*, 178.

57. Charles Goldman, "An Interview With Roger Corman," *Film Comment*, 7, no. 3 (Fall 1971): 49.

58. Gray, *Roger Corman*, 49.

59. Medjuck, "Interview," 6–7.

60. Fred Olen Ray, *The New Poverty Row: Independent Filmmakers as Distributors* (Jefferson, NC: McFarland, 1991), 25.

61. Tom Weaver, *Science Fiction Stars and Horror Heroes: Interviews with Actors, Directors, Producers, and Writers of the 1940s Through 1960s* (Jefferson, NC: McFarland, 1991), 54.

62. Roger Corman, *How I Made a Hundred Movies in Hollywood and Never Lost a Dime* (New York: Random House, 1990), 27.

63. Tom Weaver, *Eye on Science Fiction: 20 Interviews with Classic SF and Horror Filmmakers* (Jefferson, NC: McFarland, 2003), 24.

64. Gray, *Roger Corman*, 51.

65. *Roger Corman: Hollywood's Wild Angel*, Videocassette (Blackwood Productions, 1985).

66. Tom Weaver, *Science Fiction and Fantasy Film Flashbacks: Conversations with 24 Actors, Writers, Producers, and Directors From the Golden Age* (Jefferson, NC: McFarland, 1998), 65.

67. Janet Staiger notes that "most studios considered (B-movies) the training ground for younger staff" in the 1930s and 1940s. David Bordwell, Janet Staiger, and Kristin Thompson, *The Classical Hollywood Cinema: Film Style and Mode of Production to 1960* (New York: Columbia University Press, 1985), 325.

68. Corman would direct one further film in 1990, *Frankenstein Unbound*.

69. Weaver, *Attack*, 180.

70. Corman, *How I Made a Hundred Movies*, 31.

71. *The Rough Guide to Cult Movies* (London: Rough Guides, 2004), 61.

72. Arkoff, *Flying Through Hollywood*, 79.

73. Ray, *New Poverty Row*, 25.

74. "Shoot Features Two Together," *Variety*, 1 May 1957, 10.

75. Arkoff, *Flying Through Hollywood*, 74.

76. Weaver, *Attack*, 180.

77. "Film Unions and the Low-Budget Independent Film Production—An Exploratory Discussion," *Film Culture* 22–23 (Summer 1961): 136, 148.

78. Weaver, *Attack*, 180.

79. Tom Weaver, *Science Fiction Confidential: Interviews with 23 Monster Stars and Film-makers* (Jefferson, NC: McFarland, 2002), 139.

80. David Del Valle, "An Intimate Interview with Sam Arkoff," *Cult Movies* 36 (2002): 22.

81. Thomas Doherty, *Teenagers and Teenpics: The Juvenilization of American Movies in the 1950s* (Philadelphia: Temple University Press, 2002), 29.

82. Palmer, *Paul Blaisdell, Monster Maker*, 35; Arkoff, *Flying Through Hollywood*, 40.

83. Staehling, "Interview: Samuel Z. Arkoff," 261; Arkoff, *Flying Through Hollywood*, 34–35.

84. Corman, *How I Made a Hundred Movies*, 31.

85. Arkoff, *Flying Through Hollywood*, 41.

86. "Dual Bills in New Uptrend; Even 'Solid South' Gives In," *Hollywood Reporter*, 10 August 1956, 1, 4.

87. Arkoff, *Flying Through Hollywood*, 46; Mark Thomas McGee, *Roger Corman: The Best of the Cheap Acts* (Jefferson, NC: McFarland, 1988), 11.

88. Arkoff, *Flying Through Hollywood*, 47; "Terror's Boston Profit Kick—'Day'-'Phantom' Twinned $45,000," *Variety*, 25 January 1956, 9.

89. McGee, *Fast and Furious*, 98.

90. "AIP Offers Package: Dual Bill, One Story," *Motion Picture Daily*, 20 November 1958, 2.

91. Kristin Thompson and David Bordwell, *Film History: An Introduction* (New York: McGraw-Hill, 1994), 382.

92. Arkoff, *Flying Through Hollywood*, 41.

93. "Summer B.O. Tops All Years," *Hollywood Reporter*, 24 August 1956, 1; 4.

94. Arkoff, *Flying Through Hollywood*, 87.

95. McGee, *Fast and Furious*, 66.

96. Staehling, "Interview: Samuel Z. Arkoff," 262.

97. Arkoff, *Flying Through Hollywood*, 84. The major studios did use this saturation approach at times in the 1950s, but not as a standard practice as per the way that AIP distributed their films.

98. "Terror's Boston Profit Kick—'Day'-'Phantom' Twinned $45,000," 9, 85.

99. Palmer, *Paul Blaisdell, Monster Maker*, 96–97.

100. "Industry Needs to Emphasize 'Hard-Sell' Angle: LaVezzi," *Motion Picture Daily*, 20 August 1958, 1–2.

101. Advertisement, *Blood of Dracula/I Was a Teenage Frankenstein*, *Motion Picture Daily*, 21 November 1957, 8.

102. Hy Hollinger, "Is Carny Come-On Necessary?—Exploiteer Pans Those Who Snoot," *Variety*, 5 November 1958, 15.

103. "Nicholson's 'Cross-Eyed' Speech and 'Variety' Star at Mich. Meet," *Hollywood Reporter*, 24 September 1958, 18.

104. "AIP Will Release 12 during May, June, July," *Motion Picture Daily*, 25 April 1958, 2.

105. Arkoff, *Flying Through Hollywood*, 86–87.

106. "Don't Kill Thrill-Chill Mill: 4,000 Dates Live on 'Exploitation,'" *Variety*, 26 March 1958, 5.

107. "Roger Corman Sets 10 to Nourish Filmgroup," *Variety*, 18 February 1959, 3.

108. "American International's $15,000,000 Financing of 30 1959 Features," *Variety*, 15 October 1958, 3.

109. "Am.-Int'l Lifts Its Production Sights to Single-Bills," *Hollywood Reporter*, 6 April 1950, 3.

110. "American International's 'Big Singles' While Still Double-Packaging Gore," *Variety*, 8 April 1959, 15.

111. "American International Shoots 500G Bankroll, Unprecedented Budget," *Variety*, 6 August 1958, 3.

112. "On Being a Teenage Werewolf: An Interview with Herman Cohen," *Films & Filming* 6, no. 12 (September 1960): 15.

113. "Is It Becoming 'I Was a Teenage Bore?': N. Herman," *Variety*, 11 November 1958, 4.

114. "'Horrors of Black Museum' Jolly Good British Chiller," *Hollywood Reporter*, 16 April 1959, 3.

115. "'Black Museum' Sets Record Here for AIP," *Hollywood Reporter*, 14 August 1959, 3; "Cheap 'n' Quick No Longer Goes in Horror Films," *Variety*, 20 May 1959, 4; "On Being a Teenage Werewolf," 35.

116. Arkoff, *Flying Through Hollywood*, 91; "Am. Int'l Turns Cold on Chillers," *Hollywood Reporter*, 3 June 1959, 1, 4.

117. Arkoff, *Flying Through Hollywood*, 92.

118. Greene, "Sam Arkoff: The Last Interview," 15.

119. Quoted in Gray, *Roger Corman*, 72; McGee, *Roger Corman*, 115.

120. Corman, *How I Made a Hundred Movies*, 79. The director also saved money by reusing footage of a burning castle from *House of Usher* in multiple films. Corman rationalized that "since one roaring blaze looks as good as another in a long shot, I cut the *Usher* sequence into the other films. It certainly didn't occur to me back in 1960 that people someday would rent these films . . . watch them back to back, and notice the same flaming rafters crashing down in different movies" (82).

121. Arkoff, *Flying Through Hollywood*, 230.

122. Ibid., 244.

CHAPTER 5   SMALL SCREEN, SMALLER PICTURES

1. Jane Stokes dubs the two media as "rivals" in her book *On Screen Rivals: Cinema and Television in the United States and Britain* (New York: St. Martin's Press, 2000). "One of the most well-rehearsed narratives" in film and television, writes Christopher Anderson, "depicts the broadcasting and motion picture industries as antagonists locked in a struggle over the hearts and minds of a fickle public" (*Hollywood TV: The Studio System in the Fifties* [Austin: University of Texas Press, 1994], 13). Even scholars in the 1950s adopted a combative rhetoric when describing the relationship between film and television, with Professor Kenneth McGowan of the University of California describing in 1957 how "TV invaded the field of film production" ("Screen Wonders of the Past—and to Come?" *Quarterly of Film, Radio and Television* 2, no. 4 [Summer 1957]: 390).

2. Douglas Gomery, "Failed Opportunities: The Integration of the US Motion Picture and Television Industries," in *American Television: New Directions in History and Theory*, ed. Nick Browne (Langhorne, PA: Harwood, 1994), 25–26.

3. Kerry Segrave, *Movies at Home: How Hollywood Came to Television* (Jefferson, NC: McFarland, 1999), 17.

4. Thomas F. Brady, "Hollywood Gets on Television's Bandwagon," *New York Times*, 2 May 1948, 85.

5. "Rank's $300,000 Package of 70 Brit. Pix for TV," *Variety*, 6 July 1949, 2.

6. Douglas Gomery, *Shared Pleasures: A History of Movie Presentation in the United States* (Madison: University of Wisconsin Press, 1992), 247.

7. Segrave, *Movies at Home*, 37. Michele Hilmes also challenges Segrave's claim by noting in *Hollywood and Broadcasting: From Radio to Cable* (Chicago: University of Illinois Press, 1990) that CBS ran Monogram films in 1951 from 8 to 9 P.M. under the banner of *Film Theatre of the Air* (158).

8. "Will Feature Films Reshape TV?" *Business Week*, 24 November 1956, 136.

9. "TV Unit Gets 175 Pictures," *Motion Picture Herald*, 25 August 1951, 16. Republic Pictures established a subsidiary company called the Hollywood Television Service to broker its film sales and made the provision of only two screenings per year with the sale of 175 films to Los Angeles station KTTV in 1951.

10. "Says TV Films Killing 'B's' and Reissues," *Motion Picture Daily*, 13 December 1950, 1.

11. Abel Green, "Sarnoff on Hollywood Vs. TV: Sees All Cinemas Adding TV To Pix," *Variety*, 29 August 1951, 1, 22.

12. "Says TV Films Killing 'B's' and Reissues."

13. Val Adams, "Where Old TV Films Come From," *New York Times*, 11 June 1950, 105.

14. "TV Dries Up Old-Pix Sources," *Variety*, 7 November 1951, 60.

15. Adams, "Where Old TV Films Come From," 105.

16. "Republic Sells 125 Films to TV," *Motion Picture Daily*, 21 August 1951, 1; "Republic Sells 174 Films to Television," *Motion Picture Daily*, 23 October 1951, 1.

17. Murray Horowitz, "Republic to Make Fewer but Bigger Pictures: Yates," *Motion Picture Daily*, 31 June 1952, 4.

18. Gomery, *Shared Pleasures*, 248. RKO was sold by then-owner Howard Hughes in 1954 to the General Tire & Rubber Company, which also owned WOR.

19. William Lafferty, "Feature Films on Prime-Time Television," in *Hollywood in the Age of Television*, ed. Tino Balio (Boston: Unwin Hyman, 1990), 240.

20. "TV Dries Up Old-Pix Sources," 60.

21. "Divided Opinion on Old Pix as Steady TV Lure," *Variety*, 3 October 1951, 7.

22. Thomas F. Brady, "Some Film-Makers Turn to Television," *New York Times*, 6 December 1950, 56.

23. "TV Dries Up Old-Pix Sources," 3.

24. "Selznick Exploring Tele for His Films," *Variety*, 31 October 1951, 3; William R. Weaver, "Selznick Studying TV Market for Reissues," *Motion Picture Herald*, 11 August 1951, 33.

25. "TV Dries Up Old-Pix Sources," 60.

26. Hilmes, *Hollywood and Broadcasting*, 159–160.

27. William Boddy, *Fifties Television: The Industry and Its Critics* (Chicago: University of Illinois Press, 1992) 71.

28. "Will Feature Films Reshape TV?" 136.

29. In her essay "The B Film and the Problem of Cultural Distinction," Lea Jacobs argues that if B-movies possess a lowered cultural status, it is largely the result of institutional factors in the 1930s. "We tend to assume that a film's position within the double bill was determined in the planning and financing of production," says

Jacobs. Instead, she makes the case that the status of the B-movie "was determined much more complexly within the system of distribution and exhibition" (*Screen* 33, no. 1 [Spring 1992]:1–13).

30. Hilmes, *Hollywood and Broadcasting*, 159.

31. "Tailor-Made 'B' Pix for Post-Theatre Video," *Variety*, 5 September 1951, 5.

32. "Eagle-Lion Bulging with VidPix Lensing," *Variety*, 14 November 1951, 5.

33. Thomas M. Pryor, "Republic Planning to Make TV Movies," *New York Times*, 6 November, 1951, 35.

34. Thomas M. Pryor, "Monogram Sets Up Video Subsidiary," *New York Times*, 7 November 1951, 37.

35. "Eagle-Lion Bulging."

36. George W. Woolery, *Children's Television: The First Thirty-five Years, 1946–1981. Part II: Live, Film, and Tape Series* (Metuchen, NJ: Scarecrow Press, 1985), 410.

37. Val Adams, "Television in Review," *New York Times*, 31 August 1953, 15.

38. Gerard Jones, *Men of Tomorrow: Geeks, Gangsters, and the Birth of the Comic Book* (Jackson, TN: Basic Books, 2004), 259.

39. " 'B' Gallopers Slow Thataway as TV Cues Boneyard Exit of Hoss Opry," *Variety*, 29 April 1953, 7.

40. "TV Eyes $250,000,000 in Old Pix," *Variety*, 28 February 1951, 3.

41. "No Profit Anymore in B (for Bad) Pictures, Warner Tells Guild," *Variety*, 11 November 1953, 1.

42. "AIP Promises Exhibs 10-Year TV Clearance; Hikes Slate to 36," *Hollywood Reporter*, 17 December 1957, 1.

43. "Nicholson's 'Cross-Eyed' Speech and 'Variety' Star at Mich. Meet," *Hollywood Reporter*, 24 September 1958, 18.

44. "Corman Calls On Guilds to Block Sales of Newer Pix," *Hollywood Reporter*, 2 January 1958, 3.

45. "Am. Int'l Takes TV-Film Plunge," *Hollywood Reporter*, 18 March 1959, 1.

46. "Will Feature Films Reshape TV?" 136.

47. Richard Corliss, "Made-from-TV Movies," *Time*, 30 May 1994, http://www.time.com/time/magazine/article/0,9171,980805-1,00.html.

48. The 1950 film *The Goldbergs* was based on a 1949 television series of the same name, yet the latter was itself adapted from a long-running radio program. The *Captain Video* serial is therefore a pioneering film in terms of how it adapts a program originating in the medium of television. Serial producers have in fact routinely demonstrated a distinct flexibility in how they have approached their product, with such 1930s efforts as *The Return of Chandu* (1934), *The New Adventures of Tarzan* (1935), *The Lost City* (1935), *Shadow of Chinatown* (1936), *Flash Gordon* (1936), *The Clutching Hand* (1936), and *Buck Rogers* (1939), among others, having been recut into shorter, feature-length versions for theatrical release.

49. "More TV Stars for Theatres," *Variety*, 11 May 1955, 3.

50. Thomas F. Brady, "Some Film-makers Turn to Television," *New York Times*, 6 December 1950, 56.

51. Stokes, *On Screen Rivals*, 3.

52. Segrave, *Movies at Home*, 42–43.

53. Jack Gould, "A Plea for Live Video," *New York Times*, 7 December 1952, X17.

54. Rod Serling, "TV in the Can vs. TV in the Flesh," *New York Times*, 24 November 1957, 49.

55. While there were certainly live programs in a variety of different genres, the quality of their special effects was often not as good as that of filmed shows, particularly with science fiction programs. The live show *Tom Corbett, Space Cadet*, for instance, displays effects that are often not as sophisticated in execution as those of *Rocky Jones*.

56. Serling, "TV in the Can vs. TV in the Flesh," 49.

57. "Fromkess Plans to Resume on 'Ramar,'" *Variety*, 16 March 1955, 35.

58. "Hollywood Tie-Up," *New York Times*, 17 April 1955, X5.

59. "Majors Burrow Deep in TV," *Variety*, 16 March 1955, 5.

60. Jack Gould, "TV Films Boom Hollywood into Its Greatest Prosperity," *Variety*, 3 July 1955, 1.

61. Nick Browne estimates that between fifty and one hundred independent companies existed between 1948 and 1953 ("The Rise of the Telefilm," in Browne, *American Television*, 12).

62. "The Movie Makers Look for Gold on the TV Screen," *Business Week*, 23 April 1955, 154.

63. Fred Hift, "TV Ogles Hollywood, Object: Matrimony," *Motion Picture Herald*, 2 December 1950, 13.

64. William R. Weaver, "William's TV Films May Go to Theatres Instead," *Motion Picture Herald*, 16 June 1951, 33.

65. Thomas M. Pryor, "Lippert Cancels Films for Video," *New York Times*, 13 July 1951, 12.

66. Jack Gould, "The Video Freeze," *New York Times*, 3 October 1948, X9; Boddy, *Fifties Television*, 51.

67. "Vitapix, Princess Plan First Runs Made-for-TV," *Broadcasting, Telecasting*, 7 September 1953, 34.

68. "Will Vitapix Create a TV Film Revolution?" *Sponsor*, 11 January 1954, 93.

69. Boddy, *Fifties Television*, 65.

70. Lafferty, "Feature Films on Prime-Time Television," 248–249.

71. J. P. Telotte, *Disney TV* (Detroit: Wayne State University Press, 2004), 95.

72. Anderson, *Hollywood TV*, 150.

73. Thirty-six of the series thirty-nine episodes featured this three-part structure, with the remaining three episodes resolving their narratives in a single episode. Regarding the first airing of the show, some fans even claim that it debuted as early as December of 1953. See Jeffery Davis, *Children's Television, 1947–1990* (Jefferson, NC: McFarland, 1995).

74. Telotte, *Disney TV*, 22.

75. See Wheeler Winston Dixon, *Lost in the Fifties: Recovering Phantom Hollywood* (Carbondale: Southern Illinois University Press, 2005).

76. Woolery, *Children's Television*, 410; Davis, *Children's Television*, 29; Dixon, *Lost in the Fifties*, 40–41. Dixon describes how this "stock music" was "stripped off the films' soundtracks" by MUTEL founder David Chudnow and "then reorchestrated and rerecorded in Paris to improve the audio fidelity of the tracks." MUTEL also used the

same music on several other television programs in the early 1950s, such as *Captain Midnight*, *Racket Squad*, and *Adventures of Superman*.

77. For further details on the show's mode of production, see Gary Grossman, *Superman: Serial to Cereal* (New York: Popular Library, 1977).

78. The exception is Disney's *Zorro* films, which feature posters that include a small line of text at the bottom declaring the film to be "Adapted from the Original Television Series." The production values of Disney's shows were much better than those of most independent shows, however, such that film audiences often paid to see the Disney brand as much as they did to see a particular story or character.

79. An alternative strategy was to use the titles of individual episodes as the name of a MFTVM, with the assumption being that audiences likely wouldn't be able to remember every episode's title and might therefore think that the film contained a new story.

80. For a larger overview of the postcolonial critiques of *Ramar of the Jungle*, see Dixon, *Lost in the Fifties*.

81. Given that episodes of *The Virginian* were themselves seventy-five minutes long and ran in a ninety-minute television time slot, the show would seem to have been ideally suited to the MFTVM treatment. Still, the films' producers regularly combined two episodes of the show to make such films, often so as to allow for the appearance of more top-billed actors. The 1967 film *The Meanest Men in the West*, for instance, combines one episode from the show's first season in which Lee Marvin appears, along with a 1967 episode starring Charles Bronson.

82. *To Trap a Spy* (1965), *Spy in the Green Hat* (1966), *One Spy Too Many* (1966), *The Spy with My Face* (1966), *One of Our Spies Is Missing* (1966), *The Karate Killers* (1967), *How to Steal the World* (1968), *The Helicopter Spies* (1968).

83. See Gomery, *Shared Pleasures*; Stokes, *On Screen Rivals*; and Hilmes, *Hollywood and Broadcasting*.

84. "Cineplex Big Screen Available to Xbox Gamers," *CBC*, http://www.cbc.ca/technology/story/2008/08/13/tech-cineplex.html.

85. Lafferty, "Feature Films on Prime-Time Television," 235.

CHAPTER 6   BIG *B*, LITTLE *b*

1. David Sterritt and John Anderson, eds., *The B List: The National Society of Film Critics on the Low-Budget Beauties, Genre-Bending Mavericks, and Cult Classics We Love* (Cambridge, MA: Da Capo Press, 2008), xiii.

2. A Google search of the terms "War of the Worlds," "1953," and "B-movie," for instance, finds the George Pal film described as a B-movie by such media outlets as MTV and the *Washington Times*, along with a variety of fan sites and message boards. See in particular "War of the Worlds Has History of Freaking Earthlings Out," http://www.mtv.com/movies/news/articles/1504903/story.jhtml, and Gary Arnold, "Directors' Visions Face 'Worlds' War," http://washingtontimes.com/entertainment/20050624–090438–2164r.htm.

3. David Spaner, "No Cuddly E.T. in War of the Worlds," *Vancouver Province*, 29 June 2005, B3.

4. Mark Kermode, "Be Afraid, Very Afraid—Again," *Observer*, http://observer.guardian.co.uk/review/story/0,6903,1519728,00.html; *Dark Horizons*, http://www.dark-

horizons.com/reviews/war-n.php; Smart Popcorn, http://www.smart-popcorn.com/review/835/.

5. Eleanor Ringel Cater, "Platoon," in Sterritt and Anderson, *The B List*, 145.

6. Sterrit and Anderson, *The B List*, introduction to pt. 8, 143. *Platoon* cost $6 million to make, while the highest-grossing film of 1986—*Top Gun*—cost $15 million.

7. Douglas W. Churchill, "Hollywood on the Wire," *New York Times*, 30 June 1935, X3. See the introduction for a more extensive overview of these categories regarding B-filmmaking in the 1930s. Indeed, the three tiers presented in this chapter might alternatively be labeled as major studio, large independent, and small independent, but the use of these same terms has been avoided given that the economic relationship between all three was significantly different in the 1950s, as were the players involved in the latter two categories.

8. "Review: Earth vs. the Flying Saucers," *Variety's Film Reviews*, vol. 9, *1954–1958* (R. R. Bowker, Daily Variety Ltd., 1983).

9. Leonard Maltin, *Leonard Maltin's 2005 Movie Guide* (New York: Signet, 2004), 403.

10. David Bordwell, Janet Staiger, and Kristin Thompson, *The Classical Hollywood Cinema: Film Style and Mode of Production to 1960* (New York: Columbia University Press, 1985), 325.

11. "Cinema Success Story," *New York Times*, 14 April 1935, X4.

12. Bernard F. Dick, "From the Brothers Cohn to Sony Corp.," in *Columbia Pictures: Portrait of a Studio*, ed. Bernard F. Dick (Lexington: University Press of Kentucky, 1992), 9–10; Bordwell, Staiger, and Thompson, *Classical Hollywood Cinema*, 328.

13. J. P. Telotte, "Film Noir at Columbia," in Dick, *Columbia Pictures*, 107; Leonard Maltin, *The Art of the Cinematographer: A Survey and Interviews with Five Masters* (New York: Dover, 1978), 108–109.

14. Maltin, *Art of the Cinematographer*, 108.

15. Bordwell, Staiger, and Thompson, *Classical Hollywood Cinema*, 328.

16. Dick, "From the Brothers Cohn to Sony Corp.," 241–251.

17. Bernard F. Dick, *The Merchant Prince of Poverty Row: Harry Cohn of Columbia Pictures* (Lexington: University Press of Kentucky, 1993), 131.

18. *The Astounding B Monster Archive*, http://www.bmonster.com/reviews_cult.html (*Blackhawk*, 1952) and www.bmonster.com/horror8.html.

19. "$300,000 Picture's Gross Expectancy Same as $1-Mil Film—Katzman," *Variety*, 1 May 1957, 17.

20. "Zombie Pix Upbeat & Durable—20 Now or Near; Many Tandemed," *Variety*, 6 May 1956, 11.

21. Bill Warren, *Keep Watching the Skies! American Science Fiction Movies of the Fifties*, vol. 1, *1950–1957* (Jefferson, NC: McFarland, 1982), 257.

22. Dick, *Merchant Prince*, 139.

23. Mark Thomas McGee, *Beyond Ballyhoo: Motion Picture Promotion and Gimmicks* (Jefferson, NC: McFarland, 1989), 79–80. In *Lost in the Fifties: Recovering Phantom Hollywood*, Wheeler Winston Dixon makes the case that Sears's work was not in fact dull or inept, but rather quite proficient (Carbondale: Southern Illinois University Press, 2005).

24. "$300,000 Picture's Gross Expectancy Same as $1-Mil Film—Katzman," *Variety*, 1 May 1957, 17. The exact budget of *Earth vs. the Flying Saucers* proves difficult to find,

largely due to the fact that "Columbia's budgets are less available than those of Fox and Warners, which donated production files to universities" (Dick, *Merchant Prince*, 160).

25. "Universal's 'Weirdies' Ain't Crazy; $8,500,000 Since '54 a Lot of Clams," *Variety*, 3 April 1957, 3.

26. "Today's 'B' Returns $450,000: Economy a Must on L'il Films," *Variety*, 8 August 1956, 5. Allied Artists occasionally released films in the high-end budget range, such as *Invasion of the Body Snatchers* (1956, budget of $382,000), but more often released films that were of middle-end budgets such as *Attack of the 50 Ft. Woman* (1958, $88,000 budget) and *The Atomic Submarine* (1959, $135,000 budget), as well as Roger Corman's *Attack of the Crab Monsters* and *Not of This Earth* (both 1957, with respective budgets of $70,000 and $100,000). A distinct difference in production values can be seen between these middle-end films and those of *Body Snatchers*, with director Don Siegel having spent three days filming the climactic night-for-night shots. As demonstrated elsewhere in this chapter, middle- and low-end films frequently used cheaper day-for-night lighting techniques, often with mixed results.

27. Gene Fernett, *American Film Studios: An Historical Encyclopedia* (Jefferson, NC: McFarland, 1988), 45.

28. John "J. J." Johnson, *Cheap Tricks and Class Acts: Special Effects, Makeup and Stunts from the Films of the Fantastic Fifties* (Jefferson, NC: McFarland, 1996), 45.

29. "Review: Earth vs. the Flying Saucers."

30. Raymond Fielding, *The Technique of Special Effects Cinematography* (New York: Hastings House, 1968), 330, 335.

31. Johnson, *Cheap Tricks and Class Acts*, 78.

32. Ibid., 95.

33. Fielding, *Technique*, 23, 269, 273.

34. Ibid., 236–238.

35. Johnson, *Cheap Tricks and Class Acts*, 92.

36. "'Teen-Age Werewolf' Grosses $1,720,000," *Hollywood Reporter*, 30 August 1957, 1.

37. Sam Arkoff, *Flying Through Hollywood by the Seat of My Pants* (New York: Birch Lane Press, 1992), 64.

38. "Review: I Was a Teenage Werewolf," *Motion Picture Herald*, 13 July 1957, 27.

39. Warren, *Keep Watching the Skies!* 350.

40. "Review: I Was a Teenage Werewolf," *Variety's Film Reviews*, vol. 9., *1954–1958* (R. R. Bowker, Daily Variety Ltd., 1983).

41. "On Being a Teenage Werewolf: An Interview with Herman Cohen," *Films & Filming* 6, no. 12 (September 1960): 15; Arkoff, *Flying Through Hollywood*, 62; Tom Weaver, *Science Fiction Stars and Horror Heroes: Interviews with Actors, Directors, Producers, and Writers of the 1940s Through 1960s* (Jefferson, NC: McFarland, 1991), 73.

42. "Nicholson Boosts Budgets and Slate; Adds 3 Producers," *Hollywood Reporter*, 10 April 1957, 2.

43. "Hollywood Production Pulse," *Variety*, 27 March 1957, 18.

44. Weaver, *Science Fiction Stars*, 74.

45. "'Dragstrip Girl' Next Golden State Picture," *Hollywood Reporter*, 21 December 1956, 2.

46. Arkoff, *Flying Through Hollywood*, 43–45, 50, 55.

47. "'Teenage Werewolf' to Roll," *Variety*, 14 January 1957, 3. The other articles on the same page are entitled "Liz Scott, Wendell Corey Join Presley Film Cast" and "Hitchcock Gets Checkup."

48. Arkoff, *Flying Through Hollywood*, 62–63.

49. "Action-and-Horror Staple Stuff; 20,000,000 Thrill-seekers (12 to 25) Backbone of Exploitation Pix," *Variety*, 6 March 1957, 20.

50. Arkoff, *Flying Through Hollywood*, 61.

51. Tom Weaver, *Attack of the Monster Movie Makers: Interviews with 20 Genre Giants* (Jefferson, NC: McFarland, 1994), 53.

52. See Warren, *Keep Watching the Skies!* 349. Warren provides no specific sources in support of his research, however.

53. Weaver, *Attack*, 57.

54. Arkoff, *Flying Through Hollywood*, 62.

55. Weaver, *Science Fiction Stars*, 70–73.

56. Weaver, *Attack*, 57.

57. Weaver, *Science Fiction Stars*, 71.

58. Weaver, *Interviews with B Science Fiction and Horror Movie Makers: Writers, Producers, Directors, Actors, Moguls, and Makeup* (Jefferson, NC: McFarland, 1988), 319; 321.

59. Weaver, *Science Fiction Stars*, 71.

60. Weaver, *Interviews*, 66.

61. Weaver, *Science Fiction Stars*, 71.

62. Weaver, *Interviews*, 321.

63. Weaver, *Science Fiction Stars*, 73–74. In contrast, while filming *She-Wolf of London* for Universal, director Jean Yarbrough refused to allow his cast and crew to go to any of the Christmas parties that were going on while he was shooting retakes on December 24, 1945. Yarbrough closed the film's set so as to prevent any distractions (Michael Brunas, John Brunas, and Tom Weaver, *Universal Horrors: The Studio's Classic Films, 1931–1946* [Jefferson, NC: McFarland, 1990], 556).

64. Weaver, *Science Fiction and Fantasy Film Flashbacks: Conversations with 24 Actors, Writers, Producers, and Directors from the Golden Age* (Jefferson, NC: McFarland, 1998), 223.

65. Weaver, *Science Fiction Stars*, 71. With some Bs occasionally able to work with resources above and beyond their budgets (such as through friendships as in the case of LaShelle), it might even be argued that there are middle-end B-movies with certain high-end tendencies, and other such taxonomic combinations. LaShelle's work here is still limited, however, by the reduced economic resources of the middle-end B-movie. Were he to have used the resources of a high-end B-movie on *Werewolf*, he could have undoubtedly avoided some of the film's aesthetic limitations detailed in this chapter.

66. Randy Palmer, *Paul Blaisdell, Monster Maker: A Biography of the B Movie Makeup and Special Effects Artist* (Jefferson, NC: McFarland, 1997), 147.

67. Weaver, *Science Fiction Stars*, 72.

68. Warren, *Keep Watching the Skies!* 351.

69. "I Was a Teenage Werewolf," http://www.incredibletvandmovies.com/werewolf.html.

70. Weaver, *Science Fiction and Fantasy*, 222.

71. Weaver, *Science Fiction Stars*, 76.

72. Bob Burns with John Michlig, *It Came from Bob's Basement!* (San Francisco: Chronicle, 2000), 36–37.

73. Johnson, *Cheap Tricks and Class Acts*, 160.

74. Thomas Doherty, *Teenagers and Teenpics: The Juvenilization of American Movies in the 1950s* (Philadelphia: Temple University Press, 2002), 132; Warren, *Keep Watching the Skies!* 351.

75. Weaver, *Science Fiction Stars*, 70, 73.

76. Fred Olen Ray, *The New Poverty Row: Independent Filmmakers as Distributors* (Jefferson, NC: McFarland, 1991), 1.

77. http://www.horror-wood.com/warren.htm; "The Films of Jerry Warren," http://www.angelfire.com/ca3/jerrywarren/; Weaver, *Science Fiction Stars*, 386; Ray, *The New Poverty Row*, 1.

78. Weaver, *Interviews*, 370; Warren, *Keep Watching the Skies!* 294.

79. Roger Ebert, *Roger Ebert's Movie Yearbook 2007* (Riverside, NJ: Andrews McMeel, 2006), 423.

80. Kristin Thompson and David Bordwell, *Film History: An Introduction* (New York: McGraw-Hill, 1994), 381.

81. "Review: Plan 9 from Outer Space," *Motion Picture Herald*, 8 August 1959, 42.

82. "Review: Bride of the Monster," *Motion Picture Herald*, 1 September 1956, 40.

83. Thompson and Bordwell, *Film History*, 381.

84. Weaver, *Science Fiction and Fantasy*, 167.

85. Rudolph Grey, *Nightmare of Ecstasy: The Life and Art of Edward D. Wood Jr.* (Los Angeles: Feral House, 1992), 12; 54.

86. Weaver, *Science Fiction Stars*, 396.

87. Weaver, *Interviews*, 380; Ray, *The New Poverty Row*, 19.

88. Palmer, *Paul Blaisdell, Monster Maker*, 217.

89. Furthermore, whereas directors like Jacques Tourneur are celebrated for their ability to disguise the lack of production values through suggestive shadow-play in a B-film like *Cat People* (1942), 1950s B-movies brought forth a rethinking of what low-budget cinema was capable of, and whether it even needed to attempt to disguise the relatively limited nature of its production values and special effects in the same manner as Tourneur. The culmination of this notion is 1999's *The Blair Witch Project*; of which audiences were patently aware of its extremely low-budget nature, yet that did not take away from their positive response to the film. Indeed the fact that the film looks (and essentially was) nonprofessional was one of the major factors that audiences reacted to.

90. Weaver, *Interviews*, 370–373, 380.

91. Ibid., 370.

92. Ibid., 371.

93. Ray, *The New Poverty Row*, 2; Warren, *Keep Watching the Skies!* 294.

94. Weaver, *Interviews*, 370–371, 374.

95. Weaver, *Science Fiction Stars*, 389.

96. Weaver, *Interviews*, 90, 374.

97. "Review: Man Beast," *Variety's Film Reviews*.

98. Weaver, *Interviews*, 377.

99. Geoffrey O'Brien, *Castaways of the Image Planet* (Berkeley, CA: Counterpoint Press, 2002), 103–104.

CHAPTER 7   NOTES FROM THE UNDERGROUND

1. See Parker Tyler's *Underground Film: A Critical History* (New York: Grove Press, 1970) and Xavier Mendik and Steven Jay Schneider's edited collection *Underground U.S.A.: Filmmaking Beyond the Hollywood Canon* (London: Wallflower Press, 2002), for example. There were certainly significant figures making underground films throughout the 1950s, such as Morris Engel and Lionel Rogosin, with John Cassavetes acknowledging both as influences on his own work at the end of the decade.

2. "Film Unions and the Low-Budget Independent Film Production—An Exploratory Discussion," *Film Culture* 22–23 (Summer 1961): 149.

3. Vincent Canby, "Film's Poverty Row Now in N.Y.—Fast-Buck Lurids sans Union Card," *Variety*, 17 February 1960, 1, 6.

4. Colin Young, "The Hollywood War of Independence," *Film Quarterly* 12, no. 3 (Spring 1959): 4–15.

5. Colin Young and Gideon Bachmann, "New Wave—or Gesture," *Film Quarterly* 14, no. 3 (Spring 1961): 11–12.

6. Stephen R. Bissette, "Curtis Harrington and the Underground Roots of the Modern Horror Film," in Mendik and Schneider, *Underground U.S.A.*, 41.

7. P. Adams Sitney, *Visionary Film: The American Avant-Garde, 1943–1978*, 2nd ed. (Oxford: Oxford University Press, 1979), 341–342.

8. Ray Carney, *Shadows* (London: British Film Institute, 2001), 24.

9. *Cassavetes on Cassavetes*, ed. Ray Carney (London: Faber and Faber, 2001), 71.

10. Carney, *Shadows*, 28.

11. *Cassavetes*, 61.

12. Carney, *Shadows*, 39.

13. Ibid., 40–41, 45; *Cassavetes*, 98.

14. Gavin Lambert, "A Line of Experiment," *Sight & Sound* 19, no. 11 (March 1951): 444.

15. Beverly Gray, *Roger Corman: An Unauthorized Biography of the Godfather of Indie Filmmaking* (Los Angeles: Renaissance Books, 2000), 59. In contrast to AIP's use of new talent, in the 1930s and 1940s many directors at such Poverty Row studios as Producers Releasing Corporation had already made films at a major studio. Before coming to PRC, Edgar G. Ulmer directed *The Black Cat* (1934) for Universal, and he had also worked as F. W. Murnau's assistant in Germany in the 1920s. Other directors such as William Beaudine, Christy Cabanne, Lew Landers, and Jean Yarbrough regularly moved between making B-films for Poverty Row studios and for Columbia, RKO, and Universal. Many of these veteran directors moved primarily into television in the 1950s, as a new breed of rookie directors entered the field of B-movie production.

16. Quoted in Gray, *Roger Corman*, 105.

17. Martin Scorsese, Audio Commentary, *The Last Temptation of Christ*, 1988, DVD (Criterion Collection, 2000).

18. *Cassavetes*, 289.

19. Roger Corman, *How I Made a Hundred Movies in Hollywood and Never Lost a Dime* (New York: Random House, 1990), 186.

20. Scorsese, Commentary, *The Last Temptation of Christ*.

21. Tom Weaver, *Interviews with B Science Fiction and Horror Movie Makers: Writers, Producers, Directors, Actors, Moguls, and Makeup* (Jefferson, NC: McFarland, 1988), 21; Mark Thomas McGee, *Fast and Furious: The Story of American International Pictures* (Jefferson, NC: McFarland, 1984), 191.

22. Corman, *How I Made a Hundred Movies*, 34.

23. Mark Harris, *Pictures at a Revolution: Five Movies and the Birth of the New Hollywood* (New York: Penguin, 2008), 175; Gregory D. Black, *The Catholic Crusade Against the Movies* (Cambridge: Cambridge University Press, 1998), 225–227. *The Pawnbroker* was not the first film to be released without the MPAA's seal of approval—United Artists' *The Moon Is Blue* (1953) and RKO's *The French Line* (1954) were also released without the seal, for instance. It is the successful appeal of *The Pawnbroker*'s initial rejection, however, that signaled the beginning of the end of the Production Code just a few years later.

24. See, for instance, J. David Slocum, *Violence and American Cinema* (London: Routledge, 2001).

25. See Joe Bob Briggs, *Profoundly Disturbing: Shocking Movies That Changed History!* (New York: Universe Publishing, 2003), 86–87. Briggs notes that *Blood Feast* remained in distribution for up to fifteen years, earning a total of $7 million by the late 1970s.

26. See Eric Schaefer, "Resisting Refinement: The Exploitation Film and Self-censorship," *Film History* 6 (1994): 293–313, for further details on how many low-budget independent producers approached the Production Code in the 1930s and 1940s.

27. "'Blood Feast' Arrest: Hold House Manager on 'Delinquency' Angle," *Variety*, 1 April 1964, 8.

28. See Kevin Heffernan, "Inner-City Exhibition and the Genre Film: Distributing 'Night of the Living Dead' (1968)," *Cinema Journal* 41, no. 3 (2002): 59–77, for a larger analysis of the release of Romero's film.

29. See, for instance, Thomas Schatz, *Hollywood: Critical Concepts in Media and Cultural Studies*, vol. 1 (London: Taylor and Francis, 2004), 11; Geoff King, *New Hollywood Cinema: An Introduction* (London: I. B. Taurus, 2002).

30. Paul Monaco, *The Sixties: 1960–1969*, History of the American Cinema series (New York: Charles Scribner's Sons, 2001), 27.

31. *Visions of Light: The Art of Cinematography*, American Film Institute, DVD, 1992.

32. Estimates of *Sweet Sweetback's Baadasssss Song*'s final box office total have ranged from $10 million to $15 million depending on the source. In describing how Van Peebles "changed the direction of black movies," Donald Bogle lists the conservative estimate of $10 million (*Toms, Coons, Mulattoes, Mammies, and Bucks: An Interpretive History of Blacks in American Films*, 4th ed. [New York: Continuum, 2001], 238).

33. Ray Greene, "Sam Arkoff: The Last Interview," *Cult Movies* 36 (2002): 17.

34. Lewis Jacobs, "A History of the Obscure Quickie," *New York Times*, 30 December 1934, X4.

35. "Film Unions," 150.

INDEX

ABOUT THE AUTHOR

BLAIR DAVIS is an assistant professor with the College of Communication at DePaul University and received his PhD from the Department of Communication Studies at McGill University. He has had essays featured in *American Horror Film: The Genre at the Turn of the Millennium* (2010), *Caligari's Heirs: The German Cinema of Fear After 1945* (2007), *Horror Film: Creating and Marketing Fear* (2004), *Reel Food: Essays on Food and Film* (2004), and such journals as the *Historical Journal of Film, Radio and Television* and the *Canadian Journal of Film Studies*.